MUDRAS for YOUR HEART
8 WEEK GUIDEBOOK

HEAL Your LOVE MATRIX

SABRINA MESKO

Author of International Bestseller HEALING MUDRAS

By Sabrina Mesko

HEALING MUDRAS
Yoga for Your Hands
Random House - 2000 Original edition - Mudra Hands Publishing 2012 New Edition

POWER MUDRAS
Yoga Hand Postures for Women
Random House - 2002 Original edition – 2012 Mudra Hands Publishing - New Edition

MUDRA - Gestures of POWER
DVD - Sounds True

CHAKRA MUDRAS DVD set
HAND YOGA for Vitality, Creativity and Success
HAND YOGA for Concentration, Love and Longevity

HEALING MUDRAS - New Edition in full color:
BOOK I. ~ For Your Body BOOK II. ~ For Your Mind BOOK III. ~ For Your Soul

MUDRA THERAPY
Hand Yoga for Pain Management and Conquering Illness

YOGA MIND
45 Meditations for Inner Peace, Prosperity and Protection

MUDRAS for ASTROLOGICAL SIGNS Volumes I. ~ XII.
MUDRAS for ARIES, TAURUS, GEMINI, CANCER, LEO, VIRGO,
LIBRA, SCORPIO, SAGITTARIUS, CAPRICORN, AQUARIUS, PISCES
12 Book Series

LOVE MUDRAS
Hand Yoga for Two

THE HOLISTIC CAREGIVER
A Guidebook for at-home care in late stage of Alzheimer's and dementia

MUDRAS AND CRYSTALS
The Alchemy of Energy Protection – *The Holistic Mudra Series Book I.*

MUDRAS for PTSD
The Alchemy of Energy Protection – *The Holistic Mudra Series Book II.*

YOUR SPIRITUAL PURPOSE
Intentions and Choices – *The Holistic Psychology Series Book I.*

The Holistic Mudra Series

MUDRAS for YOUR HEART
8 WEEK GUIDEBOOK

HEAL Your LOVE MATRIX
SABRINA MESKO
Author of International Bestseller HEALING MUDRAS

Book Three

The material contained in this book has been written for informational
purposes and is not intended as a substitute for medical advice,
nor is it intended to diagnose, treat, cure, or prevent disease.
If you have a medical issue or illness, consult a qualified physician.

A MUDRA Hands™ Book

Published by Mudra Hands Publishing
an Imprint of

ARNICA PRESS
www.ArnicaPress.com

Copyright © 2018, 2023 Sabrina Mesko

Written by Sabrina Mesko
Illustrations by Kiar Mesko
Photos by Mara
On the Cover: MUDRA for Nurturing Your Heart

Manufactured in the United States of America
ISBN: 978-1-955354-36-3

All rights reserved. No part of this book may be reproduced or transmitted in any form or by any means, electronic or mechanical, including photocopying, recording, or by any information storage and retrieval system, without the prior written permission from the Publisher.

NO AI TRAINING: No portion of this work may be used for training artificial intelligence without written permission from the author. Any use of any part of this publication to "train" generative artificial intelligence (AI) technologies to generate text is expressly prohibited.

A Happy Heart is Your Birthright!
Love is the Purpose, Cause and Meaning of all Your Lifetimes,
Find It and Cherish It Forever…

TABLE OF CONTENTS

Introduction – What is your Love Matrix? 13
How to Use this Book 15

I. About Mudras ~ HOW TO PRACTICE 17
Mudras in Ancient Times 17
What are Mudras 17
How do Mudras Work 18
Aura, Chakras and Nadis 18
Healing Breath 19
Posture & Eyes 19
Meditation 20
Concentration 20
Visualization 20
Affirmations 21
How long should I Practice? 22
Mudras and Mantras 22
Your Hands and the Cosmos 23
Benefits of Your Mudra Practice 24

II. Week One – YOUR LOVE MATRIX 27
Love is the teacher of life 29
Your Love Matrix – Chakra Review 30
Your singular understanding of love 33
Love in your childhood 34
Your unique experience of a "normal" life 35
Your early family years – the golden example 36
Challenges offer growth 38
Your first love — traces of past-life love 39

The Love Matrix Chakra scale 42
The golden thread in your love relationships retrospective 44
Choices, expectations and consequences 45
You, love and fear 47
Confusing signals 48
Your mission 50
Your Assignment 51
Your Workspace 52
MUDRA for Developing Meditation 56
MUDRA for Emotional Balance 57
MUDRA for Self-Reflection 58
MUDRA for Taking Away Hardships 59
MUDRA for Releasing Negative Emotions 60
MUDRA for Self-Healing 61

III. Week Two – YOUR MIND AND LOVE 63

Learning from your past 63
The role of your mind in love 65
Fear and your mind 66
Your fears when you are single 68
Questions of your past to create your future 70
Fears in a relationship 72
Finding courage 74
Who are you in a love relationship 75
Contentment 77
Inner peace 79
Self-confidence 79
Self-reliance 80
Can you trust yourself? 82
What do you want? 84
What is your offering? 85
Your Assignment 86
Your Workspace 87
MUDRA for Mental Balance 91
MUDRA for Overcoming Anxiety 92

MUDRA for Tranquilizing the Mind 93
MUDRA for Facing Fear 94
MUDRA for Preventing Stress 95
MUDRA for Self-Confidence 96

IV. Week Three – YOUR HEART AND LOVE 99
Your natural frequency level and love 99
Forgiveness 102
Healing old wounds 103
Heart and mind – the unlikely partners 105
Rescue yourself first 108
Recognize your heart's longing 109
Vulnerability and attraction of an open heart 111
The empowered heart 112
Making space in your life and heart 112
Your Assignment 114
Your Workspace 115
MUDRA for Healing a Broken Heart 120
MUDRA for Help With a Grave Situation 121
MUDRA for Opening Your Heart 122
MUDRA for Love 123
MUDRA for Happiness 124
MUDRA for Uplifting Your Heart 125

V. Week Four – YOUR SOUL'S JOURNEY OF LOVE 127
The deeper needs of your soul and heart 127
Your soul path and love 133
Your ancient relationships 136
Recognize your past loves 138
Your soulmate 141
Your Assignment 143
Your Workspace 144
MUDRA for Nurturing Your Heart 149
MUDRA for Trust 150

MUDRA for Self-Identification 151
MUDRA for Powerful Insight 152
MUDRA for Willpower of Manifestation 153
MUDRA for Receiving Universe's Law 154

VI. Week Five – YOUR LOVE RELATIONSHIP 157

What to do, if the two of you are very different. 161
Come rain or shine 162
Love and other dimensions 164
Your merged energy fields 165
Love and perfect timing 167
The beginning rules and habits 169
The creation of energy components 172
Rose colored glasses 173
Yes, people change …when they are ready 175
Communication – the golden bond in a relationship 176
The consequences of silence 178
Your Assignment 180
Your Workspace 181
MUDRA for Contentment of Your Heart 186
MUDRA for Balanced Speech 187
MUDRA for Patience 188
MUDRA for Wisdom 189
MUDRA for Balancing Yin & Yang 190
MUDRA for Two Hearts 191

VII. Week Six – HEALING PHYSICAL LOVE 193

Energy shifts and cellular imprints 194
The power of subtle energy in intimacy 196
The timeless cord 197
The ancient issue of trust 198
The congested energy field of friction 200
Detaching the cord 201
The honest state of your relationship 203

Recognizing old habits and conquering triggers..204
Resolving conflict and healing..206
Misuse of physical intimacy..207
Merging of your energy fields 208
Your physical connection and spirituality..209
Your Assignment..210
Your Workspace 211
MUDRA for Feeling Your Energy Body..215
MUDRA for Creativity...216
MUDRA for Diminishing Worry 217
MUDRA for Inner Security..218
MUDRA for Sexual Balance...219
MUDRA for Rejuvenation..220

VIII. WEEK SEVEN – ALIGNING HEARTS AND MINDS..................223
The great gateway between your mind and heart..228
Synchronizing and purifying your minds 230
Listening..232
Speaking ~ verbal communication 233
Sharing...235
Reaching out...236
Adapting..236
Compromise and boundaries..237
The heart...238
Your Assignment..241
Your Workspace 242
MUDRA for Calming Your Mind 246
MUDRA for Powerful Energy 247
MUDRA for Inner Integrity.. 248
MUDRA for Empowering Your Voice...249
MUDRA for Power of Projection..250
MUDRA for Relaxation & Joy 251

IX. Week Eight – AWAKENING YOUR SPIRITUAL LOVE 253
Attune your spirits 258
Acceptance 260
Awareness 261
Transformation 262
Find your karmic purpose 264
Recognize your soul contract 266
Overcome Earthly limitations 267
Ascension of soul union 268
Your Assignment 271
Your Workspace 272
MUDRA for Divine Worship 276
MUDRA for Illuminating Your Heart 277
MUDRA for Evoking Your Intuitive Voice 278
MUDRA for Heightened Awareness 279
MUDRA for Universal Energy & Eternity 280
MUDRA for Victory 281

MUDRA INDEX 282

About the Author 285

Introduction – What is your Love Matrix?

Welcome to this beautiful healing journey for your heart. Love is the singular most important aspect of your life. No matter what kind of worldly riches or success you're pursuing or achieving, it all means absolutely nothing, if you don't experience love.

We long for love so fiercely from beyond this Earthly existence, that it brings us back countless times. It may seem there are other reasons for our continued return to this Earthly plane, but nothing can compare to the indestructible power of love.

Love has so many manifestations, expressions and nuances, it can hide in plain sight and scream in absolute silence. Love is not tangible, it is not captured in a diamond or a house, it can't be evaluated, bought, kept in a box and preserved. Love is invaluable and eternal.

When you enter this life, you are born into a certain set of circumstances. You learn about love in endless possible configurations. The love between your parents, their love for you, love of family, larger social environment, your country of birth and residence, and finally your experience of romantic love, defines and affects your perception of what love is. If you learn to feel the love within your heart freely, wholly and openly, that is all that truly matters.

> **Your love matrix is the unique combination of information, perception, experiences and your understanding of love. It is your love template, a subtle energy pattern of past and current lifetimes, that belongs to only You.**

Your Love Matrix remains with you throughout your life and gathers new information, which causes changes, shifts, growth and exposes weakness, fear and challenging aspects of your evolutionary process. Whenever you experience a new kind of love, such as love for a child, your Love Matrix takes on a new form. Since we are made of frequency, it is clearly perceivable that this Love Matrix holds a certain subtle energy information that others can feel and sense, but not necessarily see. We are all a part of an incomprehensibly immense matrix within yet another larger matrix, all interwoven and interconnected. Understanding the role of your own frequency field amidst this grand-scale maze is of greatest importance, because the most important project of your life is you. Knowing, understanding and loving yourself is the first step. Next comes the intimate heart-centered interaction with your chosen mate.

The simple yet complex purpose of this book it to know and understand your heart. Once you heal your heart, the great gateway between the lower material plane and the higher frequency field opens and your love becomes unstoppable.

The heart is the center of your being, the seat of your soul. Its delicate subtle frequencies are highly magnetic and perceptive. They send out signals to your soul mate and aim to reconnect again and again. The human experience of love offers spiritual evolution, but also causes suffering and pain. But love itself is never pain. Following your heart and finding love through lifetimes requires bravery, courage, devotion, sacrifice, patience, compassion, tolerance, loyalty, kindness, respect and resilience. Giving up on love means giving up on life. Love can find you anywhere in the world. No matter how young or old, love will always reconnect you to the soulmates that share your heart's story.

I hope his books helps expand the awareness of your beautiful heart, so that you may experience happiness in every possible way. Understanding yourself will help you understand others. Loving yourself will make it possible to love others. What is required is your complete faith and trust in Divine love, the greatest power of all.

And if for whatever reason love seems to have eluded you until now, never doubt in knowing, that you are loved beyond measure. Keep the faith that love will find you, perhaps when you least expect it. And always remember that the Divine Power, Universal Light, or your God, loves you beyond imagination. It is with you every heartbeat and remans so beyond this short Earthly journey. Love is eternal, as is your soul.

My dear Spiritual Voyager, I hope you will enjoy this journey with a happy heart…
Sabrina

HOW TO USE THIS BOOK

Mudras speak the language of love better than countless words, and clearer than any musical instrument. They carry the ancient power to uplift and transport you into a state of harmonious bliss, and are irreplaceable in helping you heal the wounds of your heart.

This book will heal your heart, regardless where you are in your love or your relationship status. The journey will transform and purify your own experience of love and all its complex nuances. Before you can attract, experience, and cultivate a fulfilling and harmonious love relationship, you need to be aware of who you are and what your heart needs and desires. On this eight-week intensive journey, you'll discover the hidden, forgotten secrets of your heart, so you can heal, open up and magnify your ability to give and receive love.

Each chapter will take you through specific steps to help you recognize and understand your Love Matrix. During this fascinating journey you will decipher and eventually harmonize this invisible map that affects every singular aspect of your life. You are a fascinating being, with unique experiences, needs and desires. Your ability and longing for love is what defines you and shapes your life.

Love is not something planned. The Universe sends it your way when you least expect it. How you navigate thru the experience, how much courage, fear, affection or detachment you exhibit, will influence and play a crucial role in all relationships of your life. Love is the most essential human emotion. If you distance yourself from love, you'll be roaming thru the hallways of denial, sadness, loneliness and loss of joy for life. Exploration, openness and the ability to receive as well as give love, will open up the gateways to the love you deserve, desire and long for.

Every step of this heart healing journey applies to you, regardless of your unique situation. If you are single, you will examine your general disposition, fears and expectations in love relationships. You will heal old wounds, make space for new love, and gain wisdom and practical tools to navigate thru your vulnerabilities. Reviewing your past love experiences and unique circumstances that made you who you are, will help open up your heart's compartments that are locked up. Perhaps you feel too sensitive, frightened, or in denial about what contributed to your past unfulfilling experiences. Now you will discover the purpose of these lessons. Taking responsibility for your choices, honest review of your expectations as well as offerings, will reveal valuable clues. Now it's time to regroup, realign your energy body, and establish a healthier, more balanced pattern to attract your future, beautiful and fulfilling love relationship.

If you are in a relationship, this journey will offer powerful tools to examine your contribution to any challenging dynamics that you are facing. You will learn to create a neutral space for growth and healing in a new direction that is healthier and more fulfilling for you and your partner. Recognize your choices that lead you to where you are. Remember, disharmony offers an opportunity for improving and overcoming challenges. Fine-tuning your compatibility thru various life changes and shifts is essential. Deepening your love is the reward. Finding spiritual synchronicity is the ultimate aim.

A long-term relationship will undoubtedly encounter numerous transformations and necessary adjustments, and by conquering the differences and mastering the reinvention of new balance together, your bond will grow stronger, and your mutual love frequency will ascend higher.

If you are in a new relationship, it is an important time to immediately recognize and remedy any possible undesirable or incompatible aspects, consciously communicate your needs, and balance both of your hearts in a newly created, equally proportioned dynamic. Fearless honesty from the beginning will promote longevity and help you overcome seemingly insurmountable differences. Where there is love and a will, there is certainly a way.

As always, Mudras offer an incredibly powerful tool for positive transformation, regardless of your current relationship and love situation. They require nothing more than a few minutes of quiet time, sitting in peace, placing your fingers in various beautiful Mudra positions, and connecting with your higher self. This will transport you into an entirely different energy space and even the most challenging feelings will diminish within minutes. You will enter a new dimension of inner calm, understanding and higher love.

Mudras hold the key to experiencing unconditional and highest manifestation of love. Practice them daily and unveil the ancient mysteries and secrets of your heart. Mudras carry all the answers you'll ever need. All that is required is discipline, and an open heart.

I. ABOUT MUDRAS
HOW TO PRACTICE

Mudras in Ancient Times

Mudras originated in ancient Egypt over 5000 years ago and were used by High Priests and Priestesses in sacred healing rituals. Mudras seem quite easy to do, but are immensely powerful and effective when practiced correctly and with precision. There are countless examples of Mudras and hand gestures in iconic figures, sculptures and depictions from all continents of the world. Mudras are truly universal and can be found in every culture on Earth. In addition to advanced work with Mudras, the Priests and Priestesses of Ancient Egypt used numerous other sensory healing modalities such as crystals, advanced healing sound frequencies, color therapy and aromatherapy. I have written about the ancient healing Mudra techniques combined with various modalities in my *Holistic Mudra Series* and online mentorships. However, in this book, I share with you the specific transformative effects of Mudras for your Heart and healing your Love Matrix.

What are Mudras?

Mudras are sacred ancient healing hand gestures that use various intricate positions of fingers, hands, and arms. They carry very specific power activating formulas and can be used with ease, accuracy and assured success. Mudras are clear, simple, yet inexplicably powerful tools for self-healing and empowering your overall physical, mental, and emotional state of well-being while magnifying your spiritual attunement. They are ancient codes to help you recharge, redirect, and reconfigure your subtle energy patterns.

How do Mudras Work?

From an energy anatomy perspective, Mudras work with precision of hand and finger placement. Our fingertips are connected to countless subtle energy currents – Nadis, that affect our entire physical, mental, emotional and energy body. Mudras are very easy to do, and can be practiced by anyone who can move their fingers, arms and hands. Simply by joining your fingertips in specific combinations, you are directly affecting, opening, cleansing, recharging and reactivating your subtle energy currents and Chakra centers. Proper Mudra hand placement is of utmost importance, specifically in relation to your body. A Mudra held above your head will affect you differently than the same Mudra positioned in your lap. Without following these very particular hand and body related placement descriptions, Mudra practice is incomplete and often ineffective. In addition, Mudras have to be practiced with proper breathing techniques to help facilitate and expedite the healing process and the subtle energy movement. Mudras are excellent for unblocking and eliminating congested energy clusters within your subtle body.

Aura, Chakras and Nadis

Your Aura is a highly perceptive yet invisible subtle energy field and sensory engine that is acutely sensitive to outside stimuli of your immediate environment. Along your spine are seven powerful energy centers, called Chakras. In their optimal state, they are spinning in a clockwise direction. These dynamic vortexes of energy affect every aspect of a specific physical region. They affect your physical health as well as mental and emotional disposition. In addition, your Aura contains 72.000 invisible energy currents called Nadis, running through your body, like subtle energy "veins". They are an intricate part of your highly sophisticated energy field and determine your general state of wellbeing.

In addition to the seven main Chakra qualities, there are also smaller Chakras in the palms of your hands and soles of your feet. Usually the right hand is on the receiving end of subtle energy, while the left hand is naturally of more giving nature, since it is closer to your heart. The right side of your body is under the influence of the Sun, while the left side is under the influence of the Moon. As a result, the right hand affects one's mental and logical perception and is reflection of your masculine nature, while the left hand expresses your intuitive, emotional, feminine side. This placement is part of each person's subtle energy field. The ability of giving and receiving subtle energy can vary depending on the individual.

A highly sensory aware and intuitive person may be able to use both hands for intentional subtle energy transmitting, sharing, scanning, reading, healing, as well as receiving.

Healing Breath

Another very important aspect of Mudra practice is proper breathing. It has an immediate connection to your emotional state. You breathe differently when you are tired, stressed, pessimistic or when you are excited, happy and peaceful. When practicing controlled breathing, you will immediately calm down and center your entire being. During the Mudra practice, the inhalation and exhalation should always be practiced thru the nose and remain centered at the solar plexus region. Place both palms of your hands on your stomach area and feel it expand with each inhalation and contract with each exhalation. Mudras are most often practiced in a slow, long and deep breathing rhythm.

Occasionally when so noted, you may use the fast, short breath of fire, which works under the same principles, but at a faster pace. With the breath of fire, the focus is on a more forceful exhalation, generated with a strong contracting movement of your stomach muscle. Always use your own judgment in regard to your breathing tempo, and remain comfortable during your Mudra practice. If needed, return back to the long, deep breathing to complete the recommended three-minute Mudra exercise. Remember, your breath holds the delicate balance between your physical body and your Soul. It keeps you alive, connected and present in this world and impacts every second of your life.

Posture & Eyes

The proper posture during Mudra practice is essential. A comfortable position with a straight back will allow all your subtle energy centers - Chakras and Nadis, to open up and function at their best capacity. Your shoulders should be in a fixed position and must not move during your breathing. The only motion is the expanding and contracting of your rib cage, accompanying each breath. During the Mudra practice, it is best to close your eyes, and gently direct the gaze towards the Third eye center. You can also keep them half open and lightly look over the tip of your nose. You may look into the middle-far away distance and relax the eyelids. Never force your fingers, hands, body or your eyes into a painful or uncomfortable position.

Meditation

During and after your Mudra practice, you will find yourself in a state of deep meditation. It will fell natural to remain still, and enjoy the elevated state of consciousness. It is most beneficial to take advantage of this most receptive and potent self-healing state. Continue with your long, deep breathing and allow you mind to settle into a most peaceful and serene demeanor of complete stillness. There are many types of meditation and you can use Mudras in combination with various meditation techniques. I suggest you do not preoccupy yourself with what you are supposed to experience, but simply allow the natural process to override any restless inner dialogue. Meditation is essential for cultivating your daily inner-calm and will greatly help you overcome various challenging situations. Approaching life with tranquility and a deep connection with the Divine will assist you in leading a happier and healthier life.

Concentration

Firmly hold your mind on a specific desired topic and direct your closed eyes towards your Third Eye area. Gently look slightly upward and direct your gaze far into the distance. That is your focus point where you can penetrate through the limited perception and glimpse into the higher realm of infinity. If you need an answer to a specific question, inquire your Higher consciousness. Only a clear question can receive a clear answer. Do not overanalyze. If you receive no answer, let go, and know that in due time your question will be answered.

Visualization

Your mind is an extremely powerful instrument. With the practice of Mudras and meditation you will learn to bring your mind into a state of absolute stillness and focus. You can practice visualization to help envision a healthy state of your body, a serendipitous circumstance, or a favorable outcome of an event. By visualizing a calming and healing environment, you can transform your well-being, reduce stress, and improve your overall health. Visualization is equally important when you desire to attract love and abundance. Seeing yourself successful in your mind will attract circumstances and people who will help you succeed. Visualization is very easy and can be practiced anywhere. Mudra practice is an excellent opportunity to visualize the desired outcome. For example, when practicing the Mudra for Protecting your Health, visualize your body surrounded by vibrant restorative energy, filling you with brightest healing light. Create a powerful sphere where you can manifest your aspirations.

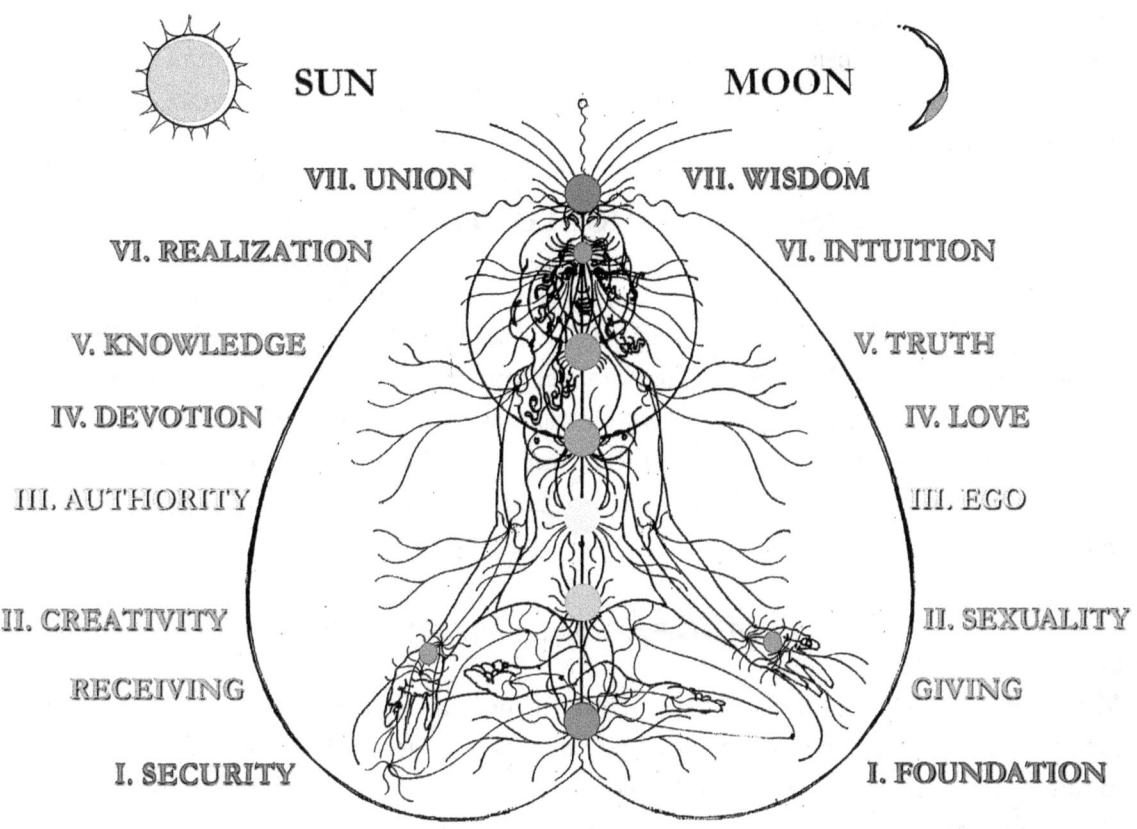

Affirmations

During the Mudra practice your mind becomes receptive and open to positive input. This is an excellent time to consciously establish a positive inner dialogue, and use an affirmation of your choice. You may say the affirmation out loud before or after the Mudra practice, or repeat it in your mind during the entire exercise. Affirmations are always practiced with an openness that allows the Universe to bring about your wish, while you make an honest effort to help this become a reality. However, once you have done your part, allow the Universe to manifest the fulfillment of your desire in whatever way is best for you, and the higher good of all. Choose affirmations in a most positive sense and avoid using any negative words. Affirm a positive outcome, a happy joyful state, optimal health and general optimism about your life. Repeat every word with true conviction, reflect on the meaning of it, while consciously embedding it into your mindset so that it becomes part of your healthy belief system and thinking pattern. A most powerful affirmation is your expression of gratitude. It carries wide reaching positive effects on all of your life circumstances. No matter how dire your situation, if you insist on finding elements you are grateful for, your effort will quickly overpower negative thought patterns in your mind. Your gratitude will attract positive and new energy into all areas of your life.

How long should You Practice?

Each Mudra needs to be practiced at least three minutes. Allow two additional minutes for sitting in stillness and meditation. As little as this may seem, do not underestimate the power of Mudras. When you develop a regular practice you will feel the positive effects faster and stronger. A longer practice option is eleven minutes for each Mudra. You may practice as many Mudras as you wish. A combined thirty-minute daily Mudra and following meditation practice is an excellent and most beneficial routine. Ideal practice time is in the morning or before going to sleep at night.

Mudras and Mantras

Mantras add a deeply transformative power of healing sound vibrations to your Mudra practice. Mantras resonate within your body in a most potent way. The hard palate in your mouth has fifty-eight power points that connect to your subtle body's energy meridians and affect your entire being. By singing, speaking, or whispering mantras, you are activating these energy points in a specific order and pattern that has a harmonious and healing effect on your physical, mental, emotional and spiritual body. The sound frequency resonates with each chakra and each cell of your body. The ancient science of mantras thus helps you reactivate and properly realign your chakras and nadis. In addition, mantras magnify your concentration, and are profoundly effective in stilling your mind. For example, when singing OM, you are affecting your entire body beginning at the First and ending at the Seventh Chakra. For a clear demonstration of the harmonious effect of sound on your body, take a long, deep breath and slowly sing A-E-I-O-U-M. Feel the sound as it travels from your lower spine and ends with powerful vibration of MMM in your forehead. The healing frequency of this sound realigns your entire body. Combining mantra and Mudra practice facilitates an experience of multidimensional healing. This technique activates your extra sensory abilities to help you recognize and work with the finest subtle frequencies that we obviously can't easily see or hear. As you sing Mantras that apply to each Mudra, consciously perceive the frequency of your own voice, traveling from your throat towards the hands and back. Feel the harmonious resonance escalate and charge you with vital life force.

Your Hands and the Cosmos

In addition to revitalizing your entire energy body, Mudras offer impressive benefits to accelerate your mental abilities, balance your emotions and elevate your state of consciousness. This specific effects occur when selected fingers are joined or kept apart, hands and palms turned in various directions, and each Mudra placed correctly in relation to your body. As I mentioned previously, Mudras are not isolated gestures, disconnected from your body's physical posture. All details such as the height and direction of the pointed fingers and palms are of the greatest importance, especially when your aim is to eliminate a challenging mental obstacle or increase a desired ability, improve a weakened state or develop and activate special gifts.

Our physical body also experiences a fascinating impact of the solar system. The right side of the body is ruled by the Sun, the male and mental aspect, and the left side is under the influence of the Moon, expressing your feminine, emotional energy. Furthermore, each finger relates to a specific planet, creating intricate network of interconnected triggers in your disposition, strengths, weaknesses, challenges as well as special abilities and gifts. This is one of the reasons why it is of significant importance which fingers connect and which hand is on top of the other, as well as where they are held in relation to your body.

Planetary Influence on Your Fingers

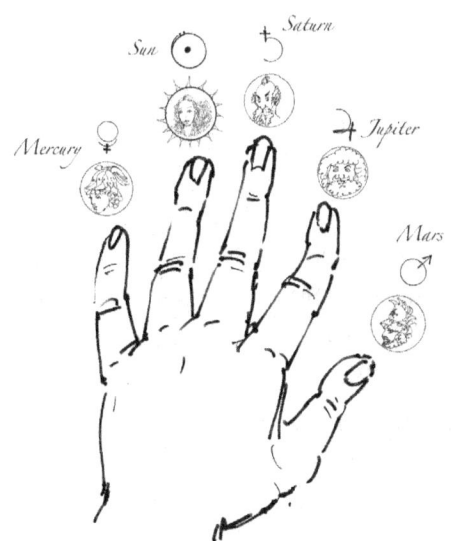

Thumb ~ MARS GOD, WILLPOWER, LOGIC, EGO
Index ~ JUPITER KNOWLEDGE, WISDOM, SELF-CONFIDENCE
Middle finger ~ SATURN PATIENCE, EMOTIONAL CONTROL
Ring finger ~ SUN LOVE, HEALTH, VITALITY, LIFE ENERGY
Little finger ~ MERCURY COMMUNICATION, CREATIVITY, BEAUTY

BENEFITS OF YOUR MUDRA PRACTICE

Emotional and mental states continuously transform and shape your energy body in response to environment, other people and events that occur in your life. You may have a mentally, emotionally or spiritually challenging day, which won't necessarily display in your physical appearance, however your subtle energy body will absorb the disruptive energy and you will feel the consequences. Likewise, you could be going through an emotionally stressful situation, which won't visibly affect your physical body, but will definitely affect your energy body.

If these dynamics continue, your physical body will eventually display dis-ease as a result of long-term stressors on finer energy levels. You won't be able to ignore your issues and keep up the facade forever. If your everyday challenges are considerable, your subtle energy body will need to compromise as well as substitute for your energy depletion. Proper practice of Mudras will help release negative energy, limit the onset of disease and promote a healthy overall functioning. The beneficial effects will magnify with regular practice.

Mudras work on the finer, subtler energy levels that are invisible to the human eye. As a result, the benefits of Mudra practice are multi layered and reach far beyond simple physical improvements.

During Mudra practice, you are connecting the energy currents from two opposite poles of the right and left side of your body. This creates an energy surge, opens up blocked nadis and increases vital energy flow for regeneration and vitality.

In complex cases with long-term challenging emotional, physical or mental issues, we need to apply Mudra Therapy™ principles, which I describe in my book MUDRA THERAPY, *Hand Yoga for Pain Management and Conquering Illness.*

At the core of any self-improvement or self-help healing modality is the need for proper evaluation about the source and deeper nature of your challenge. Simply using the *Mudra for help with Stress* will help temporarily, but will be less effective for a long term solution, unless we eliminate the source of stress and disengage in stressful situations or dynamics. Finding and eliminating the source of stress is the crucial and deciding factor.

Similarly, *Mudra for a Healthy Diet* won't do you any good, if you continue to indulge in unhealthy eating patterns. In short, there is no escaping the need to find and address the core issue of your challenge. Once that is established, you can apply Mudras that will help you overcome, reprogram and discontinue unhealthy behavior and replace it with new and healthy habits.

Finally, when specifically using Mudras for your Heart, it is essential that you recognize and identify your Love-Matrix and consciously release any negative patterns that may have been established recently or in your far-away past.

By following the intricate healing process of your subtle energy Love-Matrix structure, you will be able to recode your functioning habits and eliminate programs that are detrimental to your ability to give and receive love and enjoy fulfilling, harmonious love relationships. The newly restructured Love-Matrix will uphold an independent, balanced energy field that will resonate with your perfect counterpart and magnify your individual vibration potency. Like attracts like and once your own field is optimized, you will attract and experience the optimal physical, mental, emotional and spiritual synchronistic manifestation of love.

> **MUDRAS ARE IDEAL FOR THE PURPOSE OF HEALING, NURTURING, EVOLVING, AND ELEVATING YOUR INDIVIDUAL FREQUENCY AND ESPECIALLY YOUR LOVE MATRIX.**

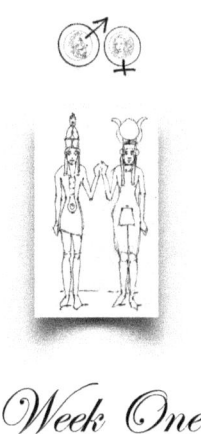

Week One

II. YOUR LOVE MATRIX

What is life without love, passion, fire, and pursuit of your heart's interests? Love comes in countless forms, it supports the engine of life, gives breath to your lungs, smile to your face, glow to your eyes, and the beat to your heart.

And even if you are a loner, and have convinced yourself that you are just fine without a love relationship, there must be another kind of love that sustains you…and it may be as simple as the love you receive from your darling pet, but it's still love. It may not be romantic love, but it is in fact love. When you cease to love, you vanish.

LOVE SURVIVES THROUGH DEATH, TIME, SPACE AND REBIRTH.

Love is immortal, the greatest power of the Universe, the most potent and effective healer of all sorrow, pain or grief. But when we lose love, it causes precisely that.

Love is a teacher. It teaches you about happiness and pain, give and take, right and wrong. And often it forces you to face the harsh reality, unfulfilled love can wound you with its sharp edges, and denied love crushes you with the weight of the loss. When love strikes with its penetrating incision, it forces and dares you to open up, so you can feel the hypnotic sting to your core, in the softest, most vulnerable and unprotected parts of you. Love reshapes your life and eventually your destiny.

Love changes your life. In order to have a chance to love, you must be willing to risk it all. And usually when you do that, you will get hurt. At least once, or twice, or three times too many. This may frighten you away, make you shy and resigned, that you'll never dare and go near that edge again. And yet, if you want to catch the magical wave of love, you must learn how to swim out into the wild ocean, jump off the cliff, do the sky dive without a parachute that guarantees a safe landing. If you avoid the risk and play it safe, love will remain only a faraway unfulfilled dream.

But when you jump into the wilderness of sea, life consumes you and love catches you again. And then you remember, why you are not meant to be alone. For that moment of pure happiness, a blissful, profoundly deep and unmistakable understanding emerges, that all that really matters in life is love. Truly, it is so.

LOVE IS EVERYTHING AND EVERYTHING IS LOVE. AND NOTHING ELSE CAN EVER REPLACE OR COME CLOSE TO IT.

This book will take you on a deep inner journey of self-exploration, to help you understand and de-cypher your unique love disposition and rare *love key* combination that you possess. This unique *heart formula*, reveals your actual life purpose, your inclinations and ability to receive and give love.

Without knowing your heart, you will never truly grasp the puzzling mystery of life. You may aimlessly wonder over the entire globe, searching for that secret answer. But unless you get to know yourself, you will never find what you are searching for. All mysteries lie within. And I don't mean within your head…but within your heart, the center of your soul's expression.

Never knowing what your heart needs, wants and desires, is a waste of life. Never daring to love is a waste of human experience. You would miss the entire point. The main part of the movie. The key to the enigma of your heart. The purpose of your human experience. Love you must and love you will, and your love shall be returned.

LOVE IS THE TEACHER OF LIFE

Love will unravel you, tear off your restrictive shield, so you'll catch the spark of realization, a glimpse into the endless ocean of the deepest mysteries of your life. This is your purpose, or undoubtedly one of them. Love is carefully wrapped into your destiny, hidden under the veil of Earthly existence, cleverly camouflaged within various prearranged relationships that offer the ideal setting to learn.

It is through love relationships that you can and will experience the raw substance of life. You can't learn about these complex dynamics living on an isolated island, on your own. You only learn by interacting, exploring, communicating, opening up and exposing your most vulnerable undiscovered and precious parts. These are the rules of the human condition. Play or go away. While in this Earthly game of life, you must learn these basic rules, the invisible boundaries, the typical human habits, the honest usual and expected mistakes, and the unintentional wounds you'll receive, or cause. Only real life relationships will offer you all that.

And while you're journeying thru these waters, do not carry foolish illusions that you are the only one experiencing challenges. Every and each human being is traveling thru their journey and meeting various obstacles, perfectly designed for each one of us. And while another person's challenge may seem ridiculously easy to you, to them, it is likely so gigantic, that they can barely manage.

> **WE ARE ALL DIFFERENT, BUT THERE IS ONE LONGING WE ALL HAVE IN COMMON…TO BE LOVED AND TO LOVE IN RETURN.**

Underneath all the camouflage, all pretense and bravery, we are desperate for loving attention, even the tiniest one bit, a simple but powerful acknowledgment from a loving soul, who sees your most precious possession - your beautiful heart. The biggest mistake you can make is to pretend that you don't need love, that you're done with it, and that you've lost all hope of finding your happily ever after. That is not so.

Love is right here, it surrounds you, it lingers in every breath and permeates every thought you create. Perhaps you are just ignoring it, or are not aware of it, you don't hear it, see it and can't touch it. And therefore you are fooled into believing that it does not exist. But it does.

My words carry the vibration of love, you are reading them and simultaneously wondering about your life and love. "Is this true?" you think. "The words touch me a bit, and I can find myself in these sentences" you think, and "Yes, I need to read more about this. I need to find my love again, understand more about it, learn further, and not give up foolishly thinking that this is all there was, is, and I can go no further."

> **YOU ARE IN THE RIGHT PLACE. WHY AM I SO CERTAIN?**
> **BECAUSE YOU ARE HERE, READY,**
> **AND YOU FELT THE VIBRATION OF MY INTENTION IN THIS BOOK,**
> **AND NOW IT SPEAKS TO YOU, WHEREVER YOU ARE IN THIS WORLD.**

So just relax, let go, and enjoy this beautiful, fascinating ride.

You know what's the most amazing part? The discovery of your heart. Mudras will bring its essence out into the open and push you to the next level regardless if you are on your own, or in a relationship. You still have much to learn, further to go, deeper to comprehend what it means to experience the ascended aspects of love. And if you're unhappy in your current situation, whatever that may be, this book will help you harmonize your dynamics and find a clear path to experiencing the love you long for.

And if you are somewhere in between, struggling thru a challenging period, feeling disappointed, afraid, and convinced or resigned to thinking that you don't need love, this book is going to push you to stop lying to yourself. It's time to look into your heart and find what you are longing for. You need to know and listen to your heart. For if you won't, who will?

YOUR LOVE MATRIX CHAKRA – REVIEW

FIRST CHAKRA

Your Love Matrix in relationship to First Chakra corresponds to your disposition toward feeling security, the ability to remain grounded, being able to provide for your basic needs and independently stand on your own two feet within your love relationship. If you depend on your partner for survival, your Love Matrix will be vulnerable in this area and will overcompensate for it in other areas, where you will overextend.

You may feel obliged to be extra accommodating, adaptable or making more effort, because you feel inadequate to survive or function on your own. If you can remove all power play, stand as equals, support and protect each other's love in a natural, grounded, mutually supportive way, your Love Matrix of the first chakra will thrive.

SECOND CHAKRA

Your Love Matrix in relationship to the Second Chakra reflects your own disposition toward creativity and most importantly, your sexuality. If you feel confident and have a healthy relationship with your physical appearance, your sexuality, attractiveness, appeal, and engage in attuned love making, your Love Matrix is strong. If there is insecurity or wounds from negative past experiences, your Love Matrix will be weak, vulnerable and prone to succumb and please others. If you are unaware of your own needs, do not feel adequate, worthy, or simply lack confidence about your physique, it will be challenging to attract and maintain and equal reciprocity balance with your partner. But if you can enjoy a naturally and mutually respectful, creative, considerate, gentle, spiritual expression of sexuality with your love partner equally, faithfully and exclusively, your Love Matrix second chakra will thrive.

THIRD CHAKRA

Your Love Matrix in relationship to the Third Chakra reveals your mind, ego awareness, self-confidence, thinking patterns and ability to understand love. If you generally relate to love through logical assessment, justifications, practicality, material advantage, appraisal and mind centered explanations, your Love Matrix is too coarse to manifest, attract and nurture a warm and loving heart-centered relationship. Mind will give way to heart and the third chakra is the crucial area for overcoming the material obsession and reaching an inner equilibrium. When you learn to lighten the mental energy and soften your stance in acceptance that love requires the surrender of ego, you will be able to experience an elevated relationship, not cemented in logic, but open within your heart. When you let go of your mind's need for control and keep your logical thinking from interrupting the pure heartfelt expression of love, your relationship will flow fearlessly, confidently, fairly and honestly and your Love Matrix third chakra will thrive.

FOURTH CHAKRA

Your heart is the centre of your Love Matrix. The Fourth Chakra is where the greatest shift occurs when you cross from the ego, material and mind perception of love, into your heart. You understand the concept of compassion, kindness, unconditional love toward yourself and your partner. Giving and receiving are equally important. Sensing the true desires of your heart will reveal your soul purpose and mission. It will attract a true soulmate, a love partner that traveled with you through many lives and is here again to continue your beautiful love story. Once you are able to detach your main frequency from the lower three chakras, you are on your way to ascension of your Spirit. Your heart is the gateway to fulfilling this destiny. If you can open your heart, accept and return love to your partner generously, compassionately, equally, your Love Matrix fourth chakra will thrive.

FIFTH CHAKRA

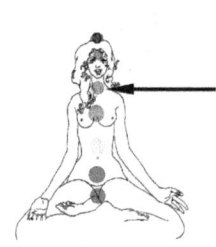

Your Love Matrix of the Fifth Chakra reveals your ability to voice your feelings truthfully, beautifully and generously. Expressing your thoughts and experiences of love directly connects with your second chakra of creativity and sexual expression. The fifth chakra is an elevated expression of your physical love. Your words, whispers, gentleness and expression of beauty will transform your partner and your relationship. You will share the ability to express love verbally in an ascended, selfless and inspiring way. If you can speak with your love partner freely, kindly, wisely and truthfully, your Love Matrix fifth chakra will thrive.

SIXTH CHAKRA

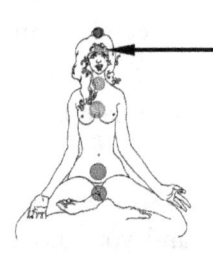

Your Love Matrix of Sixth Chakra reveals your ability to connect with your intuition. Through the experience of love, you will gain a profound understanding of the higher truth and spiritual laws. Any kind of low frequency behavior such as mind altering drugs, disruptive or addictive substances, will confuse, prevent and entirely block access to a clear heightened sense of intuition. Consciously maintaining a clear connection, free from lower three chakras and material plane disruptions, will help you attune to your partner without verbal communication. If you can intuitively connect and communicate with your hearts and minds, sensing each other's wants, needs, dreams, wishes and desires, your Love Matrix sixth chakra will thrive.

SEVENTH CHAKRA

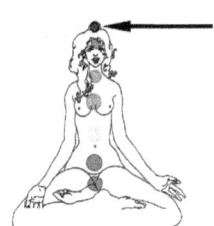

Your Love Matrix of the Seventh Chakra is a clear indicator of your ability to be attuned and consciously aware of the higher power, Universal truth, your God or the supreme being. Whatever your beliefs are, your realization of higher consciousness and your own indisputable connection with it, will elevate you into the realm of higher understanding, receiving visions, understand invisible messages, silent warnings, pure inspiration and everlasting protection. If both partners trust themselves, each other and keep unwavering faith, you will consciously merge with the universal power. You will follow and trust its guidance, understand the higher purpose and clearly sense your mission through your mutual love for each other, and your Love Matrix seventh chakra will thrive.

YOUR SINGULAR UNDERSTANDING OF LOVE

The way you understand love may be completely and entirely different from me, your friends, or anyone in this world. The way you understand love is a unique, one of a kind way.

Where is this formula to understand and fulfill your love life hiding? What influenced it to be the way it is? And who is the magical person that can unlock this treasure chest, that seems to require an expert locksmith? The way you understand and relate to love has obviously a lot to do with what you learned about it until now. And don't dismiss here one supremely important fact – your past lives.

> **YOUR LOVE EXPERIENCES FROM YOUR PAST LIVES REMAIN WITH YOU FOREVER, THEY LEAVE AN IMPRINT, AND CREATE A PUZZLE THAT NEEDS TO BE SOLVED.**

Love intertwines you with other souls that you have previously encountered and loved, or even disliked. Perhaps someone loved you and you did not love them back. Perhaps you dismissed them, carelessly wounded them, mistreated them, or made fun of them and the love for you. Or you were kind, honest, friendly and understanding, but they were less so. Whatever it was, love played a role and locked you into a complex dynamic that taught both of you important life lessons. Later on, we will learn about these incredibly complex dynamics of past life love, and how to recognize, understand, resolve or fulfill them. You past love agreements and contracts offer a deeply insightful look into the complexities of your relationships in this life. But first, we'll begin with an exploratory journey to understand your current lifetime experience of love.

LOVE IN YOUR CHILDHOOD

As always, the most influential aspect was your experience of love thru your parents. In fact the relationship between them, before you even saw the light of day, already imprinted into your cellular matrix a finely intricate model, that will always seem most familiar to you.

Whatever dynamic your parents lived thru while waiting for your arrival, you lived and experienced the same emotions on a subtle energy level, from your very beginning. A fearful expectant mother leaves the imprint of fear in her child. It is quite naive to believe that the frequency of your tiny human body could override her frequency. You may have entirely different individual frequencies, but the closeness of your physical body enveloped by your mothers, certainly affected you. This is your first information of human interaction. If the interplay between your parents was loving and harmonious, this gave you a great base, a solid beginning. If not, it prepared you for your very specific learning curve, and eventually your mission.

The concept that throughout life we unintentionally look for partners that are somehow similar to our parents, of course holds some value.

> **WHATEVER KIND OF LOVE WE RECEIVED AS CHILDREN, LEFT A DEFINING MARK ON US.**

If one of your parents was mostly absent, it is possible that you will forever try to catch up and make up for that absence with a partner, that will need to be always present. You may be overwhelmingly fearful of abandonment and will cling to your partner in unreasonable ways. This may be the case. But it is not as simple, cut and dry as that. Quite the opposite may happen as well. Perhaps because of your absent parent, you may somehow find a way to cope with this absence, resulting in feeling uncomfortable with a partner that is always present or too close. So you see, the consequences have many variables, but one thing is certain, the absence or presence of one or both parents will play an important role in your future relationships.

YOUR UNIQUE EXPERIENCE OF A "NORMAL" LIFE

If you have developed a thick, impenetrable resilience against abandonment, your partner who may like to be close and spend considerable time with you, will encounter unreasonable, inexplicable resistance. You may keep them at a distance, require much freedom, and time alone. If your partner prefers closeness and takes your need for solitude as a personal offense, you will need to work thru this, so you both understand your needs are not a direct rejection of each other, they are simply a result of your different childhood dynamics that you endured and eventually adapted to.

Let's look at it in another way. If your parent was absent, you may be used to absence, attract a partner that is absent and this may be normal for you both. If the partner needs and likes to be absent, then this may not work forever, but it may work for a short term.

On the other hand, if your parent's absence created anxiety in you, you may desire to have a partner that is very present and close. If your inclination is to experience separation anxiety when the partner is absent, it is crucial that you know and understand this basic need and challenge you have. If you don't, your expectations may be unreasonable and will create a very challenging dynamic in your relationship.

You may not know this about yourself, until the actual situation presents itself, and then it is most likely that you will not look for fault or reason for your anxiety within, but will blame the partner for their unreasonable absence, when if fact to them, this seems normal behavior.

> **YOUR REACTION AND ADAPTATION TO CHILDHOOD CIRCUMSTANCES DEPENDS ON YOUR CHARACTER AND HOW YOU DEALT WITH YOUR PARENT'S BEHAVIOR.**

If your partner is not familiar or used to you needing them around more than what seems normal to them, this may present a big problem, for they will feel suffocated while you will feel abandoned. Yes, this entire dynamic stems from your childhood circumstances.

But keep in mind, this is only one of many possibilities. There may be other reasons for your separation anxiety, whether in general sense, or just with a specific partner that involve also your past life dynamics. We will discuss these variations later, now we are looking strictly at your current life and past childhood dynamics between your parents. If your parents had a healthy, affectionate and open communication, demonstrated love freely and equally to each other and all children, you will have ideal circumstances for developing balanced expectations and behavioral tendencies in your future love relationships.

The dynamic of your parents toward you is one thing, but the dynamic between the two of them is another very important factor. If they were loving and kind towards each other, with a healthy, peaceful, affectionate disposition, you witnessed the "golden example."

> **YOUR PARENTS BEHAVIOR IS YOUR RELATIONSHIP TEMPLATE.**
> **THIS IS THE FIRST "NORMAL" FOR YOU.**

As a result, you will seek out relationships that will offer similar dynamics. Anything else won't be acceptable or feel normal to you.

YOUR EARLY FAMILY YEARS – THE GOLDEN EXAMPLE

If your parents had an abusive relationship, then sadly, that will seem normal to you. Because you have witnessed and learned to tolerate unexpected violent outbursts or mood swings, and you simply hunkered down during fights, this is how you will react to a partner that behaves similarly.

If as a child you found yourself in the role of a peacemaker, or even worse, you were the object of manipulation, tug of war, source of conflicts about your upbringing, or custody, this infused you with a sense of guilt and responsibility for any conflict. As a result, you may feel responsible for all conflicts and will behave extra leniently towards an aggressor, all in desperate attempt to reestablish peace. Depending on your character, you may go in another survival direction and feel unreasonably defensive towards anyone that criticizes you in the slightest way. The psychology of your childhood dynamics shaped your survival skills, the nature of your general disposition, and guided your response and perception of love.

The only way you can understand these fascinating and sometimes quite complex patterns, is to look deep within and remember your first impressions of what a relationship is, how people behave toward and with each other, what is said, how much affection or praise is given, and how much love is actually demonstrated. Pay specific attention if there was an unspoken price for a demonstration of love, or an inevitable pay back, perhaps an unreasonable expectation, or even manipulation. Don't forget the dynamics with siblings.

Who was standing up for you? Who set a healthy example? Who was there for you when you failed at something, when you didn't deliver something expected and felt wounded? Did you fend for yourself? Did you hide your pain? Or did you expect or force everyone to gather around you, with massive attention, and eventually fix all your mishaps? Were you so desperate for attention that you misbehaved in order to get it? Or did your siblings demand so much attention, you remained in the background and got nothing? All these details affected your overall understanding of life, love and relationship dynamics.

It is obvious and to be expected, that if you never witnessed or experienced a balanced home life, this will simply feel foreign to you. Mixed into this incredibly complex puzzle, comes your own multi-layered character that you brought into this life, and your soul's desires, tendencies and past life challenges that need to be worked thru, fulfilled and experienced. Finally, at the core and underneath it all, lie the invisible soul contracts. Nothing is as easy, everything is an unexpected, extremely complex and utterly unique blend of colors that contain all the shades of your emotional experiences up to this very moment.

> **YOUR PARENTS WERE THE GOD AND GODDESS OF LIFE FOR YOU. WHATEVER THEY DID WAS THE ONLY EXAMPLE YOU COULD OBSERVE, AND EVENTUALLY FOLLOW IN YOUR OWN LIFE.**

Your siblings and larger family completed the picture. If you are aware of unhealthy or difficult childhood dynamics, you can consciously work on and eventually overcome them, so you will not be continuing and repeating the same patterns or destructive behavior. And keep in mind, no family is perfect. And if they say they are, they are probably precisely the extreme opposite. What matters is you and your childhood family dynamics that are the base of your perception and functioning in love relationships.

CHALLENGES OFFER GROWTH

If you are unaware of a difficult childhood set-up, you may forever repeat the early life models you were shaped after, and spin in the continuous circle of disharmony and dissatisfaction.

If your parents had a happy, healthy partnership, but your life seems to be a complicated mess, then you will find answers to your puzzle in a different way. It is a bit more complex to unravel, but it can certainly be done.

Keep in mind, if your parents pretended to have a perfect relationship, but that meant that your mother kept quiet about distress, or your father tolerated unreasonable behavior by your mother, to the outside world you may have still appeared like the ideal family.

But suppressed emotions and silence are often more toxic than an open exchange, no matter how uncomfortable. In fact, relationships are quite messy and even in the best of them there may be passionate interactions and tears. There are great days and less great days, nothing is just perpetual sunshine. Life does not work that way. You may have a beautiful blissful relationship, or a period of great happiness, but eventually life will bring you a challenge, a shift, or some kind of learning opportunity.

> **WE DON'T LEARN MUCH WHEN EVERYTHING IS FANTASTIC.
> WE LEARN WHEN YOU ENCOUNTER DIFFICULTIES,
> WHEN IT GETS MESSY, UNPREDICTABLE AND UNCOMFORTABLE.**

That's a time for a test of the character. Nobody gets tested when everything is lovely, without a worry in sight.

It's like when you are riding a horse. If the horse is walking in an easy tempo, all is well, but when it breaks into an unpredictable gallop, things change in an instant. You must work harder, be stronger, hang on tight, if you want to remain in the saddle. Once you survive the challenging period, you may again return to the easy ride and most likely you will appreciate it that much more.

The growing process, the conflict and challenges in a relationship take on different flavors. Hidden frustration and unexpressed anger can be much more damaging than open warfare period, where after a short screaming match, things eventually get worked out, and everyone says their peace. Neither of two options are pleasant or comfortable. But we are all very different. Ideally, you can work thru differences in a peaceful, patient and open hearted discussion and avoid high drama. Again, it depends on the players.

Nevertheless, there are always two sides to every story, and even if one side is clearly at fault, the other side must examine their conscious participation and reasons for remaining in an unhealthy dynamic as well as their role in escalation of friction. No matter what the circumstances, situation, and countless possibilities are, in all relationships there remains a rule never to be tolerated or broken.

> **YOU SHOULD NEVER TOLERATE ABUSE, VIOLENCE, MISTREATMENT, VIOLATION, OR ANY KIND OF MENTAL, EMOTIONAL OR PHYSICAL ABUSE.**

No matter what your personal situation, I encourage you to dig deep and truly analyze the relationship between your parents, siblings and your early life and childhood dynamics. They hold the crucial key to your disposition, understanding, expectations, and acceptance of relationship dynamics, partners, love expression and interactions in general.

This self-exploratory journey is most fascinating and crucial if you want to understand and master the art of a happy, fulfilling and equally loving relationship. Even if it seems long gone, your childhood holds one of the most important keys to the happiness of your heart.

YOUR FIRST LOVE – TRACES OF PAST-LIFE LOVE

Why is this important to remember? Because at that moment in time, your soul's disposition and your character traits in relation to love manifested in their purest form. What does that mean?

However you experienced your first love, is the closest memory directly related to your last – past-life experience of love. If you felt like your life suddenly had a purpose and a meaning, this is something you brought with you.

If it made you feel out of control and you became aggressive when you did not get your way, this is your old disposition. If you disconnectedly pretended you felt nothing, or were too proud to proclaim your love, this was your old pattern. If you were afraid of your raw emotions of love, or blurted out fearlessly how you felt, and pursued your love interest in a shameless, loud and persistent manner, this is the way you were familiar with the game of love before.

Now the question poses itself: wouldn't your childhood experiences and your understanding of relationships as is related to your parent's model, dictate your first love – relationship behavior?

Not necessarily so. Your first-love experience was NOT focusing on the relationship part. It was influenced purely by the new powerful emotion of love – the greatest most healing feeling we humans can experience.

> **WHATEVER FIRST LOVE AWAKENS DEEP WITHIN YOU, CONTAINS CLEAR TRACES AND CLUES OF YOUR LIFE PURPOSE AND SOUL CONTRACTS THAT LIE AHEAD.**

Your first love was the first experience of relating to someone else outside of your immediate family, your childhood, or early life family unit. First love is usually a life altering profound experience that does not necessarily produce a fully functioning relationship, but it can nevertheless have a big effect on your life.

Therefore the experience of first love reveals more information about your far-away past, than your understanding of love as a result of your childhood experiences. Wouldn't it be logical that first love would express all your childhood scars and hardships or all unhealthy templates you may have witnessed? Again, not necessarily so.

Falling in love for the very first time is you experiencing your optimal frequency. You are in an altered, most uplifted subtle energy state. This immediately reconnects you with your far away memory of your past life love when you last felt that way and found yourself in a similar situation. Love never dies and neither does your subconscious, soul memory of it. In case of your first love, your soul memory takes over and becomes stronger than the memory of your current life's childhood. It overpowers your childhood templates, but follows the ancient pattern of how you loved in your most recent previous life.

Most often we tend to disregard the nature of our first love and describe it as foolish, childish, naive or silly. But it holds very valuable information.

THE EXPERIENCE OF YOUR FIRST LOVE IS YOUR CLEAREST SOUL FREQUENCY INDICATOR.

If you are capable of loving and ascending into a considerably higher frequency, your soul has the ability to naturally ascend to that level.

Of course, the first love most likely won't be the happily ever after. In fact that is a rare occurrence. First love has a very specific purpose. It reminds your soul of the most important emotion, your heart's longing, and re-awakens your higher frequency field. This helps you remember your life purpose, deepest desire and the essence of your heart's wish.

THE LOVE MATRIX CHAKRA – SCALE

Take a look at this scale to help you understand your past and current Love Matrix pattern in connection with the subtle energy fields of each chakra. When there is a desire for a love relationship, other factors may emerge and disrupt the flow. Your traumatic childhood or ancient, past-life love patterns may overrule your heart and pull you in a different direction, away from love. This gap between your old fear-based choices and the true desire of your heart, will eventually surface in your current relationship, causing friction. The old and unresolved energy blockages must be removed so that your Love Matrix can thrive.

CHAKRA ONE

SURVIVAL – This is the base of your love relationship. It assures your survival and feelings of safety, security and protection.
QUESTION: Does this aspect overrule other relationship dynamics for you?
PAST LIFE CHALLENGE: You feared for your survival and prioritized it above all.
CURRENT LIFE: You base your relationships on a very limited criteria.

CHAKRA TWO

CREATIVITY – This is the center of creative sexual attraction and procreation. It rules the merging of your physical and subtle energy bodies and establishes a subtle energy cord.
QUESTION: Does this aspect represent the purpose of a relationship for you?
PAST LIFE CHALLENGE: You may have been unable to control your desires.
CURRENT LIFE: Your understanding of love is limited to satisfying basic physical urges.

CHAKRA THREE

MIND ~EGO – This is the seat of power play, ego and control over the relationship.
QUESTION: Are you able to let go of control and be fearless in love?
PAST LIFE CHALLENGE: Your challenging circumstances resulted in conflict or fear.
CURRENT LIFE: Your unresolved emotions may cast a shadow over your relationship.

CHAKRA FOUR

LOVE – This is the seat of your soul, the ultimate center of love.
QUESTION: Are you able to open your heart, and give as well as receive equally?
PAST LIFE CHALLENGE: You were hurt, disappointed and have closed off your heart.
CURRENT LIFE: You may be emotionally unavailable.

CHAKRA FIVE

COMMUNICATION – This is your communication center of truth and honesty.
QUESTION: Are you able to voice your needs, wishes, dreams as well as dislikes?
PAST LIFE CHALLENGE: You suffered harsh consequences for speaking the truth.
CURRENT LIFE: You may be unable to speak and tend to suffer in silent expectation.

CHAKRA SIX

INTUITION – This is the center of otherworldly attunement and sixth sense. It facilitates the partners to communicate regardless the distance of time, space and dimension.
QUESTION: Are you longing for deep connection and a spiritual merging of two souls?
PAST LIFE CHALLENGE: You were abandoned and lost the sense of inner knowing.
CURRENT LIFE: Your carry over of deep inner doubts may interfere and prevent an open channel of communication on the subtle level of higher attunement.

CHAKRA SEVEN

DIVINE UNITY – This is the center of higher awareness of Spirit within your union.
QUESTION: Do you believe in destiny of your beautiful love?
PAST LIFE CHALLENGE: You tragically lost your love and consequently your faith.
CURRENT LIFE: You carry unfounded, persistent fear of abandonment, loss of love.

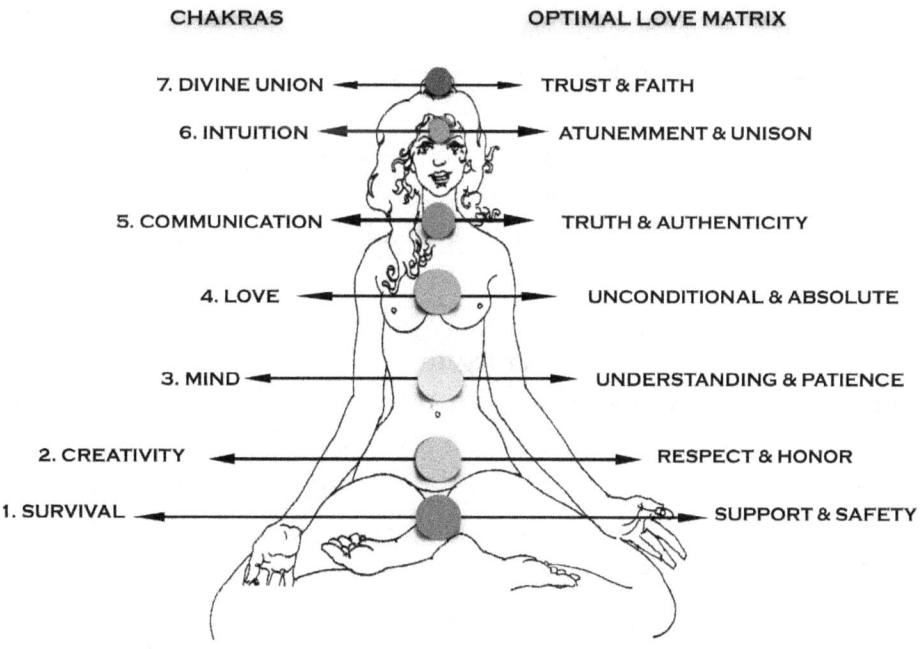

THE GOLDEN THREAD
IN YOUR LOVE RETROSPECTIVE

This is not about recalling all your relationships in a sense of remembering intricate details. This is about finding the golden tread, your love formula, the way you function in a relationship – love dynamic.

There are basically two fundamental polar opposites when it comes to your behavior in love. The two opposites are **love and fear**, the great dividers that we all encounter throughout our life. The basic purpose is to discover and see which one of those two principles dominates your personality, your actions, choices, thinking patterns, principles and certainly your decision-making. There is no clearer indicator as to how you will act in the matters of love.

The main question that presents itself is this:

> **DO YOU CONTINUOUSLY MAKE YOUR DECISIONS ABOUT LOVE AND PARTNERSHIPS BASED ON EMOTIONS OF FEAR OR LOVE?**

This is the way to reexamine your past relationships. Did you find love when you were in fear for your existence, being alone, not fulfilling expectations, own survival or pending failure? Or did you find relationships when you followed your heart, took risk of overwhelming proportions, broke the expected society rules and dismissed other people's unreasonable selfish expectations, against the odds accomplished the impossible, the daring, the risky, and the dangerous – all for the love of another.

Did you make any sacrifices for love, or did you just accept what came your way, played it safe and remained practical, logical and intellectual about it? Did you allow one painful experience to taint and discourage you from ever following and opening your heart again? Did you begin with love, but end up in fear?

What is your main motivator that wins in regard to anything in your life, is it fear or love? This will provide many answers as to why you experienced what you did, why you perhaps never experienced a deeper relationship, or why you experienced a lot of heartache. And let's be clear, it certainly does not mean that by always acting purely for love, your relationships were a happy, carefree ride.

It just indicates that up until now, the partners you selected did not function within equal love-fear principles. If you acted from your heart and ended up with a heartache, that means you did not receive love in return, so your partner was not coming into your relationship purely from love. It could have been a million other reasons, perhaps the desire for a partner out of practical, societal, or purely physical needs, but your hearts were not synchronized in a harmonious vibrational balance of love.

> **IF YOU ARE IN A GREAT RELATIONSHIP, YOUR HEARTS ARE NOT SYNCHRONIZED IN FEAR, BUT IN LOVE.**

If your relationship has very challenging issues, then one of you functions more in fear than the other, and this is causing an imbalance. And if your fear dynamics are synchronized, you are feeding off each other and sustaining the unhealthy dynamic of fear, so surely there is very little happiness, just mostly conflict and various manifestations of fear and its close relative – anger. Obviously, love and fear play a crucially decisive role in all love relationships.

Which side feels more familiar to you? This is where you energetically function. Now you can examine your past and see how these two sides interacted in your experience of love and how they brought you where you are today. This should help clarify when you wish to blame others, for now you can clearly see, that you need to take responsibility for your situations and experiences, because you attracted a partner that helped you learn a specific lesson, as a result of your choices. Now, you are ready to make a change, and create a balance of these two mighty polar opposite powers.

CHOICES, EXPECTATIONS AND CONSEQUENCES

You are like a puzzle, so learn how to disassemble and reassemble it a few times, and you'll get the point of who you are and what you're all about. You may have had luck and found a great partner, one that compliments your complex balance of love and fear. Or you may have repeatedly made poor choices with people who did not match your disposition, that's when you experienced pain and sorrow with a heartache.

This part will reveal the key about who you are. Only when you understand and know yourself, will you be able to truly understand and know someone else.

If you are a practical person, these choices may seem obvious to you. But it's not that easy. Have you had the experience of falling in love and loving someone without any swaying of your heart at all, or considering their circumstances and what's important to you in your life?

Certainly if security is extremely important to you, your partner's financial situation will overrule love. The practical part of fearing poverty will win, and you will justify your decision for the relationship. Nobody is criticizing you, we are just being really honest and clear. After all, nobody knows this except you.

But in such a case, where you chose a partner with financial stability and have perhaps sacrificed and negotiated with yourself to give up feelings of love for the exchange of security, you will always have this negotiation in your life. Realistically, you can not expect this person to fulfill all your other expectations, especially powerful feelings of love, if other factors influenced your choice. In fact, fear of lack played a decisive role. Love was a distant second, or maybe even further down the line.

You may not experience equal passion with them, as you would with a more soul energy compatible partner, however, your choice made sense to you and your particular needs at the time. In such a case, you cannot complain about missing a certain quality in your partner later on. You gave it up consciously in exchange for security. You made a choice that seemed best for you at that moment. But of course life has many moments and eventually everything catches up to us.

These are very real choices, and if your life presents you with a situation where your own financial security is the highest priority, your choice will make sense and will serve you right. But most likely somewhere in the very hidden corner of your mind and heart, you will secretly wonder how your life would have turned out, had you found a partner you loved simply by following your heart, and not material needs.

**COMPLAINING ABOUT A PARTNER
THAT LACKS SPIRITUAL AWARENESS,
WHEN YOU DID NOT CONSIDER THIS IN THE BEGINNING,
IS UNFAIR TO THE PARTNER AND DISHONEST WITH YOURSELF.
YOU CHOSE THEM BY PRIORITIZING DIFFERENTLY AT THE TIME.**

You can certainly learn to love someone with time, as has been done through the ages in arranged marriages, but most likely your relationship will provide a different actual experience.

Of course, you may choose a partner for their financial stability and under unexpected series of events their situation may shift, change, and then you will reap the consequences of your decision in a very challenging way. You may end up without love in addition to no material security.

> **IF LOVE BROUGHT YOU TOGETHER,
> YOU WILL ENDURE THROUGH ALL THE UPS AND DOWNS OF LIFE
> WITH A BETTER CHANCE OF RELATIONSHIP SURVIVAL.
> IF MONEY WAS THE ATTRACTION,
> YOUR RELATIONSHIP WILL FALL APART IF WEALTH DIMINISHES.**

These are very basic examples. One can extend this kinds of dynamics to countless other practically oriented reasons for relationships such as: power, control, societal position, career advancement, or simply a desire to have children. When any of these mentioned factors take the priority over love in a relationship, it is to be expected that eventually, you will recognize and may suffer from lack of what relationship should always be based on – love.

Not choosing a relationship based on love will always catch up to you in one most crucial aspect – there will be a lack of love. Therefore the relationship will not be a love relationship, but an asset relationship. And where there is no love, there will be no real happiness.

YOU, LOVE AND FEAR

Now, let's examine how the two opposite sides of love and fear trickle down into other elements of everyday life. Fear is connected to loss of control, lack of comfort, not having enough, competitiveness as well as greed. And let's not forget the immediate relative of fear - anger, and the ultimate source of all fears - fear of dying. There is no room for those character traits in the field of love. Love is related to compassion, kindness, happiness, gentleness, generosity, selflessness, harmony, the desire for partnership, for giving, nurturing, tenderness, sharing what you have, enjoying life's precious moments and achieving dreams together with a partner. This all belongs to love. It's a great package.

> **IN THE WORLD OF TRUE LOVE,
> YOU ARE IRREPLACEABLE.**

If you prioritize these principles, you will eventually attract a similar, compatible and loving soul. If you function in fear, you will attract a person who will also look at the relationship in a fearful, less courageous and heart loving way. If you are looking for material aspects, so will your partner, and eventually in that world, everything is replaceable, including you. This does not mean that a relationship based on pure love won't eventually shift or outgrow itself and you may have to part ways, this is entirely possible. But chances of survival and preserving what you have are certainly significantly greater than in relationship that's based on fear.

> **DO NOT TRY TO CONVINCE YOURSELF THAT YOU BELONG TO CAMP
> LOVE, IF YOU BELONG TO CAMP FEAR.**

And let's reiterate that you may have done and chosen everything with your heart and still experienced a misfortune. Perhaps fate or destined complex set of circumstances dealt you an incredibly challenging situation, where you lost your greatest love. However, as all of you who have experienced such profound disappointment know, the indescribable opportunity and fortune to have experienced true, profound love will remain with you forever. In some ways you are much more fortunate than those who never felt this kind of profound love. You know that nothing will ever replace the love you lost, but perhaps life will offer you another opportunity at a different kind of beautiful love. One should always remain open for delightful surprises from the Universe.

CONFUSING SIGNALS

There is also a very real possibility that you function well in the love principle, yet you have attracted a fear based person. How is that possible, you wonder? Well, in your subtle energy profile, there are elements that can sway you in the direction of fear. Even though you basically function from your heart, you still carry unresolved fear. Perhaps you fear that you may remain forever single or nobody will love you for you?
Or that if you fall in love again, you will get hurt?

So you may know all about heart love, but are overwhelmed from an old heartache and drowned in fear. Maybe you are enveloped by fear and the right partner cannot find you. They are deterred away from you, by your disruptive layer of fear infused frequency.

Perhaps your fear made a mark anyway, and even though you followed your heart, it was underlined with fear. And since your new partner maybe functions mainly under principles of fear, it felt like a balanced match of love. But in fact it was not. The moment crucial decisions or choices will come up, this will become apparent. Review your life choices in an honest and very objective way. What was your overall state when you embarked on a relationship? Take a look at both two principles in mind. Now you'll understand better what happened, why something occurred or why you always felt something was amiss. These are extremely valuable realizations, that no one else can do for you. Now that you understand your past choices and present situation as a result of your general disposition and the nature of your heart, you can begin finding and creating a new balance within your relationship. If you are currently alone, this is an ideal time to regroup, reposition and consciously create a new pattern.

You are not going to look at this as past mistakes and missed opportunities, you shall look at it as uncovering interesting and crucial information about yourself, so that you can recognize and break thru the imaginary self-imposed limitations. You can personally choose to consciously develop your ability to love and overcome fear. This is your goal, and no matter what your current situation, this can be absolutely accomplished. The crucial necessity is your self-realization, so you become infused with confidence and can overcome a fear based belief system that prevents you from opening your heart. This applies to you when you are single or in a relationship.

> **WHEN YOU HAVE A DESIRE TO IMPROVE CONFLICTING ASPECTS IN A RELATIONSHIP, YOU NEED TO FIRST ESTABLISH THE POSITIVE DISPOSITION WITHIN YOURSELF AND THEN SEE HOW YOUR PARTNER RESPONDS.**

If you implement your change in a subtle, peaceful and loving way, chances are they will follow your lead and perhaps together you will overcome fearful tendencies. Communication is the key, and Mudras are your solution. The personal inner balance between love and fear is an example of the countless subtle, incredibly complex dynamics that are recorded in your energy Love Matrix.

YOUR MISSION

Remembering childhood dynamics or past relationships will undoubtedly bring up a lot of emotional issues, sometimes comfortable and pleasant and other times less so. This is necessary to experience, in order to consciously reclaim your past and extract the most important grain of wisdom gained – the hidden lesson, the cleverly intertwined overall theme that may have repeated itself a few times. This is your challenging aspect that you can overcome and resolve in order to ascend and move higher in your experience of love. It will be easier for you to consciously improve, strengthen and elevate your love after releasing old conflicts, pain or confusion. In order to do so, you have to take a courageous look at those dynamics you carry and then willingly let them go. One of the biggest challenges for you will be to find and cultivate clear objectivity, not slip back into a victim mode, or refuse to take responsibility for your choices that may have not been wise. This personal review of your past experiences can be accomplished privately, on your own. Self-discovery offers a wonderful feeling of accomplishment and facilitates accelerated positive progress. Watch out for your automatic perception of people, past or potential partners, and basic relationship dynamics that are a clear result of your childhood role models.

If you were brought up to think you can't trust anyone, this will remain in your "program." If you believe that partners always have ulterior motives or want to take advantage of you, that will again persist in your program. If you naively think nobody ever tells a lie, this will linger in your program and expectation as well as assumption of others. Pay attention to your reflex answers and look at your current life situation from all possible angles, as if you were another person, and someone such as yourself was telling you their story. Be objective, non-judgmental and recognize your inhibitions, expectations or automatic exclusions and narrow mindedness. When you recognize your limited thinking pattern, you will be able to willingly let it go, extract the inaccurate past imprint and consciously shift your behavioral habits into a more self-empowering disposition that serves you better.

Every day study and practice a new weekly set of Mudras, as suggested. It will help you prepare for your transformation process of love and relationships. Observe how different you feel before and after the practice, how your perspective changes, your pent up emotions are less overwhelming, less suffocating, fears are less intimidating and sorrow is dissipating. Notice how you handle various challenges, become stronger, more conscious and don't feel like a helpless victim of challenging circumstances or your past. Every day presents new possibilities and new opportunities. You are on your way!

YOUR ASSIGNMENT

AFFIRMATION

> TO FIND LOVE IN THIS WORLD,
> YOU MUST FIRST FIND IT IN YOUR HEART.

DIARY

In order to recognize, reprogram and overcome challenging dynamics, your self-exploratory journey requires your conscious involvement and thinking process. It is not important that someone else uncovers your habits that may be unfavorable for you. What matters is that YOU find them YOURSELF. You have to discover them, understand them and as a positive consequence, a sense of deep realization will emerge. Diary work is a fantastic tool to help you track your progress, pay attention, focus and face your thoughts, inner unexpressed emotions and continuously review them later. I encourage you to keep a diary throughout this Mudra journey, answer given questions and untangle the complex story of your heart.

PROCESS

Work thru the questions, come back in a few days, see if anything changed, add it on, clarify, clean it up, and self-discover through the process.

PRACTICE

Work with the diary, answer the questions and practice the Mudras listed. Write down how you feel before and after the Mudra practice. Observe the shift in your energy field.

> **WHEN LOVE IS ABSENT, ENJOY YOUR SOLITUDE.**
> **WHEN YOUR LOVE APPEARS,**
> **COURAGEOUSLY STEP FORWARD.**
> **REMEMBER, YOU ARE MEANT TO BE LOVED.**

Your Workspace
LOVE IN YOUR CHILDHOOD

WHAT WERE YOUR CHILDHOOD EXAMPLES OF LOVE ?

Do not try to embellish how everything was glowingly perfect. Nobody has an entirely perfect childhood. There are family dynamics, siblings or events that shaped your childhood in complex, unpredictable ways. This is not about blaming your parents for your love and life challenges. This is about understanding your origins, examples you lived thru and the subtle energy imprints that remained with you until today. Write them down.

How did your mother love you?
How did your father love you?
Who gave you most love?
Who loved you unconditionally?
Did your siblings or expanded family demonstrate love?
Did your parents speak of love?
Did they demonstrate love toward each other?
What was your parent's demonstration of affection between each other?
What was your parent's demonstration of affection toward you?
Did you feel loved?
Were you ever praised?
For what?
Did you feel equally loved and paid attention to as all family members?
Was there conflict?
What replaced love?
How was love valued?
How has your childhood model of love followed you through life?

This is the Basic Love pattern that you've entered as a child.

Your Workspace
YOUR FIRST LOVE

HOW WAS YOUR EXPERIENCE OF FIRST LOVE?

Where did you meet?
How old were you?
What was going on with you at that time?
Was this a significant time in your life?
When was the moment you realized you were in love?
How did that feel?
Happy, nervous, frightened, impatient, excited, self-confident, grown up?
Did anyone know of your feelings?
Did your person of interest feel the same and returned your love?
How did they interact with you, was it pleasant or hurtful?
What and who caused it to end?
How did that make you feel?
Did you feel closure or unresolved?
Did you move-on immediately, or hope for a reunion?
Do you still carry the traces of that experience with you?

Now you understand your basic disposition to love, and perhaps even the source of deeper, unseen challenges.

LOVE CHALLENGES IN RETROSPECTIVE

What is the main thing you are looking for in a relationship?
Did you ever find it?
What did you learn from your past relationships?
Did you have a desire to find a spiritually compatible partner?
Did your partner function in fear or love?
Did you recognize and understand the difference?
Did love or fear win in your love life?
Did you send confusing signals to your partner?
Did you silently wish the partner would guess you wants and needs?

Single

What kind of partner have you attracted in your past?
Was there a repeated pattern of incompatibility?
In what areas?
What was the source of your hesitation for new a partnership?
Can you trace the cause of escalated fear, and reluctance to open up again?
Do you attract partners that are fearful or reluctant of commitment?

In a Relationship

What is the main challenge in your current relationship?
Do you see this as an old pattern that you follow?
Go back and recognize when was the first time you repeated the pattern?
How does your partner fit into this pattern?
Does it match with their own broken pattern?

You will get insight into how your past patterns affect your lack of partner, potential for a new partner, or the patterns in your love relationships today.

LAUNCHING THE HEALING PROCESS
WITH MUDRAS

We begin the practice with the basic Mudra for Developing Meditation, to help you regain inner equilibrium. This is the first step to take a pause, get centered, and re-establish your core energy vibration. Reclaiming your absolute presence and awareness will help you merge your subtle energy fields that may be disproportionately unharmonious, as a result of your specific unique Love Matrix. Merging your body, mind and Spirit, will recreate the healthy auric shield pattern, that is naturally resilient and impenetrable. Your cells remember the seed information of healthy functioning, and now you will remind your being to re-establish this healthy rhythm, and the self-healing process will begin.

YOUR PRACTICE

3 MINUTES – SHORT OPTION FOR DAILY PRACTICE
Each week, practice at least one Mudra a day for 3 minutes. Learn a new Mudra each day for six days. On day seven, practice all Mudras of that week together. Each new week, begin with the new set of Mudras, as laid out in the book. Afterwards sit still and meditate for another 5 minutes.

EXTENDED OPTION FOR DAILY PRACTICE
Each week, begin with a 3 minute practice of the first Mudra, next day add the second Mudra and so on. Your practice will extend each day for additional 3 minutes. The last day of the week, practice all 6 Mudras, this will create altogether an 18-minute practice. Afterwards sit still and meditate for another 5 minutes.

Remain disciplined with this daily practice and observe a new, pleasant feeling of inner peace that will envelop your physical body, still your mind, and soothe your heart.

The best time for Mudra practice is first thing in the morning and last thing in the evening.

LOVE AND FEAR
This can be your focus during the practice. Only you know the answers. Ask yourself:
Do I make life choices based on fear or love?
Consciously visualize living from your heart. Imagine your future life manifesting from your heart.

MUDRA for DEVELOPING MEDITATION

Sit with a straight back and keep your shoulders down, nice and relaxed. Hold the left palm open and facing the sky. Lift up your hands to the level of solar plexus and place the four fingers of the right hand on your left wrist to feel your pulse. Pressing lightly, the fingers of the right hand are positioned nicely in a straight line on the wrist of the left hand. Concentrate and completely focus on your pulse. Hands and elbows are away from your body. With each pulse-beat, repeat the mantra Sat Nam. After a minute, practice without mantra and expand your awareness to connect with the Universal heartbeat. Continue for Three minutes and relax.

BREATH
Long, deep and slow through your nose

MANTRA
SAT NAM *(Truth is God's name, One in Spirit)*

CHAKRAS
All Chakras

HEALING COLORS
All Colors

AFFIRMATION

I AM ONE WITH THE UNIVERSE

MUDRA for EMOTIONAL BALANCE

Before this practice, drink a glass of water to balance your system. Sit with a straight back and keep your shoulders down, nice and relaxed. Place the hands flat against your body, under each armpit and wrap your hands around your body as if giving yourself a hug. Keep your palms open. Close your eyes, take a deep inhale, give yourself a strong hug and lift your shoulders towards your ears for a few moments. Hold your breath, then exhale while lowering your shoulders and loosening the embrace. Continue for Three minutes, then relax.

BREATH
Long, deep and slow through your nose

MANTRA
SAT NAM *(Truth is God's Name)*

CHAKRAS
All Chakras

HEALING COLORS
All Colors

AFFIRMATION

I AM IN PERFECT BALANCE, MY HEART IS PEACEFUL

MUDRA for SELF - REFLECTION

Sit with a straight back and keep your shoulders down, nice and relaxed. Close your left hand into a fist. Wrap the right hand over the fist of the left hand. The right thumb is crossed over the left. Lift your hands and place them in front of your throat area, gently tucked under your chin. Hold for Three minutes and relax.

BREATH
Long, deep and slow through your nose

MANTRA
SAT NAM *(Truth Is God's Name, one in Spirit)*

CHAKRAS
Heart - 4, Throat - 5, Third Eye - 6

HEALING COLORS
Green, Blue, Indigo

AFFIRMATION

I STUDY AND LEARN ABOUT MYSELF, MY ACTIONS AND INTENTIONS

MUDRA FOR TAKING AWAY HARDSHIPS

Sit with a straight back, shoulders down, nice and relaxed. Close your hands into fists, while keeping the thumbs on the outside. Now swing your arms in big circles, like a pendulum. Begin with the movement holding hands outstretched to the side. Next, bend your elbows and swing fists up and forward towards you, as you inhale, then again opening your arms, stretching elbows and returning back to original position as you exhale. Left hand is going in clockwise direction, right hand in counter-clockwise direction, both fists toward you. Repeat for Three minutes and relax.

BREATH
LONG, DEEP AND SLOW THROUGH YOUR NOSE

MANTRA
HAR HARE GOBINDAY, HAR HARE MUKUNDAY
(He Is My Sustainer, He Is My Liberator)

CHAKRAS
THIRD EYE - 6, CROWN - 7

HEALING COLORS
INDIGO, VIOLET

AFFIRMATION

MY PATH FORWARD IS OPEN AND CLEAR

MUDRA FOR RELEASING NEGATIVE EMOTIONS

Sit with a straight back and keep your shoulders down, nice and relaxed. Make fists with both hands, bend your arms and bring them up in front of your heart. Cross your left arm over right while keeping your fists turned outwards. Hold for Three minutes then relax.

BREATH
LONG, DEEP AND SLOW THROUGH YOUR NOSE

MANTRA
OMM *(God in His Absolute State)*

CHAKRAS
HEART - 4

HEALING COLORS
GREEN

AFFIRMATION

I RELEASE AND LET GO
I AM FREE AND CLEAR
I AM LIGHT

MUDRA FOR SELF ~ HEALING

Sit with a straight back, shoulders down, nice and relaxed. Bring your arms up in front of your face, fingers spread and outstretched. Connect the thumbs along their length and connect the tips of the small fingers. Inhale deeply and slowly through the nose and then close off the nostrils by placing the thumb tips over them. Hold the breath for as long as you can. Release the thumbs slightly to open the nostrils and exhale. Again hold the breath for as long as possible before inhaling. Practice for three minutes.

BREATH
As described above.
CHAKRAS
Heart - 4, Throat - 5, Third Eye - 6
HEALING COLORS
Green, Blue, Indigo

AFFIRMATION

I ACTIVATE MY BODY's SELF - HEALING ABILITY

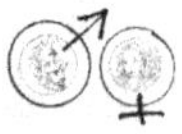

Week Two

YOUR MIND AND LOVE

LEARNING FROM YOUR PAST

Now that you've had a chance to reflect on the complexity of your fascinating life and love-journey, your newly uncovered horizon of self-knowledge is expanding. Perhaps now you can put some much needed space between your true soul-self and your various inner conflicts, created by past experiences. We all carry within our energetic make up, a detailed and exceptional library of everything that happened to us.

> **YOUR MIND REGISTERS AND REMEMBERS**
> **ALL EMOTIONS YOU EXPERIENCED, ALL VISUALS YOUR SAW,**
> **AND ALL INFORMATION YOU PERCEIVED.**

You may not remember it all precisely, even if you try to refresh and recall specific details, but no matter what, they remain part of your sensory vocabulary and play an intricate role in your understanding of life, your measure and ability to recognize pleasure and pain, joy and sorrow and conflict versus peace. These parameters are uniquely individual to you. This is what makes you one of a kind.

Now that you've uncovered your background of your own thinking process, emotional openness and spiritual receptiveness in a relationship, you are expanding the perceptive space. Suddenly, you know a bit clearer, why you are the way you are. Perhaps you can feel more compassion toward yourself and others, considering the challenges you endured, witnessed or caused. You recognize that certain things happened unintentionally, perhaps you even attracted them into your life, assuming everyone would understand your relationship expectations as you do. Relationships are about relating, sharing, and opening your life to someone else's close, intimate co-participation. It can be the most important, precious, beautiful journey you'll ever experience. But there will be lessons, surprises, expectations and disappointments. Certain aspects will work out better than you ever imagined, and others may stay unfulfilled.

> **THE MEMORY OF YOUR LOVE LIFE UNTIL THIS VERY MOMENT, REMAINS FOREVER RECORDED IN YOUR LOVE MATRIX.**

How you use this information, depends on your character and natural disposition. Do you tend to remember the good or the bad, see the glass half full or half empty, or cling to old hurt, pain and grudges forever? Or do you somehow mysteriously forget the mishaps and wrongdoings, and just remember the great, fun and beautiful side of life? This fundamental character trait is actually most important. It will decide how you sail thru life, overcome challenges, pull yourself out of impossible situations, survive while tackling your enemies, and seize the opportunities that come your way. It will also indicate how you help those in need, find solutions, answers and how you experience, act and behave thru personal relationships. Your general positive disposition will also indicate how you remember your relationships. Do you tend to over-romanticize how wonderful a past relationship was, completely erasing and forgetting the obvious serious issues that may have caused you to go separate ways? Can you objectively recognize the challenges, or do you tend to reach for the rose colored glasses, embellish the good and wash out the bad?

Perhaps you are the opposite, repeatedly dwelling on the sorrow and suffering you endured, and can't seem to remember one singular positive aspect about a person and your time together? Certainly everything could not have been all bad, or all perfect. There's always a bit of everything when it comes to love, and your own disposition will play a great role in how you experience it. Add to that the unique personality of your partner, and now you have two entirely different versions of what happened, possibly each convinced they are right. It would be wonderful, if you were both capable of cultivating a healthy ability to recognize the good, beautiful aspects, and without blame observe the challenges that occurred. Recognize the wisdom, the learning curve and the insight you gained. Then you can laugh about it later. In all these memories lies the lesson you needed. But only your mind can choose to understand, accept and incorporate the gained wisdom into your future.

THE ROLE OF YOUR MIND IN LOVE

As far as keeping track and analyzing your past and everyday life experience, your mind is a powerful player. It records and plays like a mighty orchestra to the song of your life. Your general character traits will decide how much influence over your love life is left to your mind.

If you are a mind oriented person, a big thinker, the mind is powerful and clearly at an advantage over your heart. It likes to take charge, analyze, justify, explain, and sometimes uselessly repeat the same melody again and again. If your habit is to avoid taking responsibility, your mind gladly takes over, and masterfully finds perfect excuses for you, convenient fault with others, and manages to bring you out clean and perfect, without a singular fault.

But if you lack in self-confidence, your mind can play a negative role by magnifying your shortcomings, picking at your insecurities, and sneakily blaming you for everything that ended with less than great results. It locks you up into a circle of perpetual self-blame, shrinking your confidence into a tiny marble of hang-ups. Either way, it works against your better good and spiritual progress.

If your mind is less prominent in your overall character disposition and you allow the heart to lead the way, your understanding of any experience may be more objective. Ideally, there should be an easy, peaceful balance between heart and mind, but that's not often the case. It's rather a battle for control, a full-on struggle between your heart and your mind. And the mind will fight for control every singular moment when you listen to your heart. It will wait for an opportunity for self-doubt and gallop like a wild horse running, sometimes out of control, and impossible to manage. That can only happen if you allow it to grab onto a weak emotion, and play with it. The weaker the emotion, the better and easier for your mind to take over.

If you are feeling love, and remain steady in your heart, your mind is going to have a disadvantage and will most likely lose.

> **WHEN YOU FALL IN LOVE, YOUR MIND SITS FORGOTTEN IN A CORNER WHILE YOU DON'T EVEN ASK FOR ITS OPINION.**

That's why everyone will ask you: are you out of your mind? Yes, at that moment, you are not interested in your mind. But when your heart is silenced, hidden, and ignored, your mind gets all the glory. Don't forget, your mind is a tremendous gift that needs to be appreciated and understood, but you have to learn how to use it wisely. But only your heart speaks the language of your Soul. A delicate balance must be cultivated, for you need both, mind and heart.

FEAR AND YOUR MIND

Fear is the most powerful negative emotion. Mind and fear dance a fierce tango, full of passion and persistence, aggressive possessiveness, with mighty stamina. If the drama of mind battling fear comes to the surface, you will hear a loud voice, threatening words reaching for the sky, and restless repetition of countless scenarios displaying a dark picture.

> **JUST LIKE THE MIND CAN SUCCUMB TO FEAR, IT CAN REACH FOR THE OTHER SIDE OF THE SPECTRUM, WHERE YOU AWAKEN THE STRONG WILLPOWER WITHIN AND OVERCOME INCREDIBLE CHALLENGES.**

You see, your mind can be a tremendous weapon, rescuing tool, protector and warrior. But, if left ignored, forgotten and restless, it will be up to no good, eventually bringing you down, or ruining a beautiful thing.

Let's look at fear from a perspective of energy-anatomy. The natural habitat of fear is in the Third – solar plexus area. That is the center of mind – actions, willpower, ego, anger, and of course fear, which is at the beginning and end of every negative manifestation or action. The ultimate fear of death serves as the anchor and source of all fears. The follow-up fears of dying alone, forgotten, in pain, powerless, impoverished and needy…those are serious fears.

But the truth that we all eventually die, is inescapable. And no matter how many people will sit by your side and hold your hand when you go, it will be you alone that will step thru the gates of immortality. So you see, in a way you will be alone, but it is at precisely that moment, that you may realize the ultimate truth; that you are never alone, and death is nothing to fear. You will step through the gate alone, but rest assured you will find immediate companions that await your arrival into your next dimension of existence. So the moment of aloneness is very short and filled with universal light, which is the ultimate and continuous loving companion through life and death.

The universal creative power is present always and forever. So, therefore you are never alone, even if you feel alone. You could feel alone while surrounded by thousands of admiring fans, while married with a large family, or when you are actually physically alone. Or you could never feel alone at all, even if sitting on a deserted island, seemingly on your own. When you realize this interconnectedness with the Universe, you slowly learn to let go of fear. The ground rules of fear – death and loneliness, will begin to lose their intimidating powers. If in fact you are never alone, then there is no need to fear loneliness and abandonment. Since one day each one of us will be in fact gone from this Earth, there is no point in ruining your entire life worrying about it, right?

It's like you'd go to a movie and worry about the inevitable ending. Or if you're having massive success and worry about it being over, or have a fantastic partner and worry that you will lose them. All these fears indicate a deep seated old fear from the past. Is it from this lifetime? These kinds of deep, seemingly unreasonable or unfounded fears are most likely from your past life. It is more obvious that such deep seated fear has been with you for a long while, and therefore there is no easy logical explanation for it. What can be helpful, is deep inner search and self-reflection, which will help you unravel the puzzle and cause of the fear that is haunting you.

> **ONCE YOU KNOW HOW TO RECOGNIZE AND FACE YOUR FEARS, YOU WILL IMMEDIATELY REDUCE THEM BY HALF. WHY? BECAUSE SOMETHING WE DON'T KNOW IS MUCH MORE FRIGHTENING THAN SOMETHING WE DO KNOW.**

Remember, when you watch a scary movie and someone enters the building, fearing the enemy is lurking in every dark corner? Obviously you – the viewer, are frightened because you don't know where the enemy is, you don't know how they look, and what are they going to do.

The moment you see them, the fear is arrested. It can't go any further, it just sits there. Your mind plays a huge role in how you tackle your fears. Most of all you have to be aware that you are not a helpless victim. You are and can be in charge.

This immediately shifts your stance and puts you in position of power and control. When you face the enemy frightened, they seem more frightening. When you face them fired up and resilient, you become capable of overcoming all obstacles. Think of yourself as the great warrior, who decided to come home, and be in charge again. Your reading this book is creating the perfect storm where you allow the winds of time to blow thru and wipe out everything that you don't need or like. Make space for the victorious, powerful, new, kind, lovely, light and happy mindset. At the end of the day, all it takes to get rid of the fear, is your decision to do so.

I have counseled countless individuals who battled various fears, sometimes crippling, wild, unreasonable, ridiculous, but nevertheless, very stubborn old fears. These fears were preventing them from enjoying life, and having the experience of fulfillment and everyday happiness.

> **THE MOMENT YOU LOOK AT FEAR, YOU BEGIN TO DISMANTLE IT.**
> **WITH EVERY COURAGEOUS THOUGHT, YOU MAKE IT WEAKER.**
> **QUITE QUICKLY, YOU CAN CONSCIOUSLY BLOW IT TO PIECES.**

Your mind may want to get back into the habit of fear, but with conscious decisive action to choose love and let go of fear, the old habit will soon die. You will look at your old fear with surprise how it controlled and cramped your happiness for so long. You will never take it back. You will never slip into the same old habit, because your mind will know the fear you carried has finally lost its grip on you. In fact, your fear disappeared.

YOUR FEARS WHEN YOU ARE SINGLE

When you carry old fears into a new relationships, they spoil and prevent new opportunities and suffocate your heart. You can't allow that to happen. Sometimes fear can also be a perfect excuse. You sort of hang on to the proclamation that you are afraid. This will keep you in false no-risk comfort zone, safely tucked away, excused from taking any responsibility, action, decision or stepping into something new. You may hope to evoke sympathy, pity and leniency from others, almost manipulating them into a cornered position, where no risk is required on your side, but all on theirs. In such a case, you are way too close and friendly with fear, and should honestly recognize it as a crutch, an excuse to not tackle your issues. It would be more true and fair to admit, that you are just too lazy to step forward or take a chance. You are not interested in inner character growth. Repeating to others that you were hurt and are therefore fearful, becomes really boring after a while. It is like you've made an announcement to the world and yourself that says; "I refuse to change my position and feel comfortable hiding behind my fear. I like my fear." Is that true, is that what you really want?

Well, since love and fear are on the opposite sides of the spectrum, by proclaiming your loyalty to fear, you realistically cannot expect to find love. You have made your allegiance clear and known, and now you're stuck with it. Your unresolved fears are like an old suitcase you carry around and never bother to look what's inside. Your fears may also be connected to your fresh wounds from this current life and love experiences. As a consequence you may be fearful to put yourself on the line, open up, be vulnerable again and lose it all. You may fear that precisely what happened to you before, will happen again, that you will face similar issues and challenges. And guess what? Most likely you will.

YOU WILL ENCOUNTER SIMILAR CHALLENGES IN RELATIONSHIPS, UNTIL YOU UNDERSTAND WHY YOU CONFUSE, MISREAD OR RUN FROM THE TRUE MANIFESTATION OF LOVE.

You may continue repeating the same expectation patterns, same misaligned criteria for your partners, same behavioral tendencies that do not belong into a deep loving relationship. Perhaps you will misunderstand certain actions, words, gestures or just assume they lead to what you witnessed in your childhood. Whatever it is, you will allow your fears to keep you from attracting and opening up to a new, different, healthier and more balanced experience of a loving relationship.

For example; if you are very dominated by values of the material world and judge and select your partners based on their wealth, this will keep repeating itself, until you understand that you are confusing material security with love. When you are with the love of your life, you can have more love on a deserted island living in a simple straw hut, that in a five star luxury resort where you are pampered around the clock, married to someone's bank account and feel like the loneliest person in the world.

Let us not misunderstand and make clear, that certainly one can have true love as well as riches beyond this world. On the other side of the spectrum, a person can be dirt poor and still remain in a relationship purely for survival and not love. In other words, you can enjoy material wealth and are lucky to have found true love, or you can be dirt poor and loveless.

> **LOVE DOES NOT CARE ABOUT THE WORLDLY CIRCUMSTANCES, BECAUSE LOVE IS OTHERWORLDLY.**

There are endless combinations and variations, but the question is, do you understand, recognize this, do you have a clear perception of true love, that sees beyond the Earthy trappings of this material world? If you continue to look for the same kind of partner, based on these values, this will continue to bring you the same repeated lesson, until one day you will realize that love has an entirely different value system, and has nothing to do with material wealth. In fact, love is the greatest wealth of this world.

If you are not able to offer any material comfort to a partner, does this mean that your love has no value? Absolutely not. Love is invaluable. All of us have the right to love and be loved, regardless of Earthly possessions. Love survives death and rebirth, for love is the greatest power there is. Without love you have nothing, because love is everything.

QUESTIONS OF YOUR PAST TO CREATE YOUR FUTURE

If you are single and afraid you will stay alone, instead of giving up, ask yourself:
What is your dominant fear?
Is it that you may again experience disappointment, rejection, and hurt?
What kind of partners did you seek until now?
What was the most important value system to you?
Was it popularity, monetary assets, intelligence, physical beauty?
Did you communicate your needs, express your deepest feelings?
Were you heard, appreciated and loved?
Were you trying to please them, gave them more than they reciprocated?
Did you use only your physical appearance to sustain your interactions?
Were you mentally compatible?
What was your priority: physical, mental or spiritual compatibility?

These are difficult but necessary questions, if you want to uncover the true dynamics of your past.
And finally, who made the decision to break up the relationship?
Was it you, due to uncontrollable circumstances, professional ambitions, incompatibility, boredom, disloyalty, or betrayal?

Was the ending of your relationship very painful?
How did you deal with that pain?
Did you run away from it?
Did you hide and pretend you felt nothing?
Did you get revengeful, mean, said negative things, and left with an unresolved conflict that perpetually hovers in the air?
Have you spoken or seen your previous partner since the separation?
Do you feel resolved about that relationship?

It's so easy to look like the wise person, the big strong winner, when in fact you're left with a wound the size of Grand Canyon and have not recovered since. Who is the winner now? It is never too late to shift your stance and change your life. Even if you feel a thousand years old and completely out of practice. Once you make a decision that you will abandon fear and give love a chance, you will completely change your life.

> **EVERY MOMENT WASTED IN FEAR, IS A MOMENT OF LOST LOVE.**
> **LOVE WINS WHEN YOU OVERCOME FEAR.**
> **LOVE BLOOMS IN THE PRESENCE OF A PEACEFUL MIND.**

FEARS IN A RELATIONSHIP

Some fears are quite different when you are in a relationship, but nevertheless, there are countless possibilities. If your relationship is young, you may still be dealing with the personal fears from your past. These are the fears you brought with you into the relationship, and now carry them along. Your new partner may have nothing to do with them, but you still keep hanging on to your old unresolved fears.

You may be fearful of your partner seeing you for who you really are, waking up one day and leaving you, betraying you, disliking you, or rejecting you. Or you are hiding something that you can't reveal, something not so perfect from your past, or even present. Honesty will set you free, but if you want to heal your wounds from the past, it is quite unfair to expect your new partner to do that job for you, don't you think?

> **YOU NEED TO WORK ON YOUR FEARS ON YOUR OWN, AND IF NECESSARY, SHARE THEM WITH YOUR PARTNER. BUT DO NOT EXPECT THEM TO BECOME YOUR PSYCHIATRIST, CRISIS MANAGER AND RESCUER.**

Why? Because, one day you will be healed, and then they will be out of a job. We will talk about that syndrome in future chapters.

If you are in a relationship that has endured the test of time, your fears may be very different. If you have never resolved your own personal very old fears, then they will patiently accompany you thru years of your relationship. They may diminish a bit, or become more prominent, that depends on you and how you work on them. If you ignore them and pretend they don't exist, they may pester you, but if you face and confront them, you will consciously release them. If your fears are persistent and serious, you can expect that your partner will have to shift and adapt to your fears, to either accommodate you, or to find some kind of balance with them.

For example; if you have a big fear they may abandon you, a partner may have to go out of their way to prove that they will stay with you forever. This will be a burden for them, but they will do it. If they don't make this extra effort to help neutralize your emotional handicap, this will be a perpetual cause of conflict and strain on your relationship.

Your fear will become the third person in your relationship, and we know that's too crowded, if you wish to live happily ever after. Your fear will grow and your partner's love and patience for your problem will diminish. The delicate balance of love and fear will be jeopardized. The more fears you have, the less space will be for love. The more love you have, fears will sooner or later completely vanish and you will be able to have a relationship of higher love, total inner peace and honest support for each other. There is another very challenging issue that keeps reappearing in connection with fears and relationships. Even if your relationship seems perfect to everyone that knows you, and you really have no serious challenging issues, secretly you may be chased by a fear that can appear anytime – fear of loss thru change. This is a fear that is understandable, but again quite avoidable.

Change is unavoidable,
therefore fear of change should be avoidable.

There is no escaping change, and there are simply no guarantees in life. You will change physically, you may change in your way of thinking or mindset, and you may shift and experience real bursts of spiritual growth. How is this going to affect your relationship? What if you suddenly told your partner that you feel you have an entirely incompatible view on spirituality? What if you are vastly distanced from each other? What if all that holds you together are family duties, children, financial comfort, or common property? What if you completely lose your social status, if others know that your partnership or marriage is just a sleep-walking show, and you barely speak to each other, except for the necessary small talk?

Are you afraid of changing this long established semi-comfortable dynamic that holds you both in a lifeless, passionless pattern of empty space and no joy? There is always hope and there is always a possibility to adapt, adjust and grow together in synchrony. You are here, reading thru this book, embarking onto this self-exploratory journey, because you obviously have a desire to make it work, to find a new balance and reestablish your bond. You are in the right place. First, work on yourself, your conscious release of old fearful patterns, and later, you will learn how to work on your relationship. Regular Mudra practice is a most powerful remedy to help you accomplish this goal and realign your Spirits. Mudras are a fantastic tool for every phase of your life.

FINDING COURAGE

You know very well, that a positive mindset will change your life, help heal your illness, accomplish the seemingly impossible, and strengthen your ability to manifest. And while it may sound easy to just shift gears and suddenly give up all your fears, we all know it is not a walk in the park. So what do you need, in order to make it happen?

A conscious decision, a true desire, and undoubtedly loads of courage. If I were to tell you that life happens quickly and that before you know it, the show is over, you'd probably laugh. But trust me, life does go by quickly. It goes by slowly only if you are complaining, feeling sorry for yourself, refusing to grow, or open to change. Life takes forever, if you lose hope and sit in a self-created prison. But life goes by like a lightning bolt if you are happy, having fun, laughing, observing the beauty of nature with both eyes open, and taking time for your heart.

In order to find courage, you need a cheerleader. You need someone who will tell you how wonderful you are, how strong and capable you are, how gifted and important you are in this world, and that you deserve every bit of love that comes your way. This cheerleader has to be there for you night and day, morning and evening, come rain or shine. This cheerleader is…YOU.

What I mean is that whatever thoughts are wondering thru your mind, they play an enormous role in your confidence. So instead of a pitiful inner dialogue where you criticize yourself, tell yourself that "You will never meet anyone again, never be loved again, and who in the world could possibly fall in love with you?"… instead of that negative useless chatter, you have to pick yourself up and do the opposite.

> **YES, YOU DESERVE, YES YOU WILL, YES YOU CAN,
> AND YES, ANYTHING IS POSSIBLE.**

Life is a constant process of change. Your birth was a change. Every day offers countless possibilities for a change. When you improve, you change. When you get an idea, you change. When you let go of your old fears and make room for more authentic, fearless and open-hearted love, you are consciously creating the most important change of your life. Why? Because remember, love is everything. To fear change, is to fear life itself. When you evoke your natural given courage, you conquer fear and flow in love.

Speaking from energy anatomy perspective: when you move your energy from fear based solar plexus into your heart, you naturally raise your frequency. This transition is most challenging, but truly symbolic of your spiritual evolutionary process.

> **ONCE YOU ARE IN YOUR HEART,**
> **YOU HAVE CROSSED THE MOST PROMINENT BOUNDARY,**
> **BETWEEN THE ENTRAPMENT OF ILLUSION,**
> **AND ASCENSION INTO YOUR SPIRIT CONSCIOUSNESS.**

WHO ARE YOU IN A LOVE RELATIONSHIP?

This is an excellent question. I don't mean the obvious role here, I am talking about the very complex hidden dynamics that play a decisive part in your love experience. Let me give you a few basic options to help you find the role you like to play.

ARE YOU THE LEADER OR THE FOLLOWER?

The leader does not equate with the control freak, but it is the one that leads the way, is always asked to lead and can lead. If both partners are leaders, you'll have to learn to compromise. If your partner is a follower and you are a leader, this may be great for a while, and then one day it may become beyond boring. The follower may become completely and entirely passive and your leadership qualities will expand into being forced to continuously make decisions for both of you, and this is how things can go wrong, in long-term situations. Reflect on this and give it some thought. Try to find the balance.

ARE YOU THE NEEDY ONE, OR THE CARETAKER?

Are you solving every problem while the other one lounges on the couch changing TV channels? How much fun is that for you? Do you need constant reassurance? Reflect on this.

ARE YOU THE CONTROL FREAK?

Can you relax for a bit and not be in charge the entire time? How does that feel? Do you have to always prove you're right? Isn't that a bit exhausting? Do you have a need to be constantly admired? That's a hard act to keep up. How about letting your hair down on a Sunday and just staying in pajamas with no mask on your face?

ARE YOU THE CONSTANT PLEASER?

Don't get surprised if you'll be taken advantage of sooner or later. Why? Because you'll have to learn the lesson of a rude awakening, that pleasing others does not guarantee a happy relationship. You will not be appreciated if you have spoiled everyone around you. In fact, they will become more and more demanding, while appreciating you less and less.

ARE YOU THE COMPLAINER?

Do you constantly whine and keep everyone on their toes in fear they will somehow upset you? Reflect on the true source of discontent. Perhaps you are impossible to please, because you are not pleased with yourself.

ARE YOU A MOODY MONSTER?

How pleasant is that to be around? If that's you, I can guarantee you will end up alone. Just face it, nobody will endure it for the duration. Explore reasons for your mood fluctuations, what causes them, or is this simply an old pattern to get desperate attention you need.

ARE YOU A CONFLICT SEEKER?

Do you feel bored when everything is harmonious and there's no screaming match to attend? Be aware that all you are seeking is control and attention, but in a really unhealthy and unpleasant way. Drinking other people's energy thru conflict will come back at you like a fierce boomerang. Get that nasty habit under control and stop torturing those around you.

ARE YOU A DREAMER?

Are you always day dreaming some unrealistic scenario, while your partner needs to take care of the bills, keep the roof over your head and keep your feet on realistic ground? It just means you are a bit lazy, hiding under pretense you can't, or don't know how, or don't like dealing with "Earthly stuff." Be fair and help your partner deal with the everyday messy necessities. Be responsible and carry an equal load.

ARE YOU THE CONSTANT CRITIC?

Isn't this perhaps just a self-defense mechanism, so that nobody will see your terrible flaws? Is the permanent discontent simply a reflection of your own dissatisfaction? Are your expectations unrealistic, do you compare yourself and compete with others? Do you have the ability to give compliments and recognize good and positive qualities in others?

And finally, the most essential question is this:
ARE YOU A GIVER OR A SHAMELESS TAKER?
If you are a giver, pairing with a perpetual, entitled taker will be an unfortunate combination for you. However, if you put this imbalance out in open, you could resolve it and find a fine tuned harmony. But remember, you cannot remain and overextended giver and expect the taker to curb their natural tendency. If you are a hopeless giver, you will likely attract a taker. Why? Because your imbalance is attracting a compatible dynamic that creates an energy match.

The key is to learn and balance yourself with disciplined and loving self-care. Part of this includes clear communication with your partner about your needs, and a clear boundary about what you can not give them, to replace their own lack.

> **THEY KEY TO ATTRACTING, ESTABLISHING AND MAINTAINING A COMPATIBLE RELATIONSHIP REQUIRES THAT YOU KNOW YOURSELF AND CULTIVATE A PERFECT BALANCE WITHIN.**

CONTENTMENT

This is a very important aspect for your daily life and certainly a necessary healthy relationship dynamic. Within yourself, your mind and heart, you need to find a level of contentment. This is like the basic alphabet of your life. Knowing yourself. What makes you happy, what are your desires, wishes, dreams and ambitions?

Why is this so important when it comes to relationships?
Because not knowing your basic inner longings will create a sense of tension. A desire is a crucial piece of information that helps you understand, respect and follow the mission of your soul. It is the guide to your predesigned learning experience, an intricate part of the puzzle of your life purpose. You must follow it, in order to experience what you came here to do. If you have a strong professional desire for achievement, this will forever live within you, and ignoring it will create a sense of bitterness, and repeated upset whenever you will see someone else who is doing what you want to do or accomplish. Following your desires or at least recognizing them and giving them some attention is crucial. If you have a desire

for a family life with many children, then you will not feel content until you give it a serious, conscious try.

This of course does not mean that you won't change your mind. In fact, you may realize that a desire you wanted to pursue is not interesting to you after all. A career loses its charm, or having a small army of children is less important to you, than being with the right partner. This will be your realization that will help you resolve or fulfill a desire. The final outcome is not as important as is your awareness and follow-thru, to give yourself an opportunity to experience what you want. This essential element that will create a sense of contentment within, will make you a wonderful partner. And even if you meet your partner before your desires or wishes even came thru, your own awareness and honesty with them, will help continue nurturing your sense of contentment and will never become a source of friction.

Adapting your desires to accommodate your partner will carry a price. Be honest, open and strive to compromise equally. Everything does take some sort of sacrifice, but it does not have to be a one-sided situation.

Pay attention to your and your partner's desires and cultivate a sense of contentment as a singular person. Then, you can expand that contentment into your relationship.

> **YOU CANNOT HAVE A CONTENT RELATIONSHIP,
> WHILE YOU ARE FRUSTRATED WITH YOUR OWN SELF.
> SELF-CONTENTMENT SHOULD BE CULTIVATED
> WHETHER YOU ARE SINGLE OR IN A RELATIONSHIP.**

It will help you take responsibility for your own happiness, and not burden your partner with something that is really connected to your own sense of identity and inner clarity.

INNER PEACE

Know yourself. What gives you inner peace? And what makes you restless, gives you anxiety or causes you stress?

Inner peace can be cultivated with regular Mudra practice, journal work, self-reflection and inner work. This is an essential component, which will make you incredibly magnetic and attractive to your partner. You inner peace will help them regain and maintain their own inner peace, and just being together will magnify a loving zone of powerful peace and love. Love loves calmness.

SELF - CONFIDENCE

No matter how many times your partner tells you that you are the most amazing, lovely person in the world, if you lack self-confidence, this will eventually present a drain on the relationship. Certainly if you are single and suffer from a low self-esteem, you can not expect to attract a person that will know, value or even understand who you really are.

> **IF YOU LACK IN CONFIDENCE,
> YOU WILL ATTRACT A PERSON WHO FEELS MORE COMFORTABLE
> WITH A PARTNER THAT LACKS IN SELF-CONFIDENCE.**

Perhaps it makes them feel better about themselves, more needed, like they have a purpose, and are important. If you need them in order to feel confident, they hold a certain power over you, that they obviously like. This may work for a while or even for a long time, but don't expect much potential for growth in this kind of a set up.

Why? Because, if you suddenly, overnight become very self-confident, which may absolutely happen, your partner may not like it one bit. Suddenly, they have no important position with you, may feel unneeded, unwanted and with no control or prominent role to play.

"You don't need me anymore," is what they may say to you, and you will both feel the purpose of your relationship has maybe expired. Perhaps the only way they feel confident, is if they have a less confident person beside them.

So what happens now? In all honesty, if you expect to attract a healthy, balanced, self-confident person, while you yourself lack in self-confidence, this is never going to happen. A confident person will see very quickly that your lack in confidence, and will know you are not a good match as this will be an exhausting dynamic for both, especially for them. They will become bigger, and you will disappear. They will long for an equal, and you won't be able to come close to it.

> **IF YOUR CONFIDENCE IS HEALTHY,
> YOU WILL ATTRACT A PERSON THAT LIKES YOU THE WAY YOU ARE,
> NOT HOPING TO TAKE ADVANTAGE OF YOUR POWER OR WEAKNESS,
> AND FEARING YOUR POSSIBLE PROGRESS.**

If you are in a relationship and are aware of this confidence imbalance, and are gaining in your self-confidence, keep in mind that as soon as your confidence will grow, your partner's will diminish. The less needed and important they will feel, the less confident they will become. You will need to work together, openly, to overcome this balancing act while you adjust to the growing pains of these changes.

It is always possible to overcome challenging issues, if and when you work on them together, with patience, communication and love.

SELF - RELIANCE

This is very connected to your first chakra center of inner security, and survival. If a person is in survival mode – meaning their existence is in danger, they are going thru severe hardship, or are incapable of taking care of themselves, their entire preoccupation will revolve around this one important topic. You cannot possibly expect a person that has existential issues, to be able to completely ignore these challenges, and live a carefree life, or make various choices unaffected by their problems. The existential issues will throw a shade over everything they do, think, say, and decide.

I know this may be harsh to hear, but you must be conscious of your own ability to rely on yourself. Can you? Are you able to support yourself and live a healthy, balanced life on your own? What are your main problems? Don't misunderstand me in thinking that the only time you can be happy or even begin a relationship, is when everything is perfect in your life. It does not work that way. Life is not perfect and nothing is ever without small challenges and curves in the road that require our attention.

NEVER STEP INTO A NEW RELATIONSHIP OUT OF DESPERATION.

If you do, this desperation will flavor and taint every aspect of your relationship. Again, your new partner may like the idea that you desperately need them, and they can play the big angel who saved you from the bad wolf, be the prince or princess on the white horse who came just in time. But what happens when the desperation is over? What happens when you are back in your own skin, not fearing for your existence? Your partner's role shifts. Suddenly they don't know where they belong. The overwhelming high they may have felt while they rescued you from a crisis, is now gone.

Once you don't need them anymore, this becomes an identity crisis for them and your relationship. Even if you are in a dramatic and needy situation, you can rely on yourself to be active, do whatever you can and make every effort to shift your current situation. This will send a clear signal to your potential partner that you are a fighter, a resilient Spirit, an inventive courageous being, who can face any diversity. Their help in such a case will be different, for they will expect you to recover, and actually look forward to it. This way, you will attract a person that completely understands that it can happen to anyone to have an impossibly unpredictable hardship situation, that's beyond your control and takes over your life, but your amazing character is going to get you thru. In such a case, they will recognize your most brilliant qualities, because your resilient self-reliance makes you a wonderful example.

SELF - RELIANCE IS AN ASSET, DEPENDENCY IS A CRUTCH.

What matters is how you behave under challenging circumstances. If you are in a relationship and this dynamic is already set up, and you wish to switch it, you will have to gently work with your partner so they won't get intimidated by your sudden recovery, and won't be fearful that they will lose you, once you don't need them anymore. If you are single, just make sure, you don't expect a rescuer, while you helplessly sit in a pile of self-pity. Be your wonderful self and even if you met your absolutely perfect destined partner while your world is falling apart, they will recognize the true you, your resilient self-reliable Spirit and love you for the right reasons.

CAN YOU TRUST YOURSELF?

The people that have the hardest time trusting, are the ones who can't trust themselves. Why? Because they think and know how easily one can be betrayed, since they constantly betray themselves. They may promise to themselves they will never do this or that, and yet, before you know it, they have betrayed themselves again.

They may make promises they can't keep, just because they like the sound of a promise or how it makes them feel. For a moment, they feel mighty: "I will help you," and then there is silence. "I will be there for you," and then they forget or pretend they never said anything like it. If you have issues around trust, pay attention to yourself and ask yourself: "Do I trust myself to keep the promise I make to myself?"

This promise can be about anything. Diet, exercise, completing a project, pursuing a dream, cleaning your house, being on time, a million things. You promised yourself something, and then….you realized again that you can't be trusted or relied upon. This is one kind of trust. There is also the trust about being truthful with yourself, or not repeating self-destructive habits, being weak, lazy, or simply lying to yourself.

But of course in relationships, the question of trust is of a different shade. It goes very deep, right into the core of your heart. Trusting someone with intimate information, your feelings, your weaknesses, dark secrets, things you may be ashamed of or that could harm you, expose you, and most of all, wound your heart beyond imagination.

TRUST IS A LUXURY.

Trusting someone with your private matters is a risk. If you trust too easily and have been betrayed, perhaps you need to pay attention to early signs, these tiny little invisible bells that go off in the back of your mind and you just ignore. Perhaps sometimes you don't want to hear the truth, so you don't trust yourself, when you feel these secret warning signs. That's a mistake.

When you become deeply aware of yourself, your surroundings and the people you meet, you begin cultivating instant access to your higher self. And suddenly, interesting things begin to happen. The more you progress in your inner work, the better your intuitive awareness will become. Mudras are an incredibly helpful and powerful tool in this pursuit.

> **THE DEEPER YOU LEARN TO GO WITH THE MUDRA PRACTICE,
> THE QUICKER YOU WILL GAIN ACCESS TO INFORMATION THAT CAN'T BE
> SEEN, HEARD OR TOUCHED WITH HUMAN HANDS.**

In other words, when you contemplate about trusting a person, you will almost instantly hear an inner voice or receive tangible sensation whether you can, or cannot trust them. The question is, are you going to listen?

Pay attention, your higher self will always try to warn you. But don't expect to have great intuition if you use mind altering substances or are self-destructive in any way. Your energy body cannot maintain clear or reliable immediate access to higher knowledge, if you have weakened it with unhealthy behavior. I speak about that in my book MUDRA THERAPY, *Hand Yoga for Pain Management and Conquering Illness.*

In order for your high frequency inner-intuitive-instrument to work, your energy field needs to be pristine clean. Any addictive substances that affect your cognitive behavior, will weaken your auric protective shield, confuse, numb and handicap your intuitive abilities.

> **LEARN TO LISTEN TO YOUR INNER VOICE WITHIN,
> FOR IT WILL ALWAYS TELL YOU
> WHO YOU CAN TRUST.**

However, there is always room for mistakes. But only if you are emotionally vulnerable and susceptible at that time. The weaker, more needy, afraid, insecure and lacking in confidence you are, the less likely it is, that you will be able to hear your higher self. The calmer, more centered and fearless you are, the easier you will gain access. The ultimate trust is your ability to have faith in Divine universal power that protects, guards, guides and loves you, more than you can possibly imagine.

WHAT DO YOU WANT?

This is the singular most important question you can ask yourself. Why? Because most of the people never know what they want. In the arena of partnerships, they may walk around for years saying: "I just want someone to love me, just like I am."

Sounds good, but if you don't know who you are and what are your fears, likes, desires and dreams, you are completely and entirely out of touch. And in such a case the most fantastic dream partner could appear right in front of your eyes, and you would not even recognize them. Do you know what could happen instead?

Your fears will make you hide in insecurity. Your confidence issues will make you shrivel into nothing. Your neediness will make you unappealing. Your confusion or ignorance of your desires will make you defensive, your inner restlessness will make you unaware of them, and your inability to trust yourself, will make you doubt your insane luck that you met this amazing person. So there they will be, in front of your eyes, and you will somehow or another not recognize them, not realize this is it, that you just found your greatest love. And even if you'll be lucky enough to spend some time with them, in your lost and confused ignorance, you will eventually lose them.

> **WHEN YOU DON'T KNOW WHAT KIND OF PARTNER YOU WANT,**
> **YOU COULD REALIZE MUCH LATER,**
> **THAT YOU ALREADY MET AND CONSEQUENTLY LOST THEM.**

It could take you years to come to this realization. No kidding. It could take you decades, until one evening you'll jump out of your armchair and realize: "Oh my gosh, that was the perfect person for me, and they loved me, and I was so ignorant, I didn't even know it!"

This is why it is actually extremely important to really know, what is it that you want. And I don't mean that you need to write a description of how tall your partner has to be, what color eyes they have to have and so on. That would be childish behavior. But you do need to know IF you want a relationship, WHAT KIND of relationship you want, and the main values, life principles, beliefs, and lifestyle that you would enjoy to SHARE with your partner. That is what matters. Know what you want, and ask the Universe to send them your way. They will come and what's even better, you will recognize them immediately.

WHAT IS YOUR OFFERING?

This is our final reflection for this week. In life and in love, it is important to know what you have to offer. This is necessary and will help you feel self-confident, and clearer about what kind of soul would be your ideal match, your ideal partner. When examining yourself, be honest and clear. Extreme self-criticism will not do you any favors. Again, examine what is your inner dialogue?

"I am a nothing and nobody," will not send out the right vibrational frequency. Feeling depressed, unhappy with yourself, your appearance, or your life's accomplishments, self-doubt and negative affirmations, is not where you need to go. Instead, practice this week's Mudra set to help balance your beautiful inner energy, create a peaceful inner center of peace, and open your heart to love. All the mind chatter, the old voices that can't say anything beautiful and encouraging, they need to be ignored, and cancelled out. Now, you only have space and time for creating a pristinely clear, bright and lovely atmosphere of self-confidence, trust, inner calm and self-awareness about the treasure you carry in your heart.

This is who you are, the love in your heart is your offering. And like-wise you will attract a soul that matches perfectly with your heart's energy frequency, so that together, you can sing the song of unconditional love.

> **ANYTIME IS A GREAT TIME TO WORK ON YOURSELF.**

If you have found your perfect match, this is an ideal time to realign yourself with your higher purpose, and remember the basics we learned this week. You are an individual who needs to tend to your inner dynamics on your own. You will see, each time you reintroduce a new, healed, and energized element of yourself into your relationship, it will invigorate, heal, and replenish both of you. Together you are One, however, your own individuality is important. Cherish and nurture your soul, and everything else will reflect what you emit to others and each other. Project love and kindness, and it shall be returned to you a thousand times over.

You are a beautiful human being, a precious immortal Soul, traveling thru the adventure of human life, meeting new experiences, resolving various old mysteries, exploring hidden secrets, and sharing your Light with others, to make this world a better place and help all of those that are in need of love and healing. This is who you are. Together, or on your own, you are never alone, for your Light is eternal. We are One.

YOUR ASSIGNMENT

AFFIRMATION

> FEAR IS LIKE A CLOUD THAT IS HIDING THE SUN.
> EVENTUALLY IT WILL DISAPPEAR INTO NOTHINGNESS,
> BUT THE SUN WILL ALWAYS EXIST, JUST LIKE LOVE.

DIARY

This week you have a loaded agenda. Dealing with fear will take you into the arena where your inner warrior will be called into a mighty battle. Your Diary work is an extremely important assistant in this endeavor, for if you are not clear about your fear, or it keeps changing while trying to confuse you, the written words will help lead your way. The moment you'll see your biggest fear written down, you will be shocked by its small size and weak appearance. Now you are ready to shift the direction of your usual course, and step on a new path of love. No matter what your situation, a conscious shift will change everything. If you're alone, a great door will open and love will begin to flow in your direction. If you are in a relationship crisis, your change into projecting a confident, steady and loving disposition, will disarm the worst of conflicts. Remember, it is always YOUR disposition that plays a most important role on the grand scale.

PROCESS

Work thru the questions, come back in a few days, see if anything changed, add it on, clarify, clean it up, and self-discover through the process.

PRACTICE

Work with the diary, answer the questions and practice the Mudras listed. Write down how you feel before and after the Mudra practice. Observe the shift in your energy field.

> **EVERYTHING IN LIFE NEEDS YOUR PARTICIPATION.**
> **IF THERE IS EMPTINESS, YOU ALLOWED IT.**
> **IF THERE IS LOVE, YOU CALLED IT AND IT FOUND YOU.**
> **IT ALWAYS DOES.**

Your Workspace
LOVE AND FEAR

WHAT IS YOUR GREATEST FEAR?

Only you know the answer.
Do you come from fear or love?
Do you make life and partner choices based on fear and lack?
Do you follow love and select a partner with your heart?
Do you feel that you have experienced the love you wanted?
Have you experienced deeply profound relationship in your life?
Have you experienced loss of love, and why?

Work thru the chapter and dissect your fear into a thousand pieces.
And then, dissect those thousand pieces into a thousand more.
Now you will find your Basic Fear that has prevented you from reaching the Sky.

Your Workspace

WHO ARE YOU IN A LOVE RELATIONSHIP?

Here, utmost honesty is necessary. Read thru the chapter and reflect which description sounds familiar, where you can find yourself, and recognize your challenging, overwhelming, perhaps too-demanding tendencies, or ridiculously harsh self-criticism. Find your role in your current situation. How did you co-create this?

Now you will understand your tendencies, and your role in creating your present dynamic, solo or in a pair.

ARE YOU:
- THE LEADER OR THE FOLLOWER?
- THE NEEDY ONE, OR THE CARETAKER?
- THE CONTROL FREAK?
- THE CONSTANT PLEASER?
- THE COMPLAINER?
- THE MOODY MONSTER?
- THE CONFLICT SEEKER?
- THE DREAMER?
- THE CONSTANT CRITIC?
- THE GENEROUS GIVER?
- THE SHAMELESS TAKER?

Your Workspace

WHAT DO YOU WANT IN LOVE AND LIFE?

This is a biggie. Reflect, write, think, meditate and travel into the deepest hallways of your heart. You can't possibly get what you wish if your ideas are sloppy, unclear or unreasonable. Laugh, cry and be kind to yourself.

The moment you discover what you want, and objectively analyze why you have not found it yet, relax, and know that from now on, with every minute, you are incredibly closer to getting it.

How exciting is that?

FOR YOUR MUDRA PRACTICE

SEE IT, KNOW IT, AND RELEASE IT

Now the serious work begins. This Mudra set will help you break the chains of entrapment that have limited your life. You are ready to face your fears, decipher their origins, and remove the power your focus has given them. They are only as persistent, stubborn and resilient, as you allow them to be. Now your attention is needed on the other side of the spectrum – the beautiful domain of love. Remain strong and steady and remember that you do not have to identify with fear any more. Your life is changing, because you are ready and want it so. It is your conscious choice and that decision is irrevocable.

TAKE CHARGE

The moment you allow a negative, disturbing frequency to enter your intimate energy field, you feel anxiety, nervousness and uncertainty. It takes only a moment to consciously redirect this energy to leave you, so that you can regain your steady focus, attention and unwavering inner peace, so anything that comes your way can not touch you, throw you off balance, or make you unsteady.

YOUR MIND POWER

Your mind is a powerful asset, but only when it holds the steady rhythm of a reliable advisor and wise Spirit. When your mind is tranquil, you will be free to recognize an honest, open heart, and frequency of true love. When your mind is out of control, everything is in danger, and your choices, decisions and actions are impulsively risky. Love needs courage, but not of a foolish kind. A tranquil mind is necessary, so that you can consciously connect with the universal power, and ask for protection of yourself and your loved one.

MUDRA FOR MENTAL BALANCE

Sit with a straight back, shoulders down, nice and relaxed. Bend your elbows, lift the hands up in front of your solar plexus or chest area and interlace the fingers backward with palms facing up. Fingers are pointing up and are straight. Practice for Three minutes.

BREATH
Long, deep and slow through your nose

MANTRA
GOBINDAY, MUKUNDAY, UDARAAY, APAARAY,
HARYING, KARYNG, NIRNAMAY, AKAMAY

(Sustainer, Liberator, Enlightener, Infinite, Destroyer, Creator, Nameless, Desire-less)

CHAKRAS
All

HEALING COLORS
All

AFFIRMATION

MY MIND IS IN PERFECT BALANCE AND HARMONY

MUDRA FOR OVERCOMING ANXIETY

Sit with a straight back and keep your shoulders down, nice and relaxed. Bend your elbows and raise your arms so your upper arms are parallel to the ground and extended out to the sides. Your hands are at the level of your ears, fingers spread wide and pointing up to the sky. Hold all fingers straight and apart. Start rotating your hands back and forth, pivoting at the wrists. You will go thru a period that seems difficult, but remain persistent and it will become easier. Practice for Three minutes, then relax, and enjoy the sensations.

BREATH
LONG, DEEP AND SLOW THROUGH YOUR NOSE

MANTRA
HARKANAM SAT NAM

(God's Name Is Truth)

CHAKRAS
HEART - 4, THROAT - 5, THIRD EYE - 6

HEALING COLORS
GREEN, BLUE, INDIGO

AFFIRMATION
I RELEASE ALL ANXIETY AND REPLACE IT WITH PEACE

MUDRA FOR TRANQUILIZING YOUR MIND

Sit with a straight back, shoulders down, nice and relaxed. Bend your elbows and bring your hands up to your chest. Connect the middle fingertips and stretch them outward. Bend the rest of the fingers and press them together along the second joint. Connect your thumb tips and extend them toward you. Hold for Three minutes, then relax.

BREATH
Long, deep and slow through your nose

MANTRA
MAN HAR TAN HAR GURU HAR
(Mind with God, Soul with God, the Divine Guide and His Supreme Wisdom)

CHAKRAS
Solar Plexus - 3, Heart - 4, Throat - 5, Third Eye - 6

HEALING COLORS
Yellow, Green, Blue, Indigo

AFFIRMATION
I AM SERENE, PEACEFUL AND TRANQUIL

MUDRA FOR FACING FEAR

Sit with a straight back, shoulders down, nice and relaxed. Hold the left hand in front of your navel, palm facing up, fingers together. Bend your right elbow and lift the arm up to level of your face. Face your right palm outward, as if taking a vow. Fingers are together. Concentrate on energy flowing into your hands. Practice for Three minutes.

BREATH
LONG, DEEP AND SLOW THROUGH YOUR NOSE
MANTRA
NIRBHAO NIRVAIR AKAAL MORT
(Fearless, Without Enemy, Immortal Personified God)
CHAKRAS
SOLAR PLEXUS - 3, CROWN - 7
HEALING COLORS
YELLOW, VIOLET
AFFIRMATION

I AM FEARLESS , I AM BRAVE

MUDRA FOR PREVENTING STRESS

Sit with a straight back, shoulders down, nice and relaxed. Bend your elbows and bring your forearms in front of your solar plexus area parallel to the ground. Turn the palms up and rest the back of the left hand in the palm of the right hand. Both palms facing up, fingers are held together. The rest of the fingers are straight and together. Hold for three minutes and concentrate on your breath.

BREATH
LONG, DEEP AND SLOW THROUGH YOUR NOSE

MANTRA
MAN HAR TAN HAR GURU HAR
(Mind with God, Soul with God, the Divine Guide and His Supreme Wisdom)

CHAKRAS
SOLAR PLEXUS - 3

HEALING COLORS
YELLOW

AFFIRMATION
I AM IN MY OWN SAFE SPACE OF TOTAL CALM

MUDRA FOR SELF ~ CONFIDENCE

Sit with a straight back, shoulders down, nice and relaxed. Lift your hands up to the level of your solar plexus with elbows bent to the sides. Bend the middle, ring, and little fingers of each hand. Align the middle, ring and little fingers of both hands back to back. Extend and press the index fingertips together and extend and press the thumb tips together. The thumbs are pointed towards you and the index fingers away from you. Hold for Three minutes, then relax.

BREATH
LONG, DEEP AND SLOW THROUGH YOUR NOSE

MANTRA
EK ONG KAR SAT GURU PRASAD, SAT GURU PRASAD EK ONG KAR
(The Creator Is the One That Dispels Darkness and Illuminates Us by His Grace)

CHAKRAS
SOLAR PLEXUS - 3, THIRD EYE - 6

HEALING COLORS
YELLOW, INDIGO

AFFIRMATION

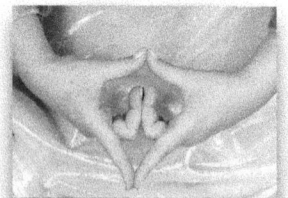

I AM READY, WILLING AND ABLE TO ACCOMPLISH MY GOALS

Week Three

YOUR HEART

YOUR NATURAL FREQUENCY OF LOVE

Now that you've analyzed your mental disposition and almost scientifically dissected it, the time has come to rise up to the occasion and meet your heart. Not only is this your emotional center, it is actually a most crucial energy center and the seat of your soul.

Why? Of course all energy centers are equally important, but the awakened state of your heart is a significant indicator of your soul's evolutionary progress.

Of course this is much more complex than it sounds. The main change and shift that you experience when you move into this region is, that the three lower energy centers are now overpowered by your genuine ability and desire to experience and share unconditional love.

To help you understand these fascinating, complex dynamics, let me explain in more detail. If your general soul frequency functions at the First chakra level of survival, your ability to love will be greatly limited, by your preoccupation with survival matters and Earth-bound energies. In relationships, this would be most obvious when a person's understanding of having a partner was solely associated with satisfying their need for survival, or material possessions and security.

> **EVEN A HIGHLY EVOLVED SPIRITUAL COUPLE MAY FACE CHALLENGING TESTS.**

Let's not misunderstand this by confusing that every person who is materially supported by a partner functions at the First chakra level. Not at all. A person could be highly evolved, function at their heart level, but the relationship dynamics were mutually agreed upon or adjusted to unforeseen circumstances where one person is the provider of material support, and the other is the nurturer, perhaps taking care of the family. Such a person would naturally more likely function at the level of the heart – unconditional giving and nurturing. Their foremost motivation is not the need to survive, although that is always present in a healthy, not overwhelming and burdensome way. But their soul desire is to establish a functioning, loving and harmonious relationship, in order to give and receive love.

Another example would be when one partner's job requires frequent traveling and the only way the partnership can work, is if the second partner adjusts their priorities to accompany them in travels. They may be financially dependent on them, however, their intention is entirely different than a person who understands and considers the basics of a relationship as a means to survive. You can have countless possibilities, where one partner materially depends on, or is significantly stronger than the other, but functions at the heart level. However, the key question is, how does the couple assure the stronger partner will not – under unexpected circumstances – suddenly abandon or abuse the position of power they have? This is the challenge that many couples face, when the dynamics unexpectedly shift, or their feelings of love diminish.

> **ONCE YOUR GENERAL FREQUENCY HAS RISEN TO THE LEVEL OF THE HEART, YOUR SPIRIT IS ON A STEADY PATH TO ASCENSION.**

If both partners function at the heart level frequency, they should be able to overcome challenges or even separation in a respectable, loving and caring way. If their core energies are different, the separation will bring out a reflex reaction, that is closest to their frequency level. If one of them functions at a significantly lower frequency, the shift and absence of love could create negative behavior or situation. The person's natural frequency is always the most important, decisive factor.

Why are we discussing these complex, energy anatomy aspects? Because they will help you recognize your own frequency. Once you do, this will provide you with clear clues, about who can be your potentially equal compatible partner. Somewhere in this maze of possibilities, you will find aspects that sound familiar to you. Something will ring a bell and make you say: "Yes, I feel like this could be me!" and then you will begin to understand why love has been perhaps challenging for you. Maybe you paid no attention to these elements and were completely lost in superficial distractions. It is possible that you looked for a completely wrong partner. Perhaps you were too harsh with the partner you have, not understanding that you function on different frequency levels. Of course it is important to remember that love knows no limitations, so it is very likely that you may fall in love with a person who is NOT compatible with you on frequency level. This will bring undeniable challenges, but you may have to go thru the experience because of past-life ties, or spiritual contracts. Most love stories are unavoidable, no matter how challenging the circumstances can sometimes prove. But your understanding of these dynamics, will help you thru any situation. This way you can adapt, and learn to find balance with a partner that may not be precisely on your level. Of course ideally, you should be on an equal level, but life is rarely ideal. And relationships are here to teach us. Remember that in any relationship where you offer harmony as well as true, deep, heart centered love, the key lies in finding your equal.

Let's continue up the chakra energy scale to broaden your understanding. If your general disposition is centered in the second chakra, you will understand ideal partnership from a narrow sexually charged perspective. Likewise, in third chakra center, your partner-ambitions will be connected with your ego and all the unpleasantries that can trap you while moving in that limited energy space. Once your main energy frequency is in the fourth center of the heart, your awareness and ability to love expands considerably. You begin to function from the heart with a generous expression of love, forgiveness, and compassionate care about others, without expecting a reward. This is what is interesting to us at the moment, since we are focusing on the dynamics of your heart.

> **THE PROFOUND EVOLUTIONARY STEP OF FUNCTIONING AT THE HEART LEVEL, IS THAT YOU ENTER THE ROLE OF A GIVER.**

This is noteworthy and wonderful, but you still have a weakness. As a giver, as many of us are, you are most likely able to give to everyone around you, shower them with care, love and attention BUT…you must learn to receive love as well. Unless you do, you will sooner or later experience depletion and eventual evolutionary stagnation. There is also a danger that your perpetual giving attracts takers and that will deplete you further. It will energetically drag you into the lower realm of the mind. This is a very important aspect to understand and consciously prevent.

FORGIVENESS

The reason why we are focusing on these energy dynamics is meaningful. Growing into or evoking the qualities of the heart will provide you with a supremely important ability to forgive. Forgiveness is not an easily attained quality or state. It requires you to release and let go of all negative, unpleasant and harmful energy dynamics.

Forgiveness can only be experienced if you abandon anger, hate, resentfulness, victim mode and other similar emotional trappings. Forgiveness will absolutely set you free. It will do more than that. It will open you up to possibilities of new love.

How can one forgive the unforgivable?
Do not focus on the words, instead, align yourself with the concept of releasing the energy tie.

> **ANY EMOTIONAL CONNECTION WITH ANOTHER PERSON WILL KEEP YOU BOUND TO THEM.**

Anger, hate, resentment, jealousy, envy…all these ugly energy connections will keep you entangled with another person until you let them go. Release is very similar to forgiving someone. You cease to hold and sustain an energy cord attached to them, you stop being connected to them, you consciously decide to not repeat and rehash the same angry, upset words and thoughts that linger in your head, and force you to stagnate in a negative field. If forgiveness seems impossible, letting go and removing them from being energetically connected to you, seems more doable and quite necessary.

The moment you loosen up the grip of negative motion and consciously decide to let it go, a very interesting situation will present itself. There will be suddenly more space in your energy field. You will feel lighter, happier, and more open. This is necessary, urgently needed and supremely healing. Any energy attachment of negative nature depletes your energy. Just remember that, and it will really help you move into forgiveness, and disposition of letting go. Until you enter the state of forgiveness, you remain energetically attached to that person, literally feeding them with your life-force. With Mudra practice you will become more sensitive to energies, and more aware of other people's attachments to your energy field. And you will understand that allowing your energy to leak towards someone undeserving, is simply not a healthy habit.

HEALING OLD WOUNDS

We have all endured emotional wounds, and some may have felt almost like straight arrows to your heart. Perhaps you even experienced them as a child, or early in life. Maybe you just experienced a fresh wound yesterday, but there it is. Old wounds leave scars, which are invisible, but not any less potent. These emotional scars create energy congestion in your energy field. Remember, all emotions are vibration, a subtle energy frequency. Emotions of love have powerful healing energy and effects, while emotions of fear have disturbing, restrictive energy consequences. All these negative energy clusters sit like a cloud in the region where they originated.

Overthinking, obsessive rehashing of life's challenges and living predominantly in your mind, will create a cloud of density around your head. Unresolved anger or fear will congest your solar plexus area. Suffering of a wounded heart will linger around your chest region. Even though you can not see these energy clusters, they can create real danger to your health. Keeping your energy field as clean as possible, free of these unresolved negative energy clusters is a necessity. Regular Mudra practice is an excellent technique to maintain yourself free of negative, congested and unresolved emotional clutter.

What to do if these wounds are old?
The solution is complex. For starters, it is imperative that you regularly and consciously let go of your negative emotions and cultivate a harmonious state of mind, body and heart. The complicated part is when the wounds are old, and may require deep spiritual work.

> **ON FINER ENERGY LEVELS,
> TIME DOES NOT EXIST,
> AS WE PERCEIVE IT HERE IN THE MATERIAL WORLD.**

This is why love can overcome separation or even death and can live on, even when someone is no longer in this realm of existence. We will get into more details about this later on. But what matters most in relation to healing old wounds, is the deeper understanding that time does not necessary heal old wounds, but rather buries them deep into your psyche, so they become a part of your belief system and your Love Matrix. Your general disposition toward love carries all these traces of old information that you have accepted as your truth, your reality, your expectation of a loving relationship.

If you were deeply wounded in betrayal, and have not released the sorrow, anger, resentment, self-doubt, insecurity or whatever heavy emotion you experienced in connection with this event, you will naturally assume that any future relationship carries a highly probable potential to inflict this kind of pain. On a subconscious level, you almost expect it. And guess what, by allowing this to be a part of your belief system, you practically attract it into your life, again and again.

How many times do you feel like you are going thru the same repeated experience with failed relationships? As long as you do not reset your perception and truly reflect upon what happened, you will carry this frequency of expected failure or wound, and will continue to attract precisely that. This fact alone should make you want to resolve and release all past negative experiences and begin anew, with a fresh, optimistic disposition.

**IN EVERY RELATIONSHIP,
REGARDLESS OF PAIN OR PLEASURE THAT WE EXPERIENCE,
WE ARE AN ACTIVE OR PASSIVE PARTICIPANT.**

It is funny how often we are quick to boast when something is pleasant or successful and proudly announce our participation in it, yet when a painful event happens, we see ourselves less as an active participant, but more as a helpless victim. We say: "This happened to me," as opposed to "I made this happen," or "I allowed this to happen."

It is not fun to face this, but it is a fact. Good or bad, you were there, right? So when pain or conflict happens, or a relationship fails, we should take a few steps back and let go of negative emotions, or seeing yourself only as a passive victim. It is time for reflection and honest admission of where and how you participated and allowed this to happen. This is not a most pleasant part of the cleansing process, but a very necessary one. And if you have a tendency to be overly self-critical, then try and expand the perception into a more objective point of view, and leave feelings of guilt off the menu. Guilt is not going to create progress, but calm reflection, honest observation certainly will. Forgiveness means also forgiving yourself, for allowing a negative experience, for making an error, hurting someone else, or hurting yourself.

FORGIVENESS IS AS WIDE AS THE HORIZON, IT NEVER ENDS.

Forgiveness allows you to breathe freely again. Let go, detach the unnecessary energy, release the strings that drain your vital force, and research old wounds from an esoteric perspective. Now, when you engage in this cleansing mission, you will create an amazing beautiful oasis of new, fresh, open space, ready to attract a positive and loving energy.

HEART AND MIND – THE UNLIKELY PARTNERS

The next step is your conscious balance between your heart and mind. These two opposites are in competition. It depends on your personal character traits, your soul's destined path, your astrological celestial planetary influences and your soul's energy matrix, how the balance between these two mighty powers lie. Ideally, there should be lovely harmony and cooperative collaboration between these two forces. This would give you the uncanny ability to navigate thru life's challenges and also be fearless enough to open your heart and experience love of the highest manifestation. Depending on your nature, you might be a more prominent thinker. If your mind loves to take over, and always needs a logical tactful explanation for everything, your heart will be forced to remain in the background, with nothing but a slight whisper, never to be heard or taken into serious consideration.

If you are all in your heart, you may give your love generously, without any reflection or restriction to anyone that shows up, and then wonder why you came up hurt and empty handed in the end. If this continues to go on, your heart will suffer continuously, while your mind will become a confused frazzle of ignored instinctual responses, that could have saved you a lot of pain ad heartache.

> **HEALING YOUR HEART IS OF TREMENDOUS IMPORTANCE,
> FOR IF YOU DO NOT KNOW HOW TO FOLLOW IT AT THE RIGHT MOMENT,
> YOU COULD LOSE THE GREATEST LOVE OF YOUR LIFE.**

Mind is an enviable asset as well, for if you learn to discern with precision, and have the ability to recognize a message from your higher consciousness that is always making an effort to guide and protect, you will experience a life filled with powerful emotional rewards. Balancing these two superpowers takes hard, dedicated inner work. The balance of your heart and mind happens in stillness of your own soul. Calming your mind will allow your intuition to reveal words of wisdom. You will hear the answers you long for, and synchronize your desire with your choices. Once your intuition is aligned and you are properly attuned, you land in a beautiful place of inner stillness. This is a magical place with a sacred melody that evokes your heart to open up, shine, and surround you with its majestic love, positively affecting everyone that comes near you. This dance of heart and mind must be performed with utmost tenderness, kindness and persistence. Learning to speak gently to yourself, your inner dialogue should reflect the kindest and most loving of words.

Speak to yourself as if you would to your nearest and dearest friend. Be supportive, patient, tender and praise the efforts made. Calmly reflect on weaknesses and approach them with a sense of deeper understanding and acceptance. Nobody is perfect, that is the indisputable truth. We all make mistakes, turn the wrong way, or make poor choices. But we learn and move forward. The more patiently you pursue your intuitive inner voice, the sooner you will make clear, reliable contact with it. The deeper your inner calm, the sooner your heart will open and awaken an entirely new part of you. If you tend to work more from the heart, learn to listen to your mind and your higher consciousness about how you lead your life. This is the Earth dimension, we are here to learn, experience and everybody, you included, will eventually learn what they have to.

Living from your heart will always open a new door and guide you precisely in the direction of your true passion. This is an excellent quality to possess, however, utilizing your higher mind will almost guarantee you success.

> **THE MORE FORGIVING AND UNDERSTANDING YOU ARE WITH YOURSELF AND OTHERS, THE FASTER YOU WILL MAKE SPIRITUAL PROGRESS.**

Let's look at an example; if you follow your heart and give a relationship a chance, because you are coming truly from your heart, it is most likely that the Universe will help you move forward, even if this particular relationship does not work out.

Why?
Because following your heart puts you closer to your destined path. Despite the possibility that the partner was not the right one for you, afterwards you may find yourself in new circumstances, new situation, new environment because you followed your heart. The new environment may be much better for your life purpose, and your journey will continue until you eventually meet the person that is meant to be your companion in life. If you do not follow your heart, but only your mind, and give up an opportunity of love because of logical

impracticalities, and justifications your mind provided, you will end up with nothing. No love, and you will simply stagnate in the same place. Nothing will change. Why?

This is the reality you must accept and recognize. There are no guarantees in life, nobody can give you a bullet proof contract and promise, you will have and accomplish everything you ever wanted. You won't know until you take a chance and give it your best shot. That's all it takes. Take a chance, and see what the Universe has in store for you. The more courageous you are, the more amazing the reward, when you finally get it. And make no mistake, you may lose ten times, get hurt, feel discouraged, broken, forgotten or cursed. But just remember, giving up is very easy.

OPENING YOUR HEART TO LOVE REQUIRES TAKING A CHANCE.

Keep going and keep opening your heart. You will see, the Universe will reward you. You will find love at the perfect predestined moment and then everything will make great sense. Using your mind to hear your heart is the magical combination. You have access to it, all that is required is your willingness to take a chance. And let's not forget, this life is a chance. You took a chance by coming back into this world, and if you are reading these words, chances are, you are somewhere warmly tucked away, enjoying the luxury of self-exploration. So why not take another chance and really make the very best of it.

It is totally and completely your decision. Likewise, if you are in a relationship, it is never too late to open your heart wider, deepen your connection and renew your commitment. By opening your heart fearlessly, you are ascending closer to the field of unconditional love.

RESCUE YOURSELF FIRST

The syndrome of wanting to be rescued is a fairy tale theme. When everything is falling apart, when the walls around you are crumbling down, when your life is in shambles, you long to be rescued. Where is the prince or princess on the white horse that will make everything better, make all the mean things go away, and fight your inner dragons? You may wish for the prince on the horse, but keep in mind a few very important details. First of all, if this prince is really experienced in fighting dragons, chances are his shield may be worn out, his horse may be of different color and he may have a few battle scars himself. If the princess that you're wishing for, is like a resilient otherworldly being, it is most likely she endured some hefty battles on her own, and might be reluctant to open her heart. Now reality sets in. What if your rescuer perhaps needs to be rescued as well?

You see, the rescuer may love to play the rescuer in perpetuity. Once you are rescued, you don't need them anymore and your dynamics will shift profoundly. If the rescuer enjoys rescuing because it makes them feel mighty and powerful, the moment the thrill is gone, they may not be so sure what to do with you next. And you won't be sure yourself either. A cabin fever restlessness may develop rapidly and your fairy tale will go up in smoke. When do you need rescuing? When you simply feel broken, discouraged, overwhelmed, too weak, or incapable of fighting life's challenges on your own. But eventually the beginning dynamic will shift and a new dynamic will ensue.

> **LOOKING TO BE RESCUED**
> **IS ONLY A BANDAGE TO YOUR WEAKNESS AND INNER DEMONS**
> **THAT YOU CAN'T, OR REFUSE TO FIGHT ON YOUR OWN.**

But one cannot control everything in life, or predict the impossible, and perhaps you will find yourself in the role of a rescuer or being rescued. If you are aware of it, and honestly communicate about it, you can mold the situation into a healthy dynamic. But it will require a lot of work. And chances are the person who needs rescuing is afraid and in survival mode. This is not ideal. Make a conscious effort to recognize all elements that have brought you into this current dynamic, so that if a person who's character is that of a rescue prince or princess finds you, you honestly share with them the intention, desire and wish to be an equal partner and not always in a lesser, needy and weaker position, because of your beginning set-up. Again, we are returning back to remembering that your best chances for cultivating a long relationship is when you find your equal. Now, don't misunderstand me, your equal may be in a temporary crisis and may need a quick rescue, but if you both recognize that an extraordinary circumstance brought you together, but you are in fact equals, despite one's current weaker position, you will be fine.

The most important thing to remember is, that you don't search for a relationship with a desperately needy, discouraged, self-confidence lacking mindset. No matter how challenging your situation, cultivate self-respect and always recognize signs of desperation you may feel. Desperation is like an annoying, old, unpaid bill that keeps coming in the mail and never seems to shrink or go away. Open the envelope, face the bill and pay it off in small portions. Tackle it head-on, and it will become meaningless and certainly not the cause of desperation.

> **DESPERATION CAN BE A RESULT OF UNATTENDED, UNRESOLVED EMOTIONS OR IGNORANT ACTIONS WITHOUT THE PARTICIPATION OF YOUR MIND.**

Have a talk with yourself and desperation will evaporate and take the need to be rescued with it. You will never be desperate again, because you have learned to rescue yourself.

RECOGNIZE YOUR HEART'S LONGING

When you endure various life's challenges, you slowly create a protective shield. This shield may turn into a wall of insurmountable proportions. Perhaps no-one can tackle it, tear it down, not even you.

If you continue on this path, you eventually adjust yourself to the needs of those around you, your work, other people's belief system and their expectations of you. Mind you, other people's expectations of you present a real danger for your heart. Why?

Because others rarely think of your heart. They usually think of their own needs and your heart doesn't have a really big space on their agenda. Molding your life's decisions, choices and belief system strictly to accommodate others, will slowly but surely suffocate your individuality and certainly your heart. The deeper desires that reside in your heart, hold a tremendously important information for you. They carry the key to your life purpose.

Whatever it is, if your heart feels a deep longing, it needs to be heard, given a chance and opportunity to be experienced. The final outcome may be entirely different from what you imagined, but by following your heart, whatever is meant to be will certainly occur.

EVERYTHING THAT YOU TRULY DESIRE AND LONG FOR, IS A CLEAR INDICATION OF SOMETHING YOU NEED TO EXPLORE.

How can you recognize that hidden voice of your heart?
The only way is in total stillness. First calm down your physical body, then your mind and finally, you will be able to hear your heart. If this seem challenging and you don't know how to go about it, you can begin by having a simple gentle, patient conversation with your heart. Not your mind, but your heart.

So ask yourself;
"How do I feel in my heart?
What does my heart tell me?
What is my answer before I give my mind a chance to analyze?
What do I long to do? What do I wish for in my heart?"
Be patient, the answer will come. You'd be surprised, but most people wish for similar things. Yes, financial stability and a few things here and there, but in the end of the end… everyone just wants love. How they express this desire can vary. And some people who are very challenged may do or say most negative things, but deep down in their heart, all they really want or need is to be loved.

ONCE YOUR HEART IS RECEPTIVE, AND YOU MOVE INTO HEART ENERGY, YOUR SUBTLE FREQUENCY IMMEDIATELY CHANGES.

This is why love heals. Love is the cure for everything. Love is the ultimate fulfilled wish that we all long for.

Why? Because we come from love and within each and every one of us, there is a deep longing to be reunited with the origin of our existence, an endless field of unconditional love, the Universal power that is within each and every one of us. And eventually, we do.

VULNERABILITY AND ATTRACTION OF AN OPEN HEART

Stoic suffering, unexpressed emotions, frozen energy states, feeling closed off…what do all these states have in common? None of them are receptive. They are literally an energy blockade that prevents any healing interaction. As an energy healer or teacher, or simply a kind and giving person, you need to be aware that when you want to help, touch or send healing energy to someone, you need to ask them for permission.

Why? Because, when they give you permission they automatically lower their defenses, and at least partially open up the gate. They become receptive, they allow the possibility of healing loving improvement. And the result? They actually experience improvement.

But they have to consciously agree, and take responsibility for participating. They become a part of their healing process. Likewise, if you want to heal your heart and open it up to loving energy, you need to ask, allow, and awaken your heart.

> **LOVE IS THE HIGHEST FREQUENCY YOU CAN EXPERIENCE WHILE ON THIS EARTHLY REALM.**

Your love frequency becomes stronger and higher. As a result you attract other similar and harmonious frequencies. This experience may at first make you feel very vulnerable and exposed.

But remember, fear will not attract a loving response, fear will only bring out more fear. On the other hand, a fearless open heart will attract another similarly fearless open heart, which will create a harmonious, somewhat equal balance. This is why feeling vulnerable is healthy, courageous and required in order to open your heart to new experiences and love. Projecting iron strength while hiding a broken, fearful heart, will not help you find love. Projecting an open heart with true qualities of your soul, will attract similar souls and a chance for friendship, interactions and potential relationships on your soul level.

THE EMPOWERED HEART

When you recognize and consciously communicate with the deep desires of your heart, you create a powerful alliance between your mind and heart. They work together and not against each other. They consult each other, have debates, listening sessions and work conferences. They try to figure out together how best to collaborate, invent new formulas, come up with a different plan, all in pursuit of your happiness. They become the unwavering, unbeatable team that will propel you further, to experience love and live the best version of your life.

When you work together with the Universe, opportunities, unexpected events and people will come into your life, because your energy field will emit great magnetism and a pleasant, attractive, and sunny disposition.

> **YOU ARE MOST ATTRACTIVE WHEN YOU ARE IN YOUR ELEMENT, HAPPY, FULFILLED, SATISFIED AND EXCITED ABOUT THE POSSIBILITIES IN YOUR LIFE.**

When you consciously cultivate this state, you will experience a truly empowered heart.

MAKING SPACE IN YOUR LIFE AND HEART

Nowadays we are encouraged to escape into the world of internet and all its trappings, the distorted illusions, mind-altering substances, and activities that take us further away from our hearts. When a few attempts at a relationships fail, we sort of invisibly make a pact, that we'll just make ourselves busy and get thru the day. Suddenly the space in your life that was meant for love, shrinks and gets smaller, until one day without even an announcement, it simply disappears. We are too busy to make time for love. We are too busy to stand still for a few minutes each day and listen to what our heart has to say. If we do that for too long, we soon completely forget we have a heart. Everything becomes just a play of necessity and running errands. The joy for life is taken away, the forgotten dreams and the deeply buried desires never to be remembered again. These are the trappings of a life distracted, wondering off on a path to nowhere.

The one thing that makes life worth living is love. Whatever way you experience it, you need to make space for it. Even if it means you have a home full of plants that you love, and they make your heart sing when one blooms, even that is an experience of love. Having a pet gives you an opportunity for boundless unconditional love and affection. Pets are tremendously healing beings, and can help sustain your heart when you are not in a relationship. And then of course there is the human person to person interaction, the one we all need. This is something that is necessary for us like air, water and the sun. It is important to consciously make space for another person, if you wish to attract them or keep them in your life. Make space and they will come. Maintain and cultivate the space and they will stay.

This week is focused on helping you remember your heart, recognize the importance of heart communication within yourself and the power that an open and receptive heart is capable of projecting.

If you are single, this is a perfect time to consciously release and let go of the old, forgive yourself and others, and make a beautiful space for a new, different relationship, nothing like the one before. It will attract an equal, someone who will share similar longings and ideas of what a happy, supportive, harmonious, loving and kind interaction requires.

> **WHETHER YOU ARE SINGLE OR IN A RELATIONSHIP,
> YOUR HEART IS YOUR OWN AND YOU NEED TO CONNECT TO IT.**

If you are in a relationship, this week is focused on reminding you to return back to your heart and re-examine your original wishes, desires and longings. In order to be content and fulfilled in a relationship, you need to pay attention to your own heart. If you don't, the nagging discontentment will creep into your relationship and pollute it with dissatisfaction. Energy cleansing and heart healing needs to be done individually as well. Learn to stand on your own, as well as together. Always remember, in order to sustain the balance in a relationship, you need two equal partners. This equality and balance is established thru energy-frequency togetherness and synchronicity. Mudras are a uniquely powerful tool to accomplish precisely that. Begin with yourself, your own inner workings. Always expand your perception beyond what you see. Close your eyes and sense what you feel, what is the inner voice that guides you, and what does your beautiful precious heart want? Pay attention and do everything you can, to fulfill its wish and desire.

YOUR ASSIGNMENT

AFFIRMATION

> YOUR HEART IS THE SINGLE
> MOST PRECIOUS POSSESSION YOU HAVE.
> ACKNOWLEDGE IT AND LISTEN TO IT EVERY DAY.

DIARY

This week you will begin the conversation with your precious heart. I know this may seem odd, but you will be surprised how much your heart has to tell you, once you listen. Usually, we don't have the tendency to take a moment and ask ourselves how the heart really feels. You could ask this question any part of your body and learn how to hear an answer. You would be surprised to find out that you feel tired, perhaps deprived of attention, and tender care. Perhaps you need to eat healthier and get more rest. Your body will tell you, but unless you listen, you won't know. Now your heart is ready to reveal what's inside, so listen well. Once you are familiar with its wishes, you can begin nurturing it with loving care. Don't expect your future or current partner to heal your heart. You need to heal it yourself. Why? Because it is YOUR heart!

PROCESS

Work thru the questions, come back in a few days, see if anything changed, add it on, clarify, clean it up, and self-discover through the process.

PRACTICE

Work with the diary, answer the questions and practice the Mudras listed. Write down how you feel before and after the Mudra practice. Observe the shift in your energy field.

> WHEN YOUR HEART SINGS,
> YOU ARE ON YOUR DESTINED PATH.
> IS YOUR HEART SINGING AT THE MOMENT?

Your Workspace
HOW DO YOU FEEL IN YOUR HEART?

Practice the Mudras, sit in stillness and be patient. In a few moments, you will feel the answer. This may surprise you, perhaps overwhelm you with tears of sadness, grief, loss or loneliness. Perhaps old hurt will resurface and an old memory will fly thru your thoughts. Whatever it is, accept it, recognize it and consciously allow it to express itself. Prepare to let it go. Now you have acknowledged the current emotional state of your heart. Write down your experience.

Your Workspace

WHAT IS MY HEART TELLING ME?

Now proceed to sense the message your heart will convey to you. It may come as a single thought, a sensation, an idea or reflection, or a message of wisdom. Your heart carries deep knowledge that will reveal sought-after answers. All you need to do, is empty your mind of all thoughts, and allow the messages to flow in. Ask your question, and an answer will come, light as a feather, and with unwavering certainty. Now you have learned to listen and establish communication with your heart.

Write down your experience.

Your Workspace
WHAT DOES MY HEART WISH FOR?

This is important for you to discover. Simply ask:
"Dear Heart, what is going to make you happy, what do you need?"
Take your time and pay attention, it will answer, perhaps with a whisper in the beginning, but after a few moments, you will hear it clearly. It has a desire. What is it? An answer will come when you're ready, and do not be surprised if your heart has many more wishes than you ever imagined. Never forget about them, follow thru and explore how you can help fulfill them. Listen well and then promise yourself you will do everything in your power to fulfill its wish. If you follow this recipe, you will find what you've always wanted.
Write down your experience.

For your Mudra Practice

LET GO OF ALL BURDENS, HEAL YOUR HEART

Before you can make space for new, you need to release the old. Anything and everything that evokes feelings of sadness, grief, sorrow, hurt, pain or heart wounds, needs to be let go and released into the Universe. While certain life experiences leave a permanent imprint of grief, making peace with them will help make them manageable. A healthy solution is not to ignore but acknowledge them, while not allowing them to take over your life. You experienced much, and learned a lot. But the purpose of life's lessons is not to overwhelm you with grief, but infuse you with wisdom of highest value, the golden principles and unwavering certainty of who you are, and what kind of love you wish and deserve to experience. Take your time and practice the next Mudra set as often as necessary, until you feel light, calm, serene and certain of the irrevocable beauty of your Spirit.

SOOTHE YOUR HEART'S WOUNDS

Your heart wounds can sometimes feel like physical pain. How high is your pain threshold? Your physical body may be able to withstand a lot, but the energy field of your heart may be delicate and highly sensitive. Nobody will ever know it, but you do. Take time for yourself and soothe your heart of all it endured, no matter how far away and long ago. Every painful experience needs to be diffused, melted, and eliminated. If you never dealt with it, it still lingers in a secret compartment of your heart, taking up valuable space. Soothe and allow your heart to heal, so it can regain its vibrancy and return to its natural higher frequency.

YOUR HEART AND MIND ARE A POWER TEAM

When you battle the inner conflict of whom you should follow, your heart or your mind, the outcome will depend greatly on your general character traits, as well as your preconceived ideas and assumptions of what is right or wrong. Those beliefs stem from the role-model behavior that you witnessed as a child. Did it prove right? Did your role models display perfect choices, behavior and a happy-end outcome? Don't you think it's time to decide for yourself? Learn to be balanced, create a field of equal opportunity for your heart and mind. They are both immensely valuable. Hear them and make a fair, bold, confident and masterful choice.

ANYBODY HOME?

You may be surrounded by a most beautiful landscape, but if you don't open your eyes, you won't see anything. You may be privy to glorious sounds, but if you refuse to listen, they will disappear into the ether. And you may be fortunate to be surrounded by love, but if you don't open your heart, nobody will be able to enter and join your burning flame. Finding, maintaining and magnifying love requires your conscious participation. Are you here? Don't settle for the role of a passive observer, but become an engaged player in the experience of life. Get your toes wet and take a swim. Open your heart and courageously welcome new waves of this healing emotion, in whatever unique way it reaches you.

LOVE IS EVERYTHING AND EVERYWHERE...

Attracting love means diminishing fear. It means having no doubts you deserve to be loved, no hang ups about how lovable you are, no hesitation to give it another chance, no useless pride when it needs to be nurtured. Attracting love means you understand that this moment is all that matters, and when everything is stripped away, and you are presented with a choice of life filled with no risk, practicality, but no love, or life with unconditional love and less Earthly clutter, you would always choose love. And when you do, you will be wealthier than you imagined. When you are surrounded by love and become love, everything else begins to flow your way. You will understand and feel with every fiber of your being, that love is truly the only experience that matters.

MUDRA FOR HEALING A BROKEN HEART

Sit with a straight back and keep your shoulders down, nice and relaxed. Lift your hands up in front of your face. Gently hold the hands together, with the tips of the middle fingers pointing towards the Third Eye area. Your hands are touching your face, the thumbs are placed around your nose and mouth. Leave some space between the little fingers and breathe through this opening. Hold for Three minutes then relax.

BREATH
LONG, DEEP AND SLOW AS IF DRINKING WATER THROUGH THE SPACE BETWEEN PALMS AND THE OPENING BETWEEN LITTLE FINGERS

MANTRA
HUMME HUM HUM BRAHAM
(Calling Upon Your Infinite Self)

CHAKRAS
HEART - 4, THROAT - 5, THIRD EYE - 6

HEALING COLORS
GREEN, BLUE, INDIGO

AFFIRMATION
I RELEASE ALL ANXIETY AND REPLACE IT WITH PEACE

MUDRA FOR HELP IN A GRAVE SITUATION

Sit with a straight back and keep your shoulders down, nice and relaxed. Bend your elbows and place both palms on your upper chest, fingers together and pointing toward each other. Gently press your hands against your chest. Feel the healing energy of your hands soothing your heart. Hold for Three minutes, then relax.

BREATH
Long, deep and slow through your nose

MANTRA
HUMME HUM, BRAHAM HUM, BRAHAM HUM
(Calling upon Your Infinite Self)

CHAKRAS
Heart - 4

HEALING COLORS
Green

AFFIRMATION
I SOOTHE MY BODY, MIND, HEART AND SOUL

MUDRA FOR OPENING YOUR HEART

Sit with a straight back and keep your shoulders down, nice and relaxed. Lift your hands up in front of your heart and create a cup, palms facing each other, all fingers spread out and pointing up. Only the upper parts of your thumbs and pinkies and the bases of your palms are touching. Keep all fingers outstretched. Hold for Three minutes and relax.

BREATH
LONG, DEEP AND SLOW THROUGH YOUR NOSE

MANTRA
SAT NAM
(Truth Is God's Name, One in Spirit)

CHAKRAS
HEART - 4

HEALING COLORS
GREEN

AFFIRMATION
I AM READY TO OPEN MY HEART

MUDRA FOR LOVE

Sit with a straight back and keep your shoulders down, nice and relaxed. Curl the middle and ring fingers into your palms. Extend your index and little fingers and cross over the bent fingers with your thumbs. Raise your arms up to the level of your head. Keep your elbows from sinking. Hold for Three minutes, then relax.

BREATH
INHALE EIGHT SHORT COUNTS, WITH ONE STRONG, LONG EXHALE

MANTRA
SAT NAM WAHE GURU
(God Is Truth, His Is the Supreme Power and Wisdom)

CHAKRAS
HEART - 4

HEALING COLORS
GREEN

AFFIRMATION
I AM LOVE, I GIVE AND RECEIVE LOVE

MUDRA FOR HAPPINESS

Sit with a straight back and keep your shoulders down, nice and relaxed. Bend your elbows and bring your arms to your sides, away from your body. Elbows are just below the level of the shoulders. Palms are facing forward. Stretch the index and middle fingers and bend the ring and little fingers, pressing them into the palms firmly with the thumbs. Hold for three minutes and relax.

BREATH
LONG, DEEP AND SLOW THROUGH YOUR NOSE

MANTRA
SAT NAM *(Truth Is God's Name, one in Spirit)*

CHAKRAS
HEART - 4

HEALING COLORS
GREEN

AFFIRMATION

MY HEART IS HAPPY, I AM HAPPY

MUDRA FOR UPLIFTING YOUR HEART

Sit with a straight back and lift your arms up to shoulder level, elbows bent and parallel to the ground. Tuck your thumbs under your armpits and keep the rest of your fingers straight and together. Your hands should be above your breasts, palms facing down. As you inhale, the distance between middle fingertips gets bigger; as you exhale, the middle fingertips should touch or cross over each other. With each inhalation feel the healing energy expand your heart and chest area.

BREATH
Long, deep and slow through your nose

CHAKRAS
Heart - 4

HEALING COLORS
Green

AFFIRMATION

MY HEART IS UPLIFTED AND FILLED WITH LOVE

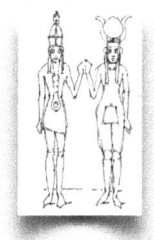

Week Four

YOUR SOUL'S JOURNEY OF LOVE

THE DEEPER NEEDS OF YOUR SOUL AND HEART

Behind all your life stories, adventures, heartache and bliss, there lies an underlying golden thread of your Soul's journey thru the many lives and loves you have experienced. No doubt that love plays a grand role in your life, whether you admit it or not. Even someone who doesn't prioritize or has very little time or luck with relationships, will not be able to experience a full spectrum of life, without a journey thru some kind of a love story.

All love stories are unique and your experiences are one of a kind. Surely there are similar situations, dynamics and outcomes, but only your unique behavior blended with your lovers particular disposition will create what you two have. The love that you experienced in this life has left a certain trace, a complex imprint, that affects you for the rest of your life. There is no questions about that. Many times a deeply emotional experience of a love relationship, changes your entire life's perspective, pulls you in a completely different direction, and lands you in a brand new, unexpected territory. You can not plan love, but love will revise your life.

> **LOVE WILL CHANGE YOUR LIFE, YOUR HEART AND YOUR LOVE MATRIX.**

Hopefully it will uplift you, teach you countless lessons and make you a better, deeper, and a more compassionate person. Of course it can also burn you and propel you into a tailspin of temporary suffering. The possibilities are truly endless. No matter what, you will transform and never see life quite the same way. Now imagine what an incredibly complex rainbow of love journeys you would see, if you combined all of your current and past life experiences together! All these adventures have contributed to who you are today, even if you don't remember the intricate details of your far away past.

> **ON YOUR SOUL LEVEL, MEMORIES OF LOVE NEVER DIE.**

Love has made you a better person, and even though you've lived thru heartaches and loss, you've courageously embarked on a new venture again and again. What is of interest to you now, is this lifetime, but what happened long ago, is something that has contributed to how you are today – especially in matters of love. The secret undiscovered details about you, hold the key to resolving the puzzle of your heart.

How can you uncover this?
Reflection, deep inner conversation with your heart, facing your old, mysterious and unreasonable fears, likes and dislikes, and recognizing your heart's desires, all this will offer you obvious clues. We have worked thru all these aspects in this book, for the specific reason of self-exploration, self-understanding, listening to your heart, and unraveling the knots that perhaps hold you captive in old patterns.

But now, let's explore beyond the easily understood challenges you are experiencing. Let us look outside the limits of time, beyond this visible world. This is a very complex investigative process. Some may think you are dabbling in the dark, but it is not so. There are certain very clear clues that you can recognize, but you have to know where to look, and pay attention. Everything we have worked thru until now, has encouraged you to dig deeper in understanding or recognizing certain habits, or pre-set formulas that you have lived by.

If this behavior can't be traced back to something that happened to you in this life, it can obviously be found in your older memory bank. It belongs to your far-away past. And even if you cannot decipher the precise details, keep in mind, that even understanding a general disposition will help you tremendously. Whatever strong desires you carry in your heart, need to be acknowledged and explored. Even if it makes no sense to others, or your current situation, you can incorporate your heart's wishes into your life here and now, and experience a deeper sense of fulfillment and inner peace. How can you accomplish this?

Recognize and eliminate any feelings of restlessness, dissatisfaction, worry, regret, anger or sadness, which resulted from ignoring your heart and not pursuing something that you want, desire or long for. In the faraway memory, you carry this information like a very valuable treasure chest, filled with clues an answers for your mission in this life. Why not pay attention and explore? At least think about it, allow the possibility of fulfilling your desires in your mind? And then, perhaps you can begin to pursue your dreams with little steps, and just see how it feels. Keep in mind, we are focusing on relationship and partnership dynamics not on general life desires, although they can be tightly interconnected.

> **IF SOMEONE WOULD ASK YOU WHAT IS YOUR IDEA OF THE IDEAL PARTNERSHIP, WHAT WOULD BE YOUR ANSWER?**

You may shock or surprise yourself at your response. Or at how undefined your answer is. Or how unreasonable and impossible you make it sound. Is your answer exaggerated? Does it linger in the unreachable, unrealistic clouds of phantasy? Is it at all possible in today's world to find what you imagine your ideal partnership should be? Knowing what you want is incredibly important. If you don't define the basic principles, you are really just lazy about exploring this opportunity.

Saying; "I just want someone that loves me," is like walking into a travel agency and saying you just want to travel. Yes, but where, and how, and for how long…and with whom? And why do you want to go here? And have you really thought about the reality of landing on a tropical deserted island in Robinson Crusoe style? That's not going to work, if you are used to comfortable hotels and prepared food, right? Likewise with your partner, know what would, could, and can work for you.

If your main desire is having a family, think about the consequences of being careless with your selection of a partner. How many people embark onto a relationship with the hurried idea of wanting a family, but zero idea of what kind of partner, the potential co-parent they envision, that they would feel compatible with? And for the rest of their life no less! So they quickly embark on a relationship, produce a few children, only to later discover that they are not in any way aligned with their partner, and disagree even about the basics of child rearing. What were they thinking? And who or what was their primary concern? It could not have been the child, that is now stuck in an unharmonious challenge between parents that don't get along.

> **KNOWING WHAT YOU WANT IS THE KEY
> TO ATTRACTING YOUR IDEAL PARTNER, WITH WHOM
> YOU'LL CREATE AN ENDURING, EXCEPTIONAL RELATIONSHIP.**

Whatever the answer of your life's main desire is, it will certainly help pursue your mission with clarity and not like a blind leading the blind. Conscious living is conscious loving. If you want to experience partnership and a free lifestyle with lots of travel and exploration, your partner will have to be somewhat open to this option, right? So, if you end up with a partner that loves a reliable nine to five office job, your unfulfilled or ignored desire will become a source of bitterness towards your partner. When in fact it has nothing to do with them, but simply with your personal desire for adventure. If you are not aware of your needs, sooner or later while you are in a relationship, this desire will creep up in a nagging, bitter expression. If you insist on ignoring your state of inner awareness, you may end up blaming your partner for something they have nothing to do with in the first place.

Taking responsibility for fulfilling your life's desires is your matter, and not your partner's duty. How you navigate, communicate, compromise and find a balance fulfilling your own, their own and your mutual needs, this will prove to be the mastery of the success or failure in your relationship. And of course, in a long-term relationship, you may continuously rediscover new desires. Perhaps at the time your relationship began, you were very young, and pretty clueless about your life's main desires. After you fell in love, your ignorance continued until perhaps years later, you had an epiphany and suddenly knew what you need in order to feel fulfilled. This can happen…and then what? You can work thru anything, any individual circumstance, turn of events, unexpected new dynamics, challenges or lucky surprises, truly anything, IF there is a desire to make it work and a willingness to compromise and communicate in a loving, kind and respectable manner.

If you love each other profoundly and want to make it work, chances are you will suceed. You can have two people that are as different as salt and pepper, fire and ice, sun and the moon, but if their love is strong, they will mold it to keep their hearts intact and blended, while finding ways to accommodate their individual needs. It is the magic of the journey, and new discoveries together that create beautiful, long lasting partnerships.

What if you partner is a loner, and needs to go to a deserted island once a year, to find their peace? If you work with this, they will go and most likely come back to you even more crazy about you than before. Because you did not steal their dream. And if this desire is unreasonable and impossible for you to accept, then find a compromise of sorts, where they get a little bit of what they need, as do you, and hopefully everybody is happy. This is really a great way to help both partners figure out their individual needs, while keeping harmony. Give it a try. If a partner is cranky and dissatisfied, forever blaming the other who prevented them from "living their dream," there is no better recipe than giving them what they wish, to see, if this is truly the reason for their discontent. You may be surprised how someone who is continuously blaming their partner for not being able to follow their dream, may remain passive and discontent despite getting their wish. Now you'll know, it has nothing to do with you. Or they may never pursue their dream, but the failure to do so is now their own responsibility, not yours. Maybe they needed to experience this. You may find out, that complaining crankiness and the habit of constantly blaming others, is simply part of their character and has nothing to do with their unfulfilled desires. This way, it becomes clear they simply have a cranky character disposition. Now you can think about how manageable this is for you. If you are a pleaser, this realization will save you from a lifetime of trying to please the impossible one.

No matter how much love two people have for each other, their personal dreams are unique. They can contain similar elements, but the singularity is guaranteed.

How compatible are your dreams?

This is the clearest indicator if it is possible to fulfill your dreams. If one partner wants to be a team, and the other loves to do everything alone, this won't work. The challenge presented can be resolved with a compromise. Do some things together as a team, and some not. Your own inner security can overcome aspects of fear, and help you understand and lovingly support your partner on their individual journey. Your deeper desires could be unusual, and perhaps difficult to understand. Perhaps you want to change professions, begin painting in midlife, or go on a month long journey, backpacking through the mountains. But if you take into consideration that these old wishes have a reason for existing, and have nothing to do with your partner, you will eliminate a massive source of conflict and prevent a crisis that happens, when someone feels trapped or robbed of their life long dreams. Your desires hold the key to your soul's journey, and your partner's desires are equally important to them, as yours are to you. Understand that their individual dreams and wishes may have nothing to do with you, but with them. Don't take them personally, understand them, observe them, talk about them and make space for your partner to pursue and fulfill them.

If you are single at the moment, this is important for you to work thru, so that when you do meet your partner, you understand who you are, what you need, and what are your wishes and dreams. Then, there will be no surprises later. You will be able to tell them right in the beginning, how important something is to you and they will recognize this as an intricate part of you. Your soul's needs are of great importance. Knowing and understanding them will offer you an almost guarantee that your communication will thrive in honesty and confidence about who you are. If you do not know who you are, you will almost surely attract the wrong person. As confused and unsure as you are, the Universe may send you an equally confused and unsure person. This is just one of many possibilities. Then there are a million other incredibly complicated possible options.

If you are in a relationship, it will be most important to establish a very secure and honest communication space, where you can share your newly discovered desires without intimidating, frightening, manipulating or blaming your partner. You can encourage each other to rediscover new layers of yourselves, and find ways to accommodate each other in reasonable and acceptable ways, so that you can experience a deeper level of self-contentment. This can then translate into a deeper, unconditional love and respect for each other. It can be incredibly rejuvenating and will offer you so much "breathing room," that your magnified love will amaze you with its depth and continuous growth.

Remember, there are no limitations in love. You can always love someone more today than yesterday, even if you believed you reached the highest level of love. Love has no boundaries and expands into infinity.

If you've ever experienced the energy sensation of Divine love, you know it feels like a powerful wave of indescribable magnitude. Human love is but a tiny drop of that ocean.

> **OUR UNDERSTANDING OF LOVE IS QUITE LIMITED,
> IN PROFOUND CONTRAST TO WHAT LOVE IS ALL ABOUT...
> LIMITLESS, NEVER ENDING, ETERNAL.
> CAN YOU TRULY FATHOM THE MEANING OF THESE WORDS?**

YOUR SOUL PATH AND LOVE

Now let's look at another very fascinating and important aspect: your ability to receive and give love. However many lives and loves you've had, here you are in this particular moment in time, with all your mysterious, unknown past experiences, and all your new hopes. And inevitably in a past life, you've had your heart broken, and you suffered through loss of love. A broken heart can be mended, eventually, and always carries the possibility of resurrection. You may not feel the same way about the next partner, and you may always carry a torch for one specific person from your past that touched you on a deep level, and left you wounded beyond words. But you will love again.

On the other hand, where there is loss, the dynamics are different from a heartbreak. Loss as a result of a person's death is challenging in very complex ways. If your love was fulfilled and you experienced a loving relationship, loss will carry a different shade of grief. You will feel sorrow, but will be more resolved, than if you've never had the chance to experience love. However, your missing and longing for the loved one will never cease.

If your loss is connected to unfulfilled, unrequited love, it will haunt you thru lifetimes, until one day, you will meet again. You may not know you carry this unfulfilled love for another soul, but when you meet them, you will certainly feel it, usually in an instant. Any and all experiences of love where there is an unfinished, unresolved and powerful emotional connection, will pull you back together in a future life.

> **LOVE IS A MOST POWERFUL MAGNET, RESILIENT AGAINST THE LIMITATIONS OF SPACE AND TIME OF THIS DIMENSION. IT DOES NOT MATTER WHERE OR WHEN, REST ASSURED, YOU WILL FIND EACH OTHER AGAIN.**

The countless stories that you've lived thru can leave you with numerous love connections that require your completion of the journey together. This can come in countless formations. But all of these experiences shape who you are, affect the decisions you make, and play a crucial role in how your life unfolds. This is not an easy, simple to figure-out puzzle. It is in fact a most fascinating riddle, one that I've dedicated a lot of time to, with my past-life Time Travel Therapy – spontaneous regression work.

If you are reading this book, you are a seeker. A seeker wants answers, and as such, you most definitely need answers about yourself, for until you know who you are and your destined journey, your mission, your purpose…until you resolve that, you will wonder about with an underlying sense of discontent.

How has your soul's path interacted with other souls thru love relationships that you experienced? Who was there in the past, who is here now, and has returned with a mission to complete your unresolved, unfulfilled story?

This are essentially the most important questions one can ask. Relationships change and perhaps in one life you are close friends, confidants, relatives, in another you are partners, in yet another you carry out an important mission. Perhaps you lost each other in a dramatic and catastrophic way, beyond your control. Maybe you sacrificed your life for one another. This is your soul's path, and the way love interacted thru your journey, holds the key to why you are here now. This puzzle holds the answer to your partner status at the moment, who that partner was, is or will be, and where does it all lead.

> **IT IS NOT SIMPLE TO UNDERSTAND
> WHO YOUR COMPANIONS THRU THE MANY LIFETIMES WERE,
> BUT WHAT'S IMPORTANT, IS TO KNOW THAT YOU HAD THEM,
> HAVE THEM NOW, AND WILL MEET THEM AGAIN IN THE FUTURE.**

Your soul's path is a mystery to be solved. You won't figure out everything, but perhaps you can, at least for now, figure out the main players. The one main player is you. When you include this decisive element into your experience of love in this lifetime, you open up the endless field of possibilities, expand your understanding of your current experience, and find the key to the answers that are most pressing.

By understanding your deeper, older possible adventures, you can change and shift your patterns, and break the seemingly challenging spell that you are under. Defining your expectations, clarifying your desires, and opening up to new, very different possibilities, will create an energy shift that will attract a surprisingly positive, healthier dynamic.

Perhaps your fear of abandonment or loss, is locked within a past life experience you had together. Maybe anxiety of a pending crisis is connected to your previous life pattern. It is possible your continuous conflict originates from a similar issue in your past life.

What if your loss of passion has to do with your personal need for a challenge?

If the unknown excites you and chaos feels familiar, you will always subconsciously create it. You need to find a different outlet where you experience suspenseful excitement, so you can stop creating chaos in your relationships. If you like a chase, or playing games, once the initial chase is over, but you still feel the same urge, you may quickly chase many great partners right out of your life. It may not be what you truly want, but it certainly is what you keep recreating. There are literally endless possibilities, but your self-understanding can transform any challenging dynamic into a more harmonious, compatible and beautiful experience. Together, you can laugh at your interesting differences and unusual longings, and figure them in harmony, not frustration and blame. Mutual curiosity about each other and respect for individuality will propel your relationship further, as you discover new adventures that you both enjoy.

Nobody ever owns anyone else. You are partners by choice and the power of love that bounds you together. If this love is ancient, don't even try pretending it's not there. If the connection is new in this lifetime, know that probably a whole lot happened to your partner in their far away past, before you ever showed up on the scene.

> **YOU AS A SOUL HAVE BEEN MARRIED, DIVORCED, ENGAGED, WIDOWED, PURSUED, BETRAYED, DESERTED AND FOUGHT OVER, AS A MAN AND A WOMAN, MANY, MANY TIMES.**

Who you are in this lifetime, is a composite of all your past experiences, and therefore impossibly complex. But love ignores all these aspects. True, powerful love is not dissuaded by anything. You may fall in love with someone who seems as different from you, as humanly possible. Love doesn't care, it's not selective. A past life connection will always recognize you on some level, no matter how, or where you hide. Unfinished, unrequited, unfulfilled love will find you, for it lives thru death and other dimensions. It will find you once again. And you may try to escape it, but you can't. Why?

> **UNFULFILLED LOVE IS PRECISELY PART OF THE REASON WHY YOU CAME BACK INTO THIS WORLD.**

YOUR ANCIENT RELATIONSHIPS

This is a most fascinating topic. But in experience of love, it is actually quite important and essential in your understanding of love relationships. By calling into this conversation the concept of reincarnation, I'd like to mention a few important aspects that play a role in helping you better understand these beautiful and fascinating dynamics.

Obviously, you have old links that you will reconnect with in this life. It is also apparent that whatever challenged you before, unless you worked it out, will be challenging once again. If trust is your issue, perhaps it originated centuries ago and here you are now, dealing with an unreasonable doubt of trust. There are endless combinations where a challenge that can't be logically connected to this lifetime, was most likely the source of your crisis before. This affects all your various relationship dynamics. Parents, children, friends in work or in a battle, countless combinations of human relationships create interactive dynamics and continue thru many lifetimes.

> **LOVE RELATIONSHIPS ARE MOST BINDING, BECAUSE TOGETHER YOU EXPERIENCED THE HIGHEST FREQUENCY POSSIBLE FOR YOU, AT THAT TIME.**

You uplifted and elevated each other's souls in the evolutionary process. This is memorable and dear to you. You helped each other ascend. And perhaps thru numerous lifetimes, you continuously help each other ascend, until one day you will reach your final self-realized destination and complete your soul's journey.

But now, let's mention the other side of the spectrum. Relationship of hate will bind you as well, force you to overcome and dig yourself out of deep karmic connections, and evolve towards the light. An interesting flow between these two polar opposites is the fact, that two people who are fiercely in love, when facing challenges, can very quickly turn that love into hate. It is like the swaying of the pendulum – love and fear, the two big polar opposites. And if love frequency is too powerful to manage and frightens you with its overwhelming force, you'll hide and run back into the comfort zone of fear, that envelops and pulls you down. You feel the crippling fear of losing the love that propelled you so high. This is why a volatile, emotionally charged couple could declare, "I love you" one minute, and in the heat of an argument proclaim, "I hate you," all within a short time span.

How can this be? When we feel profound love, it frightens us. The power of love will eventually pull you upwards, but until you can physically, emotionally and spiritually tolerate and function in the higher frequency, you will keep sliding down the slippery hillside. With time and experience, you will trust your own step and move upwards, without sliding back into the comfort zone of familiar lower frequency.

Love pushes you to grow, ascend, evolve and move upwards. Sometimes this can be challenging, but that is what a human life is all about. For this reason, we need human interaction and spiritual soul companions. We help each other on this journey. We agreed to do so before accepting this Earthly assignment.

THERE ARE SPIRITUAL CONTRACTS WE MADE, PROMISES TO BE KEPT, AND AGREEMENTS TO BE HONORED.

They contain the possibility to grow and amend the old, unresolved dynamics between each other, but all with a purpose of advancement, ascension, always striving for an upwards, soul-liberating motion. When your soul agrees to return to this Earth plane, it knows who will be waiting, meeting and connecting with them again. It is mutually agreed upon. You both agreed.

NO MATTER HOW CHALLENGING YOUR RELATIONSHIP MAY BE, YOU AGREED TO THIS ENCOUNTER, RELATIONSHIP OR PARTNERSHIP.

Now the big question presents itself:
How in the world can we find and recognize each other?

RECOGNIZE YOUR PAST LOVES

When you meet someone for the very first time, and feel like you have known them all your life…the fact is, you have known them longer than your entire current life. This is clearly a connection from before. When a jolt of force startles you the moment your eyes first meet, you experience a soul recognition. Your connection may quickly develop into a friendship, partnership, or love relationship. Keep in mind the word "may." It is entirely possible that at the time you meet, you are in challenging circumstances, married to different people, or otherwise unavailable. In such a case, nothing will happen, at least not visibly. But the energetic imprint that the person left on you will linger, sometimes for years, even till the end of your life, and beyond…until eventually, you shall meet again. It would surprise you how often older people, before they pass away, bring up precisely these kind of memories. They recall how they met someone decades ago that they felt an immense connection with, but due to circumstances they never saw them again, or their fondness for each other never had a chance to bloom. It is clear, that they are taking this memory with them, beyond the gates of human life. They regretfully remember the details of their one destined meeting, as they review their life and recognize the unfinished, unresolved, or unfulfilled dreams they still carry. What do you think happens to these unresolved feelings? They live on in some other dimension of existence and when your soul returns, these longings have another chance for fulfillment.

In my work with past life regression, I have seen countless cases of similar nature, and you can find an ocean of literature about this ever fascinating topic. It is important to help you understand yourself, your past and current relationships, as well as your unexplored, unfulfilled inner longings. All these intricate past life experiences contribute to where you are today, here and now, in regards to your heart and soul.

> **RECOGNIZING A PAST LIFE LOVE CONNECTION USUALLY CREATES AN INSTANT, OVERWHELMINGLY POWERFUL ENERGY SHIFT.**

You both feel it, but it depends how you understand it, and if you recognize and admit it. You may be synchronized and then again, you may not be. But your meeting offers all these possibilities. What happens next, is up to you. Like all things in love, this can not be planned. This happens when it is meant to happen. Your sense of familiarity with each other is really your soul's old memory of each other. It can be something visual, a physical resemblance to your prior selves, a vocal familiarity, laughter, or any specific "signal" that you recognize in each other. Before you returned to this life, you knew and agreed that you will meet again, and memorized an unusual element, that only the two of you will understand and recognize in each other. It can be almost anything, but it will be an intuitive deep memory that will awaken and get triggered in an instant when you notice it. Perhaps something in their appearance that seems so familiar and close to you, maybe an indescribable energy sensation that will pull you towards each other with irresistible force. Possibly the way you meet, the place, a song, something will throw you into a zone of your own. Your interaction will depend strongly on how and where you left off, your last memory of each other, and final state of you relationship.

Was it harmonious? In such a case you will feel at home with each other.
Was it a conflict? In such a case you will be drawn towards each other, while trying to fight it off. Perhaps you will meet thru a conflict, once more.
Did you lose each other under dramatic circumstances?
In such a case you will have an inexplicable fear of possible loss once more, even if there is no logical reason for it this time around.
Was your last interaction a fulfilled or unfulfilled experience, were you just about to begin your life together and then everything was taken away?
In such a case this mood will linger over you, at least in the beginning of your relationship, or until you overcome it and heal this wound.
Was your final interaction tragic? In such a case you may erroneously fear each other, wrongly associating each other with pending danger or suffering that you experienced before. This is a particularly challenging dynamic, because if one or both of you are afraid of this connection, you may not resolve or fulfill it this lifetime.
Was your last interaction filled with hate, conflict, or animosity? In such a case your interaction in this life may begin with conflict and end up with love. Stranger things have happened.

> **WHEN YOU ARE ENERGETICALLY BOUND TOGETHER, YOU WILL FIND EACH OTHER, PULLED TOGETHER BY AN INVISIBLE FORCE THAT MAY SEEM ENTIRELY ILLOGICAL AND SENSELESS.**

This is why often you may find two people who seem completely ill suited for each other, entangled in a dramatic love story where they both feel unhappy, but their energetic bond keeps pulling them together, until one day they will finally resolve and complete their story. There are so many complex possibilities that can repeat themselves in life. As complicated as the story was in the past, the very sensitive energy elements of that experience are again with you this time around. This is why it is impossible to explain a human love relationship with a cut and dry formula or logical explanations. Your unique story may be so old, so complex, and so interwoven with other dynamics, that it will take a lifetime to resolve, or perhaps it shall continue into the next one.

WHEN YOU ARE SUPPOSED TO MEET, YOU MOST CERTAINLY WILL.

When your story is unfinished and meant to be continued in this life, have no doubt, you will find each other, even if you are not looking. In fact, you can't look for each other, like you would look for a pair of lost shoes. You can have an open heart, so that when you do meet, you are awakened, aware and receptive. If you found each other, then this deeper understanding of possible previous interaction can help you perceive elements in your current dynamics that may be challenging or difficult. This is meant to cultivate an open mind, a gentle, accepting non-judgmental heart, and the intelligence to understand that your journey together is most certainly teaching you to overcome and grow thru human relationships. Your expanded sense of awareness will help you neutralize any source of conflict, explore the possibilities, and very often you will find most astonishing answers to your puzzling questions, precisely by taking into consideration past life experiences. Don't avoid, but instead acknowledge emotions that feel uneasy, fearful, angry or restless. Explore them, and consciously resolve them, so that nothing is holding you back and preventing you from experiencing the happiness you so wish and deserve. This requires deep inner work as a couple and an awareness of all possible dynamics that have contributed to your current situation.

And of course, there can be times when you may feel to have found the right partner, and it proves not to be so. Perhaps something deeply familiar in their visual appearance evoked sensations that this person has a deep connection with you, and with time you discover that you were wrong. But everyone will bring you an important piece of the puzzle for your evolutionary process. However, it happens often, that the true partner you finally meet, seems physically very similar to your past life partner. This is your soul memory picture of them, but you were not paying enough attention to other crucial elements. It is certainly not just the appearance of a person that plays a role in your deep connection. When you find the one you love, the physical appearance will play a lesser role in comparison to the energetic match the two of you feel. And all your preconceived ideas of how your partner should look or be, will fly right out the window.

YOUR SOULMATE

> **YOUR SOULMATE CARRIES THE VERY SPECIFIC UNIQUE HEART FREQUENCY THAT RESONATES WITH YOURS.**

This is an old memory that lives deep within you, and that frequency never changes. When you meet your past-life love, the memory that binds you together is bound by all things unseen, the untouchable, indisputable, ever lasting bond that lives on, beyond this place of time and space. You will know.

The question is, will you both recognize each other at the same time? There are endless books out there about how to call your soulmate or find you ideal partner. The truth is; there is no secret formula to do this, and it is not something you can command to occur. In fact, it is quite often naively written how easy is to attract the perfect partner, if you follow steps one, two, three and make up your mind about it. It is not realistic, true, fair or even helpful for a single person to hear how incredibly easy it is to find a mate. The single person can easily feel more discouraged and hopeless, when they fail to find a partner. The truth is, the timing of your love and your partner, when you meet, how you meet, and who they are, all of those factors are not in your hands. So if you are single, rest assured, you are not doing anything wrong, or failing at some totally easy thing that everyone else seems to manage.

It's simply a fact, that nowadays, there are more single people than ever. Do they want to be single? Some do, and some don't. Perhaps you are simply more aware of specific spiritual needs you desire to find in a partner, and don't wish to settle for less. Maybe you will meet your ideal soulmate tomorrow. Who knows? If you are single, and wish to have a compatible loving partner, you will greatly eliminate possible challenges by striving to become a self-realized being on your own. And when the stars are aligned just so, you shall meet your ideal partner, your soulmate, your match. The idea of soulmate can sometimes be very confusing. You may have numerous soulmates thru your life, even a dear friend can be your soulmate of sorts. In my upcoming book *TIME TRAVEL THERAPY*, I write intricately about the concept of soul groups that work together to accomplish what they desire or need. Soulmates can be your closest allies in life, partners, and lovers.

If you are single, this book provides you with much thinking material about what to look for in a compatible partner, instead of creating an idea of a partner that may be entirely ill suited to you. I remind you to pay attention to your heart and not the physical appearances. Look beyond the facade or materially based criteria.

But there is more to it, if you consciously look for a deep soul connection, harmonious frequency and evolutionary compatibility, you are opening an entirely new realm of possibilities. These kinds of dynamics require no words, convincing or justification. The energy simply blends in synchronicity.

LOOK FOR THE SUBTLE ENERGY COMPATIBILITY, THAT OVERRIDES ALL CRITERIA WHICH SOCIETY MAY HAVE PUSHED UPON YOU.

See the bigger picture. This is why this book is guiding you into the deepest layers of your heart and soul, for self-exploration and expansion of your love consciousness.

LOOK FOR YOUR FUTURE LOVE NOT AS A LIMITED HUMAN BEING, BUT AS AN ENLIGHTENED SOUL.

YOUR ASSIGNMENT

AFFIRMATION

> YOUR UNIQUE EXPERIENCE OF ALL PAST LOVES, HAS MOLDED HOW YOU SEE LOVE NOW. RECOGNIZE AND OVERCOME YOUR LIMITATIONS.

DIARY

This week, we take a peek beyond the gates of this dimension. Allow to consider the love stories of your past. Allow to trust that your promised love will find you, that the agreements you made with each other hold, and are kept. Allow the possibility, that everything in this life is not easily explained with logic, and open up your spirit-self, which holds all the answers to your longings, desires, and past loves. Your Spirit is guiding you every day, so that you may fulfill your heart's desires. Call on your Spirit and with the help of Mudra practice, help establish a clear channel of communication with your higher self. The answers are always available to you.

PROCESS

Work thru the questions, come back in a few days, see if anything changed, add it on, clarify, clean it up, and self-discover through the process.

PRACTICE

Work with the diary, answer the questions and practice the Mudras listed. Write down how you feel before and after the Mudra practice. Observe the shift in your energy field.

> TRUST THE UNIVERSE THAT IT WILL BRING BACK YOUR LOVE, AND YOU SHALL NEVER LOSE SIGHT OF EACH OTHER AGAIN...

Your Workspace
PERSISTENT RELATIONSHIP CHALLENGES

What is your persistent challenge in relationships?
What triggers this challenge?
Is it associated with past trauma in your childhood?
Is it associated with past trauma in your love life?
Is this trigger of unknown origin-past life?
Is this challenge always present in your life?
Does it appear in friendships?
Does it appear in working partnership?
Does it appear with family member relationships?
Is this challenge present only in romantic relationships?
Can you find the source of this challenge?
What would it take for you to overcome this challenge?
Have you made an effort to overcome this?

Now you found your main issue that causes conflict and dissatisfaction so that you can consciously learn to manage and eliminate it.

Your Workspace
OBSTACLE PREVENTING NEW LOVE

IF YOU ARE SINGLE, WHAT IS THE MAIN OBSTACLE THAT IS PREVENTING YOU FROM FINDING LOVE?

Do you feel love eludes you? Are you open to meeting new people?

Why is love often a challenge? Do you stick to old rigid ways?

Why do you keep finding yourself in similar patterns?

Why does love frighten you? Is that fear reasonable or exaggerated?

Why can't you find a compatible partner?
Do you have unreasonable expectations or demands?

Why do you always get hurt? Do you know how to set boundaries?

What is the shift you need to create to overcome your obstacle?

Are you ready to transform this dynamic?

Take the first step and the Universe will help you. Now you understand what you need to adjust, so that you **can move forward in creating a compatible partnership, that will be different from the past relationships.**

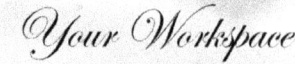
ATTRACTING YOUR FUTURE LOVE

ARE YOU READY FOR YOUR IDEAL RELATIONSHIP?

Attracting your ideal love partner requires clarity of your heart, freedom and openness, a calm self-confident mindset and spiritual trust – to name a few.

BODY:
How confident do you feel about your physical self and your appearance, to share your love with your ideal compatible partner?

MIND:
How clear is your mind, that you are fully prepared for your ideal compatible partner?

HEART:
Do you feel emotionally self-reliable, with an open and free heart to welcome your ideal compatible partner?

SPIRIT:
Do you trust that the Universe will bring you together with your ideal compatible partner that longs to meet you?

Can you see yourself in a happy, beautiful, ideally compatible relationship, in love and equally loved in return?

Visualize yourself in this kind of wonderful and spiritually destined partnership.

For your Mudra Practice

FIND YOUR ANSWERS
When you are longing to find answers about your deep, far away past, and wish to understand issues that seem to have no origin in this life, you need to engage your mind in a way that penetrates thru the walls of limitations and gain access to your higher consciousness. Answers will come, sometimes easily and other times unexpectedly, but they will come. Set aside time with the purpose and in confidence, that clarity will manifest, solutions will be offered, keys will be provided. All you have to do is ask. In stillness of your soul, you shall gain insight.

REMEMBER YOUR MAJESTIC SOUL
Before you get lost in Earthly illusion, before you completely forget who you truly are, take a few moments and remember your true essence, your inner lightness, your immortal soul, and your beautiful heart. Whenever self-doubt envelops you, or your confidence wanes, do not fret. You are loved more than you will ever comprehend. And in this life, love will always find you, for you belong with your equal, your true mate and companion in life. Remember that you should never have to beg for love, plea for kindness and affection, or cry for loving attention. The ones who love you, will always find you, just as you will always find them.

TRUST THE UNIVERSE
If you truly believe that everything is on your shoulders and that you carry the troubles of the world alone, it will overwhelm you. Always remember, that you are not alone, and the Universe will send you a partner that will dance with you equally, in a balanced and most loving way. Trust that everything will fall into a beautiful harmonious rhythm, and you will overcome the challenges that you may encounter. Trust in Divine protection, trust in each other, and trust yourself.

ALL IS WITHIN YOU
There is a male and female vibration inside you, for you have been everything and seen it all. You may remember only glimpses of your long journey, so your view is not obstructed by the sorrows of the past. The treasures of knowledge and wisdom that you carry, gift you with the capability of tremendous compassion and understanding. Nobody is to be judged, least not you and your loved one. Remove all imaginary lines of limitations, and remember

that your love is endless, and offers healing to you and your loved one. Heal the past and fly into tomorrow.

YOUR GREATEST TREASURE – YOUR HEART

When you need to find the meaning to your life – your heart holds the answer. When you wonder what is the purpose of it all, your heart knows the answer. When you follow your heart, it will bring you to your love, your ancient soul partner, and your ever present Divine protector. Your heart is the center of your human Universe. It doesn't need much, only your gentle care, attention, and your ability to listen to its whispers full of wisdom, like the jewels of infinity.

MUDRA FOR NURTURING YOUR HEART

Sit with a straight back and keep your shoulders down, nice and relaxed. Connect the thumb and index fingers, the rest of the fingers are outstretched. Lift your hands and place them over your heart area, crossing the left hand over the right. Hold for Three minutes and relax.

BREATH
Long, deep and slow through your nose

MANTRA
OMM *(God in His Absolute State)*

CHAKRAS
Heart - 4, Third Eye - 6

HEALING COLORS
Green, Indigo

MY HEART IS UPLIFTED AND FILLED WITH LOVE

AFFIRMATION

Sit with a straight spine. Make a circle with your arms arched up and over your head. Place the right palm on top of the left. Press the thumb tips together and visualize a protective circle of white light that surrounds you. Men - put the left palm on top of the right.

BREATH
Fast, short breath of fire from navel

MANTRA
HAR HAR HAR WAHE GURU
(God's Creation, His supreme power and Wisdom)

CHAKRA
Crown - 7

HEALING COLOR
Violet

I TRUST THE UNIVERSE LOVES AND PROTECTS ME

AFFIRMATION MUDRA for SELF IDENTIFICATION

Sit with a straight back and shoulders down, nice and relaxed. The left arm is at your waist, close to body, elbow bent at a 90° angle, and palm looking up towards the sky. The right arm is bent, close to body, and hand is brought up to shoulder level. Palm is facing down. The index and thumb fingertips are connected, the rest of the fingers are straight and together. Hold the Mudra and feel the energy interaction of the two palms and the balance it creates between your emotional and mental energies. Consciously expand the feeling of harmonious balance throughout your entire being. Hold for Three minutes, then relax.

BREATH
LONG, DEEP AND SLOW THROUGH YOUR NOSE

CHAKRAS
ALL CHAKRAS

HEALING COLORS
ALL COLORS

I PERCEIVE, RESPECT AND UNDERSTAND WHO I AM

AFFIRMATION
MUDRA FOR POWERFUL INSIGHT

Sit with a straight back and keep your shoulders down, nice and relaxed. Bend your elbows and raise your hands to the level of the navel. Make a gentle fist with your left hand and place it face up into the palm of your right hand. Left thumb tip is above the right. Concentrate on your Third Eye, breathe, and hold for three minutes.

BREATH
Long, deep and slow through your nose

MANTRA
SAT NAM
(Truth is God's name, One in Spirit))

CHAKRA
Third Eye - 6

HEALING COLORS
Indigo

I CALL UPON MY INSIGHT AND DISCERNMENT

AFFIRMATION
MUDRA FOR WILLPOWER OF MANIFESTATION

Sit with a straight back and shoulders down, nice and relaxed. Extend both arms and lift them in front of you at your heart level, parallel to the ground. While holding the wrists together, flex the palms, as though pushing against a wall. All the fingers remain stretched and spread out. Thumbs are pointing upwards. Keep the shoulders down, fully stretch the elbows and maintain this position for Eleven minutes, then relax.

BREATH
LONG, DEEP AND SLOW THROUGH YOUR NOSE

MANTRA
SATNAM, SATNAM, SATNAM,
SATNAM, SATNAM, SATNAM, WAHE GURU
(*Truth is God's Name, one in Spirit, His is the Supreme Wisdom*)

CHAKRA
THIRD EYE - 6

HEALING COLORS
INDIGO

I MANIFEST MY DREAMS, I MATERIALIZE MY VISION

AFFIRMATION
MUDRA FOR RECEIVING UNIVERSE'S LAW

Sit with a straight back and keep your shoulders down, nice and relaxed. Lift your left hand to your solar plexus area, palm facing up, toward the sky. Lift the right hand to heart level, palm facing down, right above the left hand. Leave enough space between the palms for a small ball. Elbows are to the side. All fingers on both hands are together and stretched, hands are lightly cupped. Hold the Mudra and concentrate on the energy between your palms. Practice for Three minutes.

BREATH
LONG, DEEP AND SLOW THROUGH YOUR NOSE

MANTRA
OMM *(God in His Absolute State)*

CHAKRA
THIRD EYE - 6

HEALING COLORS
INDIGO

I RESPECT AND RECEIVE THE LAWS OF THE UNIVERSE

AFFIRMATION

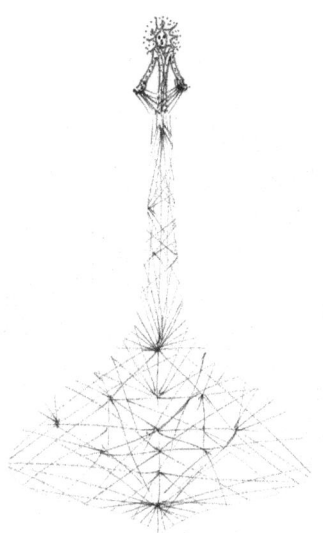

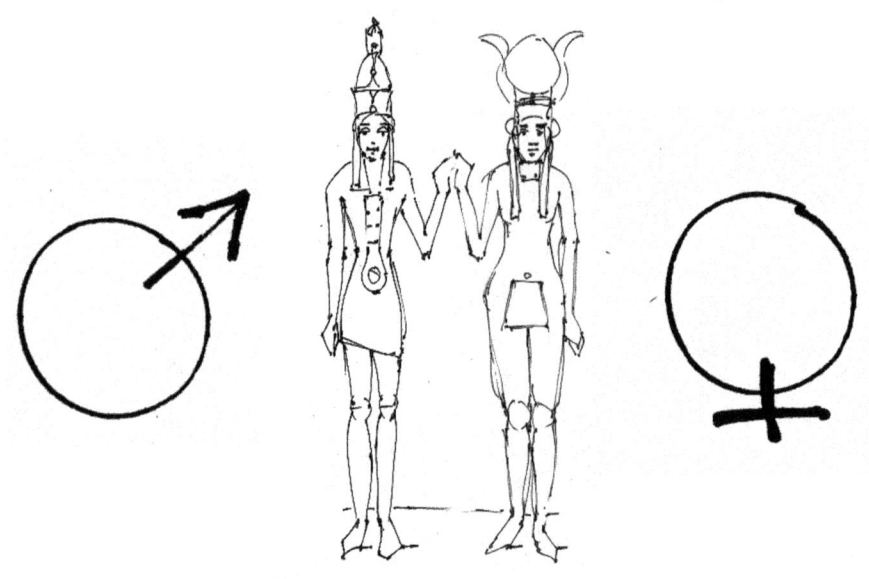

Week Five

YOUR RELATIONSHIP

In this part of our study and exploration of your unique life and love journey, we shall focus our attention on the complex dynamics within a relationship. Until now, you have reflected upon your own personal disposition and understanding of love and relationships. This is very important regardless of your relationship status. We will now continue the fascinating study of finer energy elements that are created between two souls, when they interact in an emotionally charged way within a love relationship. As we move forward and take a closer look at the countless complex energy dynamics, we will learn how to use the powerful Mudras to heal various challenges you may encounter. This part of the study will serve you in the following ways:

IF YOU ARE CURRENTLY SINGLE:

This information is of great value to you, because you will explore what a healthy relationship dynamic should and can be, before you enter a new relationship and face various possible challenges. You have the advantage of preparation. Very often, when you are single, you may focus only on finding a great partner for yourself. But I believe it is absolutely essential, that you think and research beyond just this initial objective. One must read and explore about how a loving, healthy, balanced, compatible and resilient relationship works. Yes, you could meet the most incredibly amazing partner, just as you envisioned. But have you thought about what happens beyond the initial fireworks? The next day and month… and years to come? You could meet an incredibly compatible person, recognize a powerful connection, but let's face it, if you are not ready, the opportunity will come and go. How many times have we seen this explanation for a failed relationship: one was ready, while the other partner was not. It's quite unfortunate when that happens. A beautiful opportunity lost, a sea of regrets is born, a heartache follows, that possibly lingers for years. And then if you reconnect perhaps in the future, you are faced with all the possibilities that could have been, but were not... because one of you was not ready. Now circumstances may be different, and one of you may be no longer available.

You want to avoid this kind of missed opportunities, you want to be in a beautiful harmonious place and ready to recognize, accept and offer the love that resides in your heart. This is all a part of that preparation process. In truth, this is precisely how you attract a great and compatible partner into your life! Now you will learn to recognize and consider all these important aspects when you open up your heart to meet someone new, who is wonderfully compatible. Therefore it makes sense to look beyond, and educate yourself as to what a balanced dynamic can and should be, and how to find, establish and maintain it. In addition, reading thru this part of learning to uncover your love patterns, will help reflect on your past relationships and objectively review what may have been an avoidable failure, what were your natural reflexes, defense mechanisms and where you found yourself most challenged. You can then avoid similar mistakes in the future, and find a way to overcome your weaknesses. Learn to objectively understand a challenging situation from a wiser perspective. Now, you are better prepared to recognize, prevent or diffuse similar challenges that may come up in your future relationship.

Knowing yourself better will help you express your likes and dislikes, as well as needs, wants and expectations. You can practice the Mudra set in each chapter, and become familiar with them, so that you will be well versed with the hand positions.

> **IF YOU ARE CURRENTLY SINGLE,
> YOU ARE PREPARING AND RESEARCHING
> FOR YOUR FUTURE RELATIONSHIP.**

That is a wonderful motivation that will change they way you recognize and navigate thru the relationship that awaits.

IF YOU ARE IN A RELATIONSHIP:

The next chapters will hand you powerful tools for navigating thru your journey and elevating your joint frequency. There are countless kinds of relationships, and it doesn't matter whether you have been in a relationship for a short or a long while, keep in mind that the two of you continuously create new energy field that sustains and affects you each and every day.

IF YOU ARE IN A NEW RELATIONSHIP:

Certainly, when everything is new, you may tend to oversee or embellish your partner's problematic dispositions, which could later grow and become burdensome. If you are aware of them now, and can mutually diffuse them from the beginning, you will move forward stronger and synchronized. Mudras will help you establish a resilient base so you can launch your journey from an energetically harmonious perspective and open, honest, synchronized communication.

IF YOU ARE IN A LONG TERM RELATIONSHIP:

Your time together has endured thru the years, and you have probably learned to tolerate, navigate and adjust thru some complex events, or persistent character traits in order to compromise and maintain harmony. Mudras will help you heal any unnecessary wounds, shift into a positive, nurturing and appreciative mode, and fine-tune areas that could open up, merge, and elevate your relationship to a much higher frequency level.

IF YOU ARE THE ONLY ONE IN THE RELATIONSHIP PRACTICING MUDRAS:

This is a very common dynamic. Instead of imagining and daydreaming how you wish your partner was more "spiritual" and open to this topic, approach the situation with patience and wisdom. You can study these techniques, and then later, at an opportune moment, lead your partner into one Mudra, without making a big announcement about what is happening. The partner may simply expect and understand this experience as holding hands, but you will guide the two of you into a powerful quiet stillness, sitting together for a few minutes, gazing into each other's eyes, holding a Mudra and connecting on soul level. The less of a big deal you make about it, the better.

MUDRAS NEED NO EXPLANATION WHEN PRACTICED TOGETHER, AND YOU CAN EASILY GUIDE YOUR PARTNER'S HAND POSITIONS WITH YOUR OWN HANDS.

Select a very simple, easy Mudra, and be the guide for the two of you. They are immensely powerful when practiced alone or together, but when practiced with someone that has a strong love energy connection with you, the effects are going to be immediate. Therefore you first experience does not have to be a long practice. You need only three minutes. Rest assured that sooner or later you will manage to find the perfect environment where the two of you experience Mudras for three minutes. No words, no explanations, just guide your partner thru one easy Mudra and open up your energy field in a most loving way. Direct them to be still and quiet, and breathe with you in a gentle, synchronized manner. You will both experience a powerful shift that will profoundly transform you. Chances are, your partner will love the experience and long to repeat it.

In my book LOVE MUDRAS, *Hand Yoga for Two* you can find various descriptions of the manifestation of love in relationships. However, in this book, we are looking at the deeper subtle-energy anatomy interaction that occurs in relationships, so it will help you understand these complex and fascinating dynamics from an esoteric perspective. The purpose and intention here is to broaden your outlook, and know how to interpret your past or current relationships.

Something you may have experienced in a relationship, can be easily understood when you put aside the personal expectations or hurt, and see it differently. If two people have a substantial difference in their subtle-energy anatomy and core personal frequency, they will be encountering corresponding challenges in relation to this.

> **A PERSON COULD LOVE YOU TO THEIR BEST ABILITY, BUT THEY SIMPLY CANNOT MOVE BEYOND A CERTAIN FREQUENCY LEVEL.**

This understanding will help you heal and accept your past that was perhaps challenging, and move on without holding on to resentment, anger, feelings of failure, or any other negative emotion. And most importantly, this knowledge will also help you find balance in your present situation, if you may be facing a challenge. Remember, in the future, you will be aware of these complex dynamics and will perceive your relationships better prepared and with a sense of deeper understanding and awareness.

WHAT TO DO, IF THE TWO OF YOU ARE VERY DIFFERENT

Understanding is the key that will help you diffuse conflict, frustration, resentment or anger. You will replace these negative states with an expanded perception of human nature, openness to adjust, adapt, and strive to find mutual ground that is comfortable and acceptable to both. Of course in some cases, this will be most challenging or simply not possible. But in many cases, you will be able to manage and find a harmonious way to maintain a rewarding partnership, relationship and love connection, despite your frequency difference.

Obviously there will always be some interests that you will pursue separately in order to fulfill individual desires. If one of you wants to go on a spiritual retreat, and the other prefers to go fishing with buddies, this can work if you so choose. You can respect each other and communicate your desires, follow them, and still share wonderful interactions when returning to each other. But do not expect the partner to understand your spiritual experiences, just as you might have a hard time pretending that you care about how many fish were captured. So it will be up to you to decide, if you want to remain in a relationship where you can not share your spiritual longing and discoveries. If you are harmonious and in love, have created a beautiful life with each other, a family, share a property, or even business collaborations, you may make the wise decision to accept the limitations, because the positive aspects outweigh this missing element. But if in addition to the missing spiritual compatibility, you are experiencing overall disharmony, then you might not be able to remain in this dynamic long-term. It will always be your very personal choice.

You have to consider many factors, including family, existential needs and complex dynamics that you may have established thru your life or many years together. Instead of a grand upheaval that would bring great challenges to everyone involved, you can find a compromise.

FIND A WAY TO SATISFY YOUR SPIRITUAL QUESTS AND MAINTAIN THE GENERAL STATE OF HARMONY.

This will be better for all, including family members you my be responsible for.

COME RAIN OR SHINE...

There is no perfect relationship, for we are here in this world to learn from each other. As long as your intention is to do the best you can, you are doing your job.

I have had the opportunity to counsel many lovely couples who found themselves in challenging transitions, that usually have to do with imbalance of energy dynamics. I always encourage the partners to find that core emotion that brought them together, remember it and cultivate it further. It is quite naïve and immature to immediately toss away a relationship when it encounters a challenge. This is when you are tested, when you learn and have the opportunity to grow. This is life. Without growth, there is only stagnation, which is never good.

> **LIFE IS ABOUT ADJUSTING, COMPROMISING AND FINDING THE BALANCE IN EACH GIVEN MOMENT.**

Don't dwell on yesterday and rehash the old stuff, or obsess about tomorrow and what will, could, should, or might happen. Be here, today, fully present, willing and able. Simple awareness of certain dynamics from subtle-energy perspective will help you find and improve your inner balance. You will not be taking conflict personally, you will understand it stems from energy imbalance and unintended ignorance.

Can you be the teacher and guide your way out of the dark tunnel to establish harmony?
Can you be the student and overcome pride, recognize your misstep, confusion, misinterpretation and inner fears that pushed you to overreact?
You most likely can, if you are ready, willing, able and choose to do so.

There are countless possibilities how you can manage and balance your differences, and the majority of population that has harmonious relationships functions precisely that way – with compromise and mutual acceptance of individual differences. If the discrepancies become unmanageable, or if one of you encounters a new person who is a better subtle-energy match, well then, your love relationship will most likely not last. It will change into a friendship or co-parenting or whatever is required to fulfill your joint responsibilities you may have.

But the average relationship has these kinds of challenging dynamics. It is rare and special when both of you are on the same level throughout your life together, with identical desires and always functioning on a highly compatible frequency. Usually one of you has to adjust in order to maintain the relationship dynamic.

How does this adjustment happen? Partially by rising to the occasion, but that ability is very limited, like we learned in previous chapters, one can not achieve spiritual and subtle energy ascension forcibly. Most likely, one may have to descend to accommodate the struggling partner. And when you are in love, you will do anything to maintain this enchanted dynamic, while willing to sacrifice more than necessary. This happens easily, because your compromise is on a subtle-energy level and entirely invisible.

One of you will eventually ascend thru the power of love, but until that happens, the other will descend to accommodate the partner, all for the sake of love. If you are true equals, count your blessings and cherish your amazing good fortune, for it is precious and rare.

This intensive study is about your deeper understanding of frequency interaction between two people, and accepting that everyone has a limit about how far they can ascend.

> **THE MORE EVOLVED PARTNER CANNOT FORCIBLY ELEVATE THE LESSER EVOLVED PARTNER. IT IS NOT UP TO YOU. IT IS UP TO THE INDIVIDUAL TO ASCEND WHEN THEY ARE READY.**

Now we will go thru a few more comparisons studies, which will help broaden your perspective about this important and fascinating dynamic.

LOVE AND OTHER DIMENSIONS

Let us bring our awareness to the finest energy field that exists between two people that are in a relationship. This is truly immensely fascinating. In our last chapter, we explored the spiritual aspect of your connection and the multi-dimensional layers of your past-life experiences you may have had together. We mentioned how the unresolved, or unfulfilled dynamics of love between two souls continue and live on beyond death. When these two souls return to this Earthly realm, they eventually find each other, at a precisely predestined moment.

But, before they reconnect in the physical world, they may sense each other energetically from far distances and even worlds apart. This deeper sense that resides in their subconsciousness, the knowing that they exist, will draw them together, and eventually they will find each other. What does that mean?

> **THE BINDING CORD THAT LIVES IN THE FINE ENERGY FIELD IS INVISIBLE, UNBREAKABLE AND CONNECTS THE TWO OF YOU, WHEREVER YOU ARE.**

This cord is alive and links you on a soul level. Despite the fact that it is invisible to human eyes, it is quite powerful and binds you together. When this cord is torn as a result of a break-up or separation, you may experience physical pain. Where? If you are connected by love, then in the area of your heart, if it is fear based emotions that bind you, then more in the area of the solar plexus.

The interconnectedness of your energy and physical body is ongoing and constant. As an example: when a person experiences severe heartache, they may suffer from a heart attack, or heart arrhythmia – irregular heartbeat. This is the effect of trauma to the Fourth Chakra center. When they suffer from shock connected to emotions of fear or even anger, they will most likely suffer from an upset stomach, vomiting or onset of an ulcer. This is the effect of trauma to the Third Chakra center. Different emotional states cause various physical reactions, always connected to your subtle body.

As we know, each one of us has an energy field called aura, that surrounds your physical body. The aura continuously reacts, transforms and adapts to your immediate environment. If you have ever had a professional photo of your aura, it reflected your aura at that particular moment in time. Your aura might have looked quite different later in the day. The basic energy centers, the Seven Chakras that run along your spine, and 72.000 fine energy currents called Nadis, are invisible yet mighty powerful. As you learned in the first chapter, moving your hands in various Mudra positions, affects these fine energy currents in a profound way. Take a look at the map of basic emotional dispositions that are connected with each Chakra center on page 21. It is important and helpful to understand the various energy levels and desires directly connected with them.

YOUR MERGED ENERGY FIELDS

Everything in your environment affects your aura, therefore it is important to pay attention to what you allow yourself to be exposed to. Noise, electronics, air pollution, toxins, negative people, depressing media overload, all those elements affect your energy field in an unhealthy, negative, draining and weakening way. Your aura is changing all the time, depending on your emotional, mental as well as physical disposition and environmental facts. You could be on a beautiful tropical island, but if your mental and emotional state is negative, your aura will reflect this. Or, you could be in a challenging situation, but your spiritual, emotional and mental inner strength will keep your frequency as elevated as possible, despite the challenging environmental circumstances.

As an example, a person facing great adversity could still manage to inspire and uplift others, despite tremendous upheaval or conflict. No matter what, it will affect them, but they will remain as resilient as possible and maintain a positive, loving, and calm disposition. However, do keep in mind that environment is stronger than your will, meaning; you can be a most positive and optimistic person, but if you are continuously surrounded by negative people and environment, eventually this will have a draining effect on you. Likewise, even if you are in a most negative state or energetically depleted, but find yourself in a beautiful environment, you will become at least a bit uplifted and feel somewhat better. Besides the environment, all the people you interact with and how your energy resonates, reacts, communicates or balances with theirs, will have an effect on you.

> **ALL HUMAN RELATIONSHIPS AND INTERACTIONS AFFECT YOUR AURA, HOWEVER, LOVE AFFECTS YOU IN A DEEP AND MOST PROFOUND WAY. THE CONNECTION BETWEEN TWO PEOPLE IN LOVE IS VERY POWERFUL AND FIRST HAPPENS ON FINER ENERGY LEVEL.**

Like attracts like and whatever energy frequency you vibrate at, you will attract a similar frequency. If you are in a very negative space, because of outside elements that have drained you or pulled you into negativity, you will attract a negative person. This happens regardless of your own natural frequency level. Your natural frequency level could be at the level of your heart, but if you suffer from bad environmental influence, and your frequency drops, while you engage in negative, self-destructive behavior, you will attract a person that is in a similar destructive energy space. It is very important to understand the complex energy interactions and attractions in relationships.

> **DEPENDING ON YOUR ENERGY STATE AT THE TIME, YOU WILL ATTRACT INTO YOUR ENERGY FIELD A SOUL THAT RESONATES ON A SIMILAR FREQUENCY LEVEL.**

The case I just described would attract a soul that is in fact not compatible to your soul frequency, but is attracted to the temporary depleted state of negative frequency, caused by your destructive behavior. There is a very definite distinction to make here.

Another example would be, when you do attract a true soulmate energy, but because of your past experiences, unresolved emotions, or mutual soul agreements, you are not ready, you will not resonate on a harmonious level. In such a case, you might meet, recognize each other, feel a profound connection, but it will not lead to a relationship of any resilience or longevity.

> **YOU HAVE TO RESONATE ON A COMPATIBLE FREQUENCY LEVEL IN ORDER TO BE ABLE TO SUSTAIN YOUR CONNECTION.**

Being in love does not mean you are resonating at the same frequency level. It only means that you are experiencing your highest individual frequency. This is why you feel so wonderful. You are high on love – your highest frequency is reached. Similarly, when you are feeling depleted, you vibrate at your lowest frequency.

LOVE AND PERFECT TIMING

Another example is a situation where two people meet, have a strong attraction, spend a short time together and then part ways, because they are incompatible or want entirely different things. But there could still remain a great amount of love between the two, and their soul agreement is far from over or fulfilled. But the timing was off. It could very well happen, that these two people will meet many years later, and still feel the profound connection, but this time they resonate on a similar frequency and can absolutely stay happily together, developing a relationship they were meant to have.

> **IF YOU ARE CONSISTENTLY RESONATING AT DIFFERENT LEVELS, YOU WILL NOT BE ABLE TO SUSTAIN A LONG-TERM RELATIONSHIP, DESPITE YOUR STRONG PAST LIFE CONNECTION.**

Sometimes, relationships like this will take decades or lifetimes to resolve. You may meet every few years and resolve another element, separate again, and reconnect a few years later and so on. These strong past life relationships can also be resolved in an "on and off" way. You may be permanently and deeply connected, but unable to coexist in an intimate long-term relationship.

A great example are Elizabeth Taylor and Richard Burton who clearly repeated their love story by marrying and divorcing a few times, until they gave up and finally divorced. And yet, upon Richard's relatively early death at age fifty-nine, Elizabeth clearly stated she still deeply loved him and that all relationships after him were just for company. Their love story continues, have no doubt.

A more recent example are two well known film actors of our current generation, who also rekindled their love and finally married after a broken engagement and numerous marriages and children with other spouses. After decades apart, they reconnected and were finally together, this time seemingly more compatible and mature. mature. However after a few years, they came upon similar incompatibility and again divorced. It is not an uncommon occurrence, but is a great example of how even destined love needs perfect timing. And there are endless love stories, where there is great love between two people, but the timing seems permanently off. They will return in next life, looking to find each other, once again.

The point is to understand the complexity of human love interactions and how it can shift, evolve, miss the timing, or find the perfect moment when everything seems to work in synchronicity and the two of you meet, and are able to establish a beautiful, long lasting relationship. It needs to be mentioned, that if a relationship concludes its purpose, your energies may no longer be compatible, or may hopefully transform into a deep and very valuable friendship. There are countless possibilities how your relationship begins, what is its purpose and how it concludes, resolves or goes on into eternity.

> **YOU MAY MEET UNDER LESS THAN IDEAL CIRCUMSTANCES, AT AN INCONVENIENT TIME, JUST TO FULFILL A PAST-LIFE DYNAMIC THAT NEEDED COMPLETION.**

Whatever the unusual elements at play are, the most important aspect is, that you strive to maintain or conclude every relationship on a harmonious note, if at all possible. It is clearly not the best outcome to hold regrets, anger, bitterness, or any negative emotional connections with a person that is no longer in your life. As we learned in previous chapters, forgiveness will set you free and make space for new, harmonious, happy and love-filled experiences.

By understanding your individual position when you met, or how it shifted with time, or how you are processing different life experiences, you are expanding your horizon and awareness of the complexity of human emotions within a relationship.

Let's look at the interactions between the two people in a relationship at a frequency level:

EXAMPLE: If one person's main desire is the experience of power and authority (chakra 3), and their partner is focusing on devotion (chakra 4) or speaking the truth (chakra 5), they will encounter continuous conflict of interest.

EXAMPLE: If one partner is feeling the most satisfaction in pursuing only material security, while the other partner's main desire is self-realization and less attachment to worldly possessions, this will present a continuous obstacle in finding common ground. The two people could have a strong physical attraction, but apart from that, very little in common. But if they have an old bond that needs to be experienced as a relationship, they will go thru it, however, eventually they will inevitably realize that they are on very different levels and are spiritually incompatible.

This mostly happens in our younger years, when we are not quite sure what we want. I am not implying, generalizing, or indicating here, that you cannot have a serious, committed relationship when you are very young. Love has no limitation of age, but it is the level of maturity that offers a better chance at longevity. I believe that if you meet your perfect mate early, you may be able to grow together very well and adjust to changes in a synchronized manner. This kind of pairing is quite special. But clearly, you will have a different level of maturity and self-realization, when you are in second or even sixth decade of your life. That is to be expected, after all, maybe you've lived thru some powerful experiences, perhaps parenthood, the loss of a parent or seeing your professional life thru success or failure. Later on, when we mature and know ourselves better, we will not pursue partnerships that do not offer what we wish for. In the following pages, we are giving some deep thought to the delicate balance of energy fields, different needs of each partner, and the ever changing state of your spiritual development. This brings us to the important and delicate balance at the very beginning of your relationship.

THE BEGINNING RULES AND HABITS

Now that we have reflected upon the fine energy components of interaction between two people, we will bring this principles into the very beginning of a relationship.

> **WHATEVER YOUR UNIQUE COMBINATION IS AT THE BEGINNING WHEN YOU'VE MET AND CONNECTED, REST ASSURED, IT WILL PLAY THE MAIN THEME THROUGHOUT YOUR RELATIONSHIP.**

What does that mean? However your dynamic was set when you met, will be something you will be learning about during your time together. Now things get even more fascinating. We discussed in previous chapters about the givers and takers, the rescuers and so on. Whatever your starting dynamic is, will follow you thru the relationship. If this beginning attraction is purely physical, then you will eventually be facing the facts that a relationship requires more than that.

No matter how immense your physical attraction is, sooner or later you will need to have a conversation. Here comes into question your mental compatibility. Common beliefs or interests can be an incredible stimulant that connects you, however, it takes more than mental compatibility to maintain a relationship. Physical and mental aspect aside, if you have fallen in love, you are intertwined with this powerful emotion. This can happen even if you seem quite astonishingly incompatible in other areas. How can this be? Because it may be your past life connection that has drawn you together. But this does not guarantee a happy outcome or a breezy, carefree interaction.

> **REMEMBER, IN THIS LIFETIME, YOUR RELATIONSHIP WILL BEGIN WHERE YOU LEFT OFF IN THE PAST.**

Whatever the ending was between the two of you, you will be continuing your story, overcoming challenges or completing missions, or simply experiencing togetherness, finally at peace to have found each other again. You may be very different, but you will function together despite the profound differences.

Love will bind you together like glue, until you are either more harmonious or have fulfilled and completed your agreement. A perfect example of the power of past life connections is, when two people seem very mismatched, yet they are drawn to each other in an incomprehensibly irresistible and undeniable way. The whole world can watch in shock why two such different people are together, but it truly doesn't matter what anyone says.

Love will never be understood by ignorant people, who may have never experienced the inescapable power of mutual attraction, predestined karmic love and emotional attachment of the deepest kind. If your love is extremely powerful despite your fundamental differences, you will go thru this experience, and nothing or nobody will be able to stand in your way.

> **ONLY WHEN YOU COMPLETE AND FULFILL ALL DESIRES AND ALL PAST-LIFE CONTRACT DETAILS, WILL YOU BE RELEASED.**

Here we are talking about those difficult yet very codependent, almost addictive relationships, where two people might be quite bad for each other, but are so entangled that they keep going on, despite all the upheaval and destruction they are creating together and for each other. Eventually, they will complete their mutual lesson and be free to experience healthier relationships. The point is, one can never be too judgmental about others, for we cannot even remotely imagine what these two souls have endured together, how long they waited to receive the opportunity of a long-lost reunion, and what extreme difficulties or obstacles they previously encountered.

It is important to observe others with compassion, non-judgment, and the openness to a deeper understanding of the complexity in love dynamics. If we look at another crucial indicator of compatibility, sooner or later, you will land in the complex area of spirituality. Let's say that you are physically and mentally synchronized, but if you are spiritually worlds apart, this will eventually present a great challenge. If both of you are not interested in spiritual aspects of life, you will just journey thru life, solely focused on physical and mental distractions and values.

> **IF YOU ARE SPIRITUALLY CONNECTED,
> YOU HAVE ALL THE ELEMENTS TO SURVIVE THROUGH THE MANY
> UNFORESEEN UPHEAVALS AND HOLD ON TO WHAT YOU HAVE.**

But let us keep in mind a very important point; quite often some may daydream of having a wonderful "spiritual" partner, who would be eager to meditate and pursue all sorts of enlightening endeavors, travel the world, and forget about the normal everyday life. And yes, up to a point this may sound wonderful, but you have to keep a healthy dose of reality. People usually always want something unrealistic. If the two of you are like twins doing everything "spiritual" without managing earthly responsibilities, you better be sitting on a gold mine, so you can afford to pursue such lofty existence. Balance is the key. After all, let's face it, this is planet Earth and someone has to tend to material needs as well, unless you are happy living under a tree in wilderness. Exclusive pursuit of perpetual "spiritual quests" won't pan out exactly the way you imagined. Who will support you? You have to participate and contribute to all areas of your life, otherwise your existence in this world will be compromised. Most importantly, a spiritually compatible and mature relationship is when you are able to transcend all challenges and apply spiritual principles to daily life, with all its ups and downs.

> **PRACTICING SPIRITUALITY ON A RETREAT IS A VACATION.
> BUT LIVING SPIRITUALLY EVERY DAY REQUIRES MASTERY,
> DISCIPLINE AND TRUE DEDICATION.**

THE CREATION OF ENERGY COMPONENTS

So what is the main energy dynamic that brings you together in the beginning? What is most important to you personally?

If you just envision a partner that offers you security – Chakra 1, and pay absolutely no attention to other aspects, even if you get that kind of partner, eventually you will have to learn that this is not what love is all about. If your main focus is on the physical interaction – Chakra 2, or even just the appearance that is favorably granted to everyone in their youth, keep in mind that even you will eventually look different age and not be able to "compete" in the category of such limited and superficial criteria.

Similarly, if a person picks a partner purely on their wealth – Chakras 1 and 3, when and if the main source of this attraction is gone, so will be the partner. In other words, a millionaire who is suddenly poor, most likely won't be able to keep a partner who was primarily attracted to his wealth. A person who just wanted a young, beautiful partner, in order to keep their ego – Chakra 3, in denial about the fact we are all aging every second of this Earthly life, such a person will eventually desire a new, younger, or temporarily more beautiful partner. Their ability to have a relationship is limited and does not go beyond this superficial level. Looking at this from energy frequency perspective, they operate on the Chakra level 3, and are preoccupied with material possessions and ego.

Let's keep in mind that the person who plays along this dynamic, is also on that level, meaning, that they function purely by using their very short lived temporary physical attributes to gain what they desire, including their partner. They function mostly in the Chakra 2 and 3 centers, and relate to everything as if their physical appearance is their most valuable currency, main power, and communication tool. Such a person will sooner or later hit a panic button, when eventually time catches up and no matter what they do, their fleeting physical beauty won't be compatible with someone younger and seemingly more beautiful. This is a very common occurrence, but it is interesting to look at, from a subtle energy perspective.

The Chakra 3 energy level is also about worldly power. If that power is gone, then what? And when someone feels like an adequate partner only when they have power, what happens when that disappears, perhaps overnight? These become the most crucial lessons in their life. Moving beyond Chakra 3, you are crossing the Earth binding boundary, and finally ascending into the heart – Chakra 4, where the expression and many nuances of love rule.

Now you are in the territory of the heart, and have overcome the most challenging traps of human interactions of Chakras 1, 2 and 3 where the experience of actual high frequency love is very limited. Moving into the heart center – Chakra 4, will teach you the most basic ground rules, to learn to give as well as receive. Every other beautiful nuance of love expression stems from mastering these two abilities.

ROSE COLORED GLASSES

In the very beginning of your relationship, there is a connection, a certain dynamic. There is an energetic give and take. There are the endless options; a partner that is more forgiving and less needy, or less forgiving and more needy. One is moody, while the other pleases. One is bossy, while the other is timid, one is a giver the other a taker.

> **WHEREVER YOUR ROAD TOGETHER BEGINS,
> IS WHERE YOU SHALL TRAVEL.**

What does that mean? It means that you should pay attention in the very beginning to how you behave, how much you need to tolerate, or even ignore some things that you may not like, and how capable you are to communicate your needs. Do not think it is better to be quiet, with the idea that you will deal with certain unpleasant or bothersome issues later. It does not work that way. In the beginning of a relationship we are all wearing similar rose colored glasses.

After all, you have waited for your love for such a long time, now that it is here, you don't want to see the less favorable character traits. You would rather pretend they don't exist. You want to enjoy the dreamy existence, where your loved one is simply perfect. It helps reaffirm your joyful affirmation that the ideal partner has finally arrived. You want it to work, you want it to be the very best you ever dreamed of, and your partner is about as close to perfection as you could imagine. Actually, they are even more perfect than you thought was possible. These are the rose colored glasses, and they help you maintain the magical spell of the first days, weeks, and even months. But sooner or later, surely in about three months time, the small nagging character traits will remain hidden no more, and they will creep up and become rather bothersome.

Perhaps a tiny detail, a reaction, a word, a critique, an opinion, or a judgment …something will push the red button at the back of your mind and the shrilling sound of alarm will shatter the rose colored glasses into a thousand tiny pieces, so impossibly small that they simply can't be repaired or glued together, ever again. You will get frightened, that perhaps everything is not totally perfect. But, have no fear, this is to be expected, and it is about time to admit that nobody is perfect and keeping up appearances is simply too exhausting. Now you can settle down and begin to really get to know each other.

> **IF THERE ARE PROBLEMS IN THE BEGINNING,
> SEE AND FACE THEM BRAVELY, HEAD ON AND WITHOUT FEAR.**

This will make your differences or challenges much more manageable. Just remember, what you see in the beginning is the best version of what you get. If this is compatible with you, together, you will bring the best out of each other. If it is challenging, together you may bring out the worst. But relationships are here for us to learn, grow, and overcome all obstacles. What is important is your honesty with yourself and your partner.

Whatever you allow each other to get away with, shall follow you into the relationship. If you don't like something, but are quiet and afraid to speak up, this issue will only grow and eventually, one day you won't speak it, but scream it. Why not get it out into the open right away? If you are exceptionally tolerant and forgiving in the beginning, you have set the bar so low, it will be mighty difficult to raise it and explain new rules of tolerance and boundaries.

Just be honest, in touch with your feelings, your heart and speak your mind. This will assure that together, you will give each other a fair opportunity to work thru everything and find a way to adjust, compromise, and give each other some room for the differences that you surely have. It's all about your ability to communicate.

Ask yourself:
How honest, direct, kind and diplomatic are you in a conversation with your partner?
Are you afraid of confrontations and therefore always surrender without even voicing your desires? Where does this insecurity and unproductive habit or hang-up stem from?
Find it, and remove it from your memory bank, for it does not bring you any benefits or happiness. You are both creating the dynamics…from day one. Take responsibility for your part and step up. Be present, don't sleep walk and daydream thru your conversations.

In the beginning, you have the absolute best chances of adjusting to each other and finding a mutual field of sacred harmony. Be brave, be open, be confident and be yourself. You are enough just the way you are. And you are better at playing the real you, than anyone else. Be you. And by the way, no matter how long your beautiful love story has been going on – always remember the essence of the very first moments, days, weeks that you spent together. These are your treasures, that will always bring you back to the first energy that ignited the flame of love that still burns between you two. Keep that flame alive.

YES, PEOPLE CHANGE ...WHEN THEY ARE READY

By all means, do not be naive in thinking how you will change your partner, or how they will change once something happens. You may hope forever, without success. It is a big error to enter into an intimate and complex relationship with someone that has a seriously bad, self-destructive or negative character trait, that you clearly see right away. Your hopes of a quick change or transformation will require a lot of your energy. You will be very engaged and whenever you will clearly see that despite your devoted love, monumental efforts and big hopes, there is no change, you will suffer, feel betrayed, depleted, and take it as a personal failure, because you could not help them overcome this challenging habit. You are forgetting that you are two different people and the change is up to them and not you.

IF YOUR PARTNER CAN NOT OVERCOME THEIR OWN CHALLENGES, IT IS NOT A REFLECTION OF YOUR FAILURE, OR HOW MUCH THEY LOVE YOU.

They are simply incapable of change or overcoming their inner demons. Some people may say they changed for the person they love. Perhaps they were ready to change anyway, you just gave them the final push. No matter how you look at it, they were ready, willing, able and wanted to change. It was in their time and with their free will and not yours.

Let's face it, nobody is perfect, and when you love someone you want them to see you in the best light, while being the best version of yourself. You want to please them. So if you are ready, this was what you needed, an inspiration, a motivation, a purpose. In such a case you will change.

And what happens if you lose that person, that motivated your change for the better? Will you go back to your old ways? Possibly. But again, you are responsible for your willingness, effort, discipline, and decision to change, and no one else. Do not blame others, take responsibility for your choices, actions as well as inactions. You could wait for someone to change till the end of your life and yet your waiting will have nothing to do with their final choice. Each one of us has free will and so does your partner.

Don't take this responsibility on your shoulders. But also, do not console yourself when something major and substantial is missing in your relationship, by hoping that with time they will change, and then everything will be as lovely as you imagined. What you see is what you get – for the most part. It is the best version of them. Can you live with that? Keep in mind that nobody, not even you, is perfect. The only thing that is perfect is Divine love.

COMMUNICATION – THE GOLDEN BOND IN A RELATIONSHIP

Communication is the key to loving, bonding, resolving, growing, overcoming, balancing, ascending…everything in your relationship is navigated by your ability to communicate with one another. This is where Mudras offer a most powerful, transformative and healing effect. Honestly, without communication there is really no relationship.

Have you seen people that sit together in a restaurant and have nothing to say to each other? Each one sits there with their own disconnected thoughts and nothing is shared. Have you seen people who talk to everyone else, except to each other. Each one speaks to their friends and complains about the other, but they can't seem to be able to speak to each other directly.

> **AS LONG AS YOU CAN COMMUNICATE,
> YOUR CHANCES OF MAINTAINING AND GROWING
> A BEAUTIFUL RELATIONSHIP ARE QUITE EXCELLENT.**

But some of us fear confrontation, or that the partner may see something they won't like, and so on. Well, worse than facing an unpleasant conversation is silence. It is also quite counterproductive to cultivate the habit of remaining silent, pouting away and expecting your partner to guess what you want. You may wait for a long time, or eternity. The inability to express yourself, creates an energy congestion, suffocating and taking the oxygen right out of the room, as they say. People that are incapable of communicating, conveniently escape into silence. That creates an impenetrable wall and that space grows to an insurmountable height.

When all you have in a relationship is silence, you have really nothing. Except truckloads of tension that is exhausting you and everyone else. No matter how difficult it is, communication will always ease the tension and help you move thru a period of disharmony. Quiet anger is more volatile than a five minute screaming match. But neither of them are pleasant and hopefully you can do better.

Be in touch with yourself and communicate regularly so you don't collect a big pile of resentment and unhappy dissatisfied thoughts, that eventually accumulate into a gigantic problem. Deal with this daily, breathe, release, and take responsibility for your dissatisfaction or discontent. After all, if someone behaves badly towards you, it is up to you to remind them not to do so. Unless you do precisely that, you are silently signaling to them that they can repeat their behavior, because it is acceptable to you, and there will be no repercussions. You will just tolerate anything and everything that comes your way.

> **SILENCE IS NOT SETTING A BOUNDARY, IN FACT IT IS AVOIDANCE OF SETTING BOUNDARIES.**

Are you afraid to speak up for the sake of losing your partner? Well, if you stay silent, you will surely lose them sooner or later. Remember that the sooner you speak, the better. This way you prevent a small nuisance from growing into a big issue that pollutes your beautiful space of love. Open up, be free, speak your mind and say what you desire or long for. And say what you don't like, can't tolerate and do not wish to experience. Laugh, hug, take a moment to breathe and move forward with extending an olive branch when needed, and stating firmly what you wish.

Nobody will do it for you. Only you can tell the world and your partner what you want. This unfortunate unresolved dysfunction is most visible when people hire divorce attorneys that are paid immense amounts of money. They communicate instead of the two people that a short while ago made love, had children and swore to stay together into eternity. How can this be possible? How did they communicate then? You can recognize all the challenging signs of weak communication early in the relationship, but if you are aware of this, you can immediately consciously improve and navigate thru this challenge. Even if you are in a relationship for a long time and continuously battle lack of communication, try to shift your disposition. It takes two players to participate, so if you wish to change the standstill of communication, change yourself and your behavior.

Begin to interact in a very different way than before. Not with confrontation, creating conflict, attacking, blaming, or harboring resentment. Do it in a calm conversation. When you shift and change your disposition, you transform the energy field, the frequency, and your partner will be pleasantly surprised. And maybe you've finally opened the gates to harmonious interaction.

THE CONSEQUENCE OF SILENCE

If you are suffering from a tendency to be silent when in emotional pain, you need to self-examine and review your past. Staying quiet and refusing to communicate is your misinterpreted belief and understanding that silence is a way of communicating, when in fact it is clearly not. Unless you speak, nobody can guess what you need, want, desire and wish for. Not even you. Nowhere is this more obvious than in an intimate relationship. Suffering in painful silence is also one of the primary causes of illness.

Just think of the side effects of silence on your fine subtle-energy body. If you remain quiet, the cause of your suffering has absolutely no outlet. The negative energy has nowhere to go.

> **EVERYTHING YOU ARE FEELING AND THINKING IS ENERGY. IF THIS ENERGY HAS NO OUTLET TO RELEASE AND DIFFUSE THE GROWING PRESSURE, IT WILL REMAIN STUCK SOMEWHERE INSIDE YOU AND CREATE AN UNHEALTHY CONGESTED STATE, OR ILLNESS.**

Why is this the case? Because it is not an emotion of happiness, but an emotion of anger, fear, rejection, grief and sadness. This is very important to understand. Quite often, people who have issues in relationships and do not express them, experience illness in the emotional center that is closely connected to their particular relationship dynamic. Of course, all your energy centers are connected and affected by your relationships, for there is no separation. But, some centers are obviously more vulnerable than others. Most exposed are the reproductive organs and the heart center. This does not mean that you could not get a headache as result of relationship tension, but the source of the issue will reside in your heart. And in holistic approach to healing, we always look for the emotional source of the challenge. We go to the source of problem, for therein lies your answer.

For that obvious reason, reproductive organs suffer when the communication is broken, silence is the norm, and the person remains in a relationship where they quietly suffer, but otherwise still play a passive role of a partner. This is most damaging to women when they are deeply unhappy with the relationship and their partner, yet they continue to engage in physical intercourse.

Why? Because, as the natural recipient of partners energy, the reproductive center – Chakra 2, remains congested with suppressed emotions of negative energy, while engaging in physical interaction focused in that region. The merging of the two energies doesn't offer an uplifting release and energy ascension, but quite to the contrary. It magnifies the negative energy congestion of the unexpressed anger, resentment, dislike or fear of confrontation. The energy center eventually becomes so overly saturated that its density materializes into tangible matter in the form of physical disease, such as infection, tumor, cyst or worse.

A different negative manifestation results in the heart area, where emotions of grief, sadness, betrayal or deep sorrow reside. Consequently an illness in the lungs, heart, chest and breasts region, may develop as a result of long-term emotional suffering. However, do not misunderstand and assume that every person who has reproductive or breasts health issues has a difficult partner. No, but they do carry negative energy emotional residues in these areas that are closely connected to matters of the heart and love, therefore this is where the challenge will manifest. This can be the result of any and all matters of the heart that create grief and sadness. The cause may be the negative dynamic with a partner, parent, child, or any other profound discord, betrayal, suffering, loss or grievance. The consequences of remaining silent and not expressing one's feelings, will cause this congested energy to magnify, gather and reach such level of density to materialize into an illness. It is important to know, that a continuously harmonious state of body, mind and heart is essential for your overall wellbeing.

THE STATE OF YOUR RELATIONSHIP HAS AN IMMENSE EFFECT ON YOUR GENERAL HEALTH.

YOUR ASSIGNMENT

AFFIRMATION

> SEE YOUR DIFFERENCES AS
> A GIFT OF TWO PERSPECTIVES,
> WHILE GAINING WISDOM FROM EACH OTHER.

DIARY

This week you are ready to get deep into the complex dynamics of relationship patterns. Now that you have the ability to see everything from the fascinating perspective of finer, subtler energies, you can perhaps easily understand why certain aspects may be challenging and will required some serious effort to manage. Hopefully you can adjust and compromise without taking things too personally. Most often, the differences or conflicts have nothing to do with the partners as a unit, but with each individual. Of course, being together brings out everything you still need to learn and face on your own. This is why we are such fantastic mirrors that help each other learn and grow. If you are single, this is a perfect opportunity to research all your past relationship dynamics and prepare for the right one that is coming your way. If you are in a relationship, examine your unique dynamics and what needs to improve.

PROCESS

Work thru the questions, come back in a few days, see if anything changed, add it on, clarify, clean it up, and self-discover through the process.

PRACTICE

Work with the diary, answer the questions and practice the Mudras listed. Write down how you feel before and after the Mudra practice. Observe the shift in your energy field.

> **THE MAGIC OF TWO BLENDED ENERGIES
> THAT ARE FILLED WITH LOVE FOR ONE ANOTHER,
> TRANSFORMS THIS WORLD IN PROFOUND WAYS.**

YOUR IDEAL RELATIONSHIP

WHAT IS YOUR DREAM RELATIONSHIP?

What is your expectation of your ideal relationship?
Which elements are most important?
Rate the level of importance as it relates to chakra-energy scale.

Your dream relationship must offer the following aspects, in order off importance:

1. CHAKRA – assuring security　　　　　　1 2 3 4 5 6 7 8 9 10
2. CHAKRA – sexuality　　　　　　　　　　1 2 3 4 5 6 7 8 9 10
3. CHAKRA – control, intellectual matters　　1 2 3 4 5 6 7 8 9 10
4. CHAKRA – love, expressing feelings　　　1 2 3 4 5 6 7 8 9 10
5. CHAKRA – communication, truth　　　　1 2 3 4 5 6 7 8 9 10
6. CHAKRA – respecting intuitive abilities　　1 2 3 4 5 6 7 8 9 10
7. CHAKRA – prayer and spirituality　　　　1 2 3 4 5 6 7 8 9 10

Your intention is to clarify what you expect and reflect upon your answers. Maybe you need to change a few things around to realistically create your dream relationship and attract a partner that has similar preferences. If you are in a relationship, honestly communicate with your partner about these aspects and find a mutual compromise.

Your Workspace

WHAT DO YOU WISH TO IMPROVE?

IF YOU ARE IN A RELATIONSHIP, WHAT IS THE MAIN CHALLENGE YOU WOULD LIKE TO IMPROVE?

What challenges did you face from the beginning?
Is this challenge something you experienced in other relationships as well?
Is this challenge similar to your parent's challenge?
Can you find the source of this challenge in this life, or does it seem to be an old pattern that makes no sense in current life?
When did this challenge first surface? Is it still present?
Is it an individual problem, or it surfaces only when you are together?
How do you work thru this?
Has it expanded into other areas of your relationship?
Has it caused wounds, and how do you navigate this journey?
Where can you improve? What are you missing?
What was something you cherished, but don't make time for it anymore?
Have you communicated this with each other?
Are there patterns that could be improved?
Are you committed to establishing absolute harmony with each other?
What strength does your connection offer you?
Where lies the deepest comfort you offer each other?
How can you make your relationship even better?

Now you are narrowing down the source of the challenge, so that you can isolate and work thru it, transforming it into an asset.

Your Workspace
CHAKRA COMPATIBILITY

WHAT IS YOUR CURRENT SUBTLE ENERGY STATE?

If you're currently single, what is your natural desire for relationship and life focus:
1. CHAKRA – assuring survival and material possessions
2. CHAKRA – satisfying a physical connection
3. CHAKRA – logical mind-oriented disposition, control, pride
4. CHAKRA – feeling love, your heart, giving and receiving
5. CHAKRA – communication, truth
6. CHAKRA – pursuing enlightenment
7. CHAKRA – spiritual connection and belief system

What pulls you down, and how does that affect your relationships?
What is the dynamics that attracts you?
Where is your common ground?
When do you feel most profoundly energetically connected with another?

HOW COMPATIBLE ARE YOUR CHAKRAS?

If you are in a relationship, where are you best aligned and feel a healthy sense of energy flow?
1. CHAKRA – pursuing material gain
2. CHAKRA – sexuality
3. CHAKRA – power play, intellectual matters
4. CHAKRA – merging of the hearts
5. CHAKRA – speaking and sharing your truth
6. CHAKRA – intuitive pursuits
7. CHAKRA – prayer and devotion

You can have many areas where you blend perfectly, but one takes the lead, which one?

Now you **found your basic energy dynamic,** and can consciously navigate to find and maintain the perfect balance.

MANAGING YOUR DIFFERENCES

IF YOU ARE SINGLE:
YOUR PAST RELATIONSHIP CHALLENGES?

IN YOU ARE IN A RELATIONSHIP:
HOW DO YOU DEAL WITH YOUR DIFFERENCES?
We all have differences, some bigger some smaller. Know them and fine tune a reasonably comfortable compromise to manage them.

In what areas were/are your main differences:
1. CHAKRA – assuring security
2. CHAKRA – sexuality
3. CHAKRA – control, intellectual matters
4. CHAKRA – love, expressing feelings
5. CHAKRA – communication, truth, openness, no secrets
6. CHAKRA – respecting intuitive abilities, inner knowing
7. CHAKRA – prayer and spirituality

YOUR INTENTION IS TO:
Overcome negative tendencies
Find a compromise
Establish optimal harmony and peace
Cultivate positive aspects

Now you **understand your basic habits when facing challenges. Together, you can consciously improve and establish a new way of managing your unique combination.**

FOR YOUR MUDRA PRACTICE

Mudras are perfect for relationships in many different aspects, especially when you wish to improve your communication skills. Why? Because no words are necessary, and Mudra practice is a powerful harmonizer which prevents you from falling into confrontation or discord. You merge on a fine energy level without the expectation, pressure or demand for a physical intercourse. There are no ulterior motives for your caring, attentive, and tender time together. You can sit opposite each other and enjoy eye contact, which almost immediately helps dissolve all barriers, and brings you into a field of profound inner calm, harmonious, resonant, and most loving energy. No words are necessary. From the subtle energy perspective, by practicing Mudras together, you are merging, redirecting, empowering and cleansing fine energy pathways, thus magnifying your frequency resonance and energy compatibility. You are charging up your merged energy field. Once a harmonious energy field is established with the practice of Mudras, you will be able to communicate verbally and express your feelings in a calm, productive and loving dialogue. The energy entity that you create with your partner is your home base, keep it clean of negativity and cultivate its nurturing and protective shield for your love. For a more advanced and intense experience, explore my book *LOVE MUDRAS – Hand Yoga for two.*

Mudra for Contentment of Your Heart

Sit with a straight back and keep your shoulders down, nice and relaxed. Connect the thumb and the middle finger of the right hand and the thumb and the little finger of the left hand. Relax the rest of the fingers and hold your hands a few inches apart, palms up. Hold for three minutes, then make fists with both hands and relax. Men should practice the same position with opposite hands.

BREATH
Long, deep and slow through your nose

MANTRA
SARE SA SA SARE SA SA SARE HARE HAR
(God is Infinite in His Creativity)

CHAKRA
Solar plexus - 3

HEALING COLORS
Yellow

AFFIRMATION
I NURTURE PEACE AND CONTENTMENT OF MY HEART

MUDRA FOR BALANCED SPEECH

Sit with a straight back and keep your shoulders down, nice and relaxed. Connect all the fingertips and keep them outstretched, held apart, with only fingertips touching. Lift your hands and hold them in front of your heart and throat area. Thumbs are pointing towards you, little fingers away from you and the rest of the fingers towards the sky. Elbows are out to the sides and away from your body. Hold for Three minutes and relax.

BREATH
LONG, DEEP AND SLOW THROUGH YOUR NOSE

MANTRA
OMM *(God in His Absolute State)*

CHAKRA
HEART - 4, THROAT - 5, THIRD EYE - 6

HEALING COLORS
GREEN, BLUE, INDIGO

AFFIRMATION

**MY WORDS ARE IN PERFECT BALANCE,
HARMONIOUS AND CALM**

MUDRA FOR PATIENCE

Sit with a straight back, shoulders down, nice and relaxed. Connect the fingertips of the thumbs and middle fingers. The rest of the fingers are outstretched. Lift your arms up at your sides so that your hands are at the level of your ears, palms facing outward. Hold for Three minutes, then relax.

BREATH
LONG, DEEP AND SLOW THROUGH YOUR NOSE

MANTRA
EK ONG KAR SAT GURU PRASAAD
(One Creator, Illuminated by God's Grace)

CHAKRA
THIRD EYE - 6, CROWN - 7

HEALING COLORS
INDIGO, VIOLET

AFFIRMATION

I AM PATIENT, COMPOSED AND POISED

MUDRA FOR WISDOM

Sit with a straight spine and bend your elbows to the side, parallel to the ground. Make gentle fists, with the thumbs inside and the index fingers out. Now hook your index fingers around each other. The right palm is facing down and the left toward your chest. Gently pull on the index fingers throughout the practice. Hold for Three minutes, then relax.

BREATH
Long, deep and slow through your nose

MANTRA
SAT NAM *(Truth Is God's Name, One in Spirit)*

CHAKRA
Solar Plexus - 3, Heart - 4, Third Eye - 6

HEALING COLORS
Yellow, Green, Indigo

AFFIRMATION

MY INNER WISDOM IS ANCIENT AND INFINITE

Mudra for Balancing Yin & Yang

Sit with a straight spine. Connect the thumbs and index fingers, extending the rest of the fingers and spacing them apart. Lift your right hand up in front of your chest with the palm turned outward, the fingertips pointing left. Hold the left hand below the right in front of your stomach area, palm turned inward and fingertips pointing right. Now connect the thumbs and index fingers of both hands, creating the Wheel of Life. Hold for Three minutes and relax.

BREATH
Long, deep and slow through your nose

MANTRA
OMM *(God in His Absolute State)*

CHAKRA
All Chakras

HEALING COLORS
All Colors

AFFIRMATION
I AM BALANCED IN MY HEART, MIND AND BODY

MUDRA OF TWO HEARTS

Sit with a straight spine. Connect the thumbs and index fingers, forming a circle. Extend all other fingers, keeping them spread out. Lift your arms up in front of your heart, left over right, palms facing outward, and cross your wrists over each other. Hook your pinkies together, keep all fingers extended. Hold for Three minutes and relax.

BREATH
LONG, DEEP AND SLOW THROUGH YOUR NOSE

MANTRA
SAT NAM *(Truth Is God's Name, One in Spirit)*

CHAKRA
ALL CHAKRAS

HEALING COLORS
ALL COLORS

AFFIRMATION
I SHARE THE PERFECT HARMONY OF MY HEART

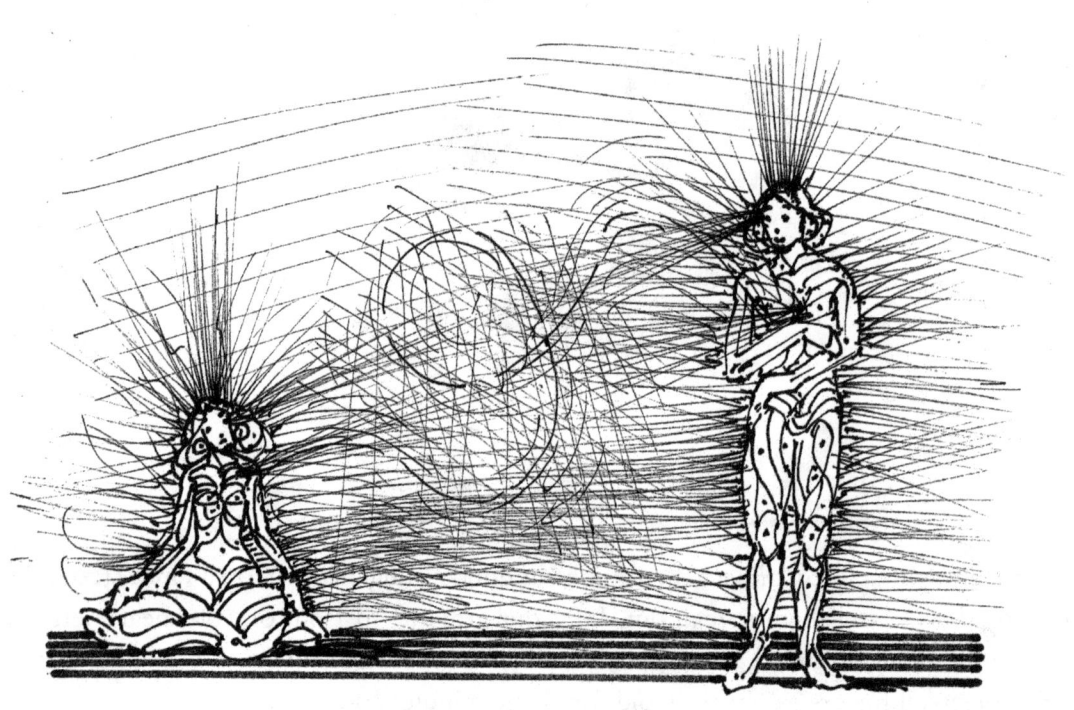

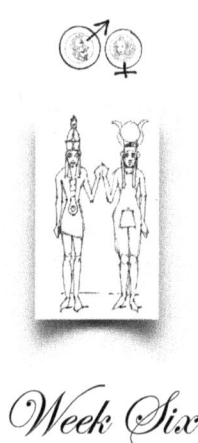

Week Six

HEALING YOUR PHYSICAL LOVE

Let us narrow our esoteric study of love and focus on one specific, powerful element of your relationship – your physical connection. We touched on this topic a bit in our previous chapters, when we discussed the fine energy components of how two people can sense each other's energy from a far distance, often without realizing that this is how fine, subtle energy works. Of course the better your awareness is, the stronger the chances, that you will sense and register someone's energy when it resonates and is attracted to your own.

> **YOU MAY HAVE A PREMONITION, A STRANGE THOUGHT, INEXPLICABLE KNOWING THAT SOMEONE WILL APPEAR, BEFORE YOU MEET THEM.**
> **YOUR AURA WILL CONNECT WITH THE AURA OF YOUR FUTURE PARTNER, BEFORE YOU EVEN MEET.**

But once you do meet, the fine energy field is practically exploding with energy shifts, adjustments, as well as combustions, while your new, joined and magnified energy field of resonance, undergoes the manifestation process. In such a case, two highly receptive and sensitive people can practically feel the electricity between them, as an otherworldly force that may feel like sparks, electric jolts and an irresistible magnetic pull. When the two of you are physically close for the first time, the air is thick with electricity and once you touch each other, you will feel an immediate, profound subtle energy shift.

ENERGY SHIFTS AND CELLULAR IMPRINTS

Emotions are a powerful energy force, and before you physically meet, your energy bodies sense and attract each other on the ethereal and astral level. Once you two finally meet in this dimension, your subtle bodies are already well acquainted with each other, and have detected an element of compatibility. This can be connected to soul recognition and a sense that you belong together. An overwhelming feeling of "being at home" will wrap you into an invisible bubble of complete stillness and peace. This is why your emotional awareness and outward projection is most important.

If you are in your true and healthy state of inner power, you will attract a soul that is compatible with you on many levels. If you are feeling down and depleted, and are functioning at a less than your optimum capacity, you will attract a person that is compatible with the lower frequency version of you.

> **DESTINY WORKS IN ITS OWN UNPREDICTABLE WAYS, AND COULD BRING YOU TOGETHER UNEXPECTEDLY, AND OFTEN NOT WHEN YOU ARE AT YOUR BEST. BUT YOU MADE A SOUL CONTRACT WITH EACH OTHER LONG BEFORE RETURNING TO THIS WORLD.**

You agreed you shall meet again in order to resolve or continue to enjoy your love journey. The most crucial question is this: are you prepared to meet, and what happens if one of you has strayed, veered off course, and engaged in some self-destructive damaging behavior?

This will have very difficult and possibly detrimental effect on your predestined meeting.
For example, if a person has a past of battling addictions, their energy sensory abilities are most likely dampened. They were escaping reality in order to avoid facing an inner challenge, thus delaying their overall process of soul evolution. In such a case, when they meet their predestined partner, they are unable to rise to the proper level and interact, as they have previously agreed.

This is quite a common occurrence. What happens next, is that despite mutual love for one another, this couple may struggle for a while to overcome their unbalanced energy fields, and get synchronized on a spiritual level. Most likely their soul agreement will not be fulfilled. But in a more positive possible outcome, they could overcome the gap in their level of self-awareness and still complete their mission. It truly depends on each individual case. What is important here to understand, is that when a relationship with a powerful soul-love connection encounters this challenge, both participants will endure a certain level of suffering, while trying to understand their dynamic and frustration caused by the lack of synchronicity. If one partner is not ready, their love will have to wait.

Another example would be, when a couple is in love, and while one person understands and recognizes the deeper aspects of the connection, the other person remains in denial, hesitant, afraid, destructive or confused. You each carry a cellular imprint of the other in your energy matrix, but that does not guarantee a happy outcome or completed mission in this current lifetime. Of course, the first meeting is always of greatest importance. When this occurs there are countless components that play a decisive role. Physical attraction is like an assurance that the two of you will interact and notice each other. This can be connected to an ancient memory of your physical appearance. The next aspect that happens has to do with the energy of soul recognition.

> **MUTUAL FINE ENERGY RESONANCE WORKS IN POWERFUL WAYS, BUT THE QUESTION IS IF YOU REALIZE, RECOGNIZE, AND ADMIT IT. CAN YOU HANDLE TRUE LOVE WHEN IT APPEARS IN YOUR LIFE?**

Once you meet, the shift instantly affects both of you. It is impossible that one of you would feel a powerful pull of attraction, while the other would feel nothing. It is simply a question of self-awareness.

Your dynamic exists, but as we said before, your maturity level has many variables. If your interaction with others is always mostly physically charged, and you do not look much beyond physical appearances, you will be much less aware of the subtle, fine energy and deeper components of an interaction.

Let's look at another example:
Two people meet, one is more mature and recognizes a deep soul-level connection, while the other person is spiritually somewhat asleep and focuses solely on physical or material, as opposed to spiritual attraction. They are completely unaware that the person they just met is a strong and important soul connection. They feel the powerful pull, but confuse the nature of attraction.

Why? Because they are inexperienced, unaware, or simply afraid and incapable of looking beyond the physical interaction. This creates a dynamic that is somewhat connected, but usually very frustrating for the more awakened partner. This is a typical example of an energy shift. The more evolved partner who immediately recognized the soul-level connection, will feel they have to do everything in their power to awaken the "sleepy" partner, and this may prove a very painful and impossible assignment. As you remember from a previous chapter, you can not force another soul to ascend. They need to grow in their own time, at their own pace. This is a most typical example of energy shift that occurs immediately, but requires some patience or may often not conclude as we hope.

THE POWER OF SUBTLE ENERGY IN INTIMACY

Physical intimacy is an extension of soul to soul communication, a beautifully delicate and powerful, transformative spiritual experience. Let's look at this dynamic in the context of intimate, physical interaction. When two people engage in physical intercourse of intimate nature and make love, a lot happens that we don't see. When you are in love, your auric field is highly charged and resonates at your highest frequency level. Imagine the powerful energy exchange that happens, when you are both in love and engaging in physical intercourse. Once you merge, your subtle energy Love Matrix is most definitely affected by your partner's. Your individual vibrations unite and resonate together, leaving a tangible imprint on one another. You create a profoundly powerful unified energy field. The energy imprint after intimate physical contact with another person, remains with you for years. This is profoundly powerful and long lasting. This is why engaging in intimate contact with multiple partners too closely together or even overlapping with each other, is highly confusing and polluting for your auric field. Your interaction is disturbed by residual presence of other people's subtle energies that linger in your auric field. This feels uncomfortable and immediately becomes unpleasant, unhealthy and energetically confusing for all involved. You can not naively imagine that you can simply take a shower and wash someone else's energy imprint off. It does not work that way. Once you have blended your energy with another, you can feel them as if they are part of you. And in fact they are. Their frequency is imprinted into yours and a powerful energy cord between the two of you is established. You can not just cancel it out, as you wish.

> **TRACES OF SOMEONE ELSE'S ENERGY FIELD IN YOUR OWN SUBTLE ENERGY LOVE-MATRIX, CAN REMAIN UP TO SEVEN YEARS.**
> **EVEN IF LOVE BETWEEN YOU IS UNFULFILLED, THE CORD REMAINS.**

THE TIMELESS CORD

The etheric cord between two people is very strong and allows both of you an immediate psychic access to each other, whether you like it or not. You have little choice in this matter, once the cord is established. You are connected by thoughts from a distance, your hearts feel the energy attachment and a physical pull, and if you are very psychically attuned, you can practically communicate without speaking. You read each other's minds and intuitively know what the other wants, feels or projects.

If your relationship is harmonious, you are like one unit, synchronized, attuned and wonderfully coordinated. Everything flows, is comfortable, and you are both surrounded by an elevating and empowering energy. You become invincible and can keep this energy cord alive no matter the physical distance of time and space. In fact, you have a guaranteed entry into each other's energy field.

Why? Because you opened your energy field, and allowed access to the deepest core of your subtle energy Love Matrix. Keep in mind, that the energy cord is not limited just to intimate relationships. You can have a cord of attachment with anyone you feel a deep connection with, but the cord is literally embedded into your Love Matrix after physical intercourse.

> **THE POWERFUL CORD CONNECTING THE TWO OF YOU CAN SURVIVE PHYSICAL DEATH, AS WELL AS THE LIMITATIONS OF TIME AND SPACE.**

In other words, the cord between two people with unfulfilled, or deep love from a previous life, can survive in the ethereal dimensional existence. If you agreed to find each other again from your previous life connection, the cord will help you accomplish this, no matter where you are in this world. Upon your rebirth, you will eventually find each other and experience a reinforced subtle energy, ethereal cord connection. This psychic bond will remain with both of you until you complete your agreement. Because the cord is very powerful, it will have a profound effect on how you experience all your relationships.

If you happen to be with the wrong person, an inner longing will continuously linger and remind you, that the person you are with, is not your destined partner. You may eventually meet them while you are in a committed relationship with someone else. That is the case when out of the blue, a married person suddenly meets someone else, that they simply cannot resist. If you take a look at both of their astrological charts, you can clearly see they have a strong karmic connection and need to resolve or continue their love story in this life. And nothing or nobody will stand in their way. We cannot judge this kind of situation, because unless you understand it from an esoteric subtle-energy perspective, you do not know all the intricate and complex details of a love story that has endured through lifetimes.

THE ANCIENT ISSUE OF TRUST

Once your unified energy field is created, optimal trust plays an incredibly important role. Why? Because the moment you do not trust each other or betray your trust, the other person will feel and sense it, even without any special effort. You will both know when the trust has been broken and will experience physical discomfort, in a way of suspicion, guilt, restlessness, fear, anger, anxiety, physical pain and hurt.

Why is this important? Because understanding and respecting each other's energy field and fine energy attachment is of profound importance. By betraying someone else, you are only betraying yourself.

> **WHEN BEHAVING DISHONESTLY,
> YOU ARE DISHONEST WITH YOURSELF.**

When your partner is incapable of honesty, you know that your relationship requires a lot of work and clear and fearless communication, examining why something happened, or why one of you feels the need to jeopardize your beautiful union. Of course these are complex topics, but as we learned in beginning of this book, if and when both of you are clear what you expect from your relationship, a betrayal of trust will most likely never happen.

Why? Because you are a mature, evolved, spiritually awakened being that understands, respects and cherishes each other's sacred energy. Knowing and understanding the fine sensitive nature of your subtle energy Love Matrix, should serve you as most powerful warning of damaging effects a physical intercourse of meaningless nature can inflict. If you consider yourself an evolved, spiritually aware person, you will understand that careless engagement in physical intercourse with someone outside of your sacred union carries long-term subtle energy consequences and will inflict damage to your individual Love Matrix.

If you justify the physical interaction with another person as meaningless entertainment, you are ignoring the fact, that no matter how strong you think you are, you will take on your temporary partner's frequency, whether you like it or not. Their energetic imprint will stick to you for quite a while. Merging of the two energy fields in this intimate capacity carries its consequences and will negatively affect and disrupt a healthy function of your main relationship.

> **WHEN YOUR RELATIONSHIP IS HARMONIOUS AND CARRIES ELEMENTS OF TRUE LOVE, YOU WILL BE UTTERLY TRANSFORMED IN OPTIMALLY POSITIVE WAY.**

Equally so, energy exchange with someone who's energy is low or draining, not equal or harmonious with yours, will carry negative consequences. Sleeping with someone just for the sake of sex, will dampen your finest senses, and freeze your soul's ability to open up and experience a truly profound spiritually charged intimate intercourse.

Why? Because if someone's habit is to engage in careless physical intercourse void of love, their soul will create a shield in order to avoid subtle-energy drain caused by ongoing multiple, unsuitable partners. Such a person may go thru the motions, but the experience of elevated love will elude them. The self-inflicted shield will not protect them from other people's energy cord attachment, but will dull their own ability to tune into and ascend to the higher level of spiritual communion with the destined beloved.

If later this person is ready to open their heart and experience a higher frequency interaction with their destined partner, it will require a serious effort to dissolve the self-created shield that numbed their sensory receptivity. In addition, they will have various energy cords from past partners attached to them, depleting their energy, taking up space and disturbing healthy and optimal energy flow with their true partner.

A practical example would be the case of a person that has found their true love, but all the previous numerous interactions with wrong partners for wrong reasons have left them scarred and numbed. As a consequence, they need to overcome and cleanse all the obstacles, before they are able to recognize, receive and open to their true love. They may carry self-destructive habits based on fear and mistakenly push away their true love, only to later regret their choices, actions and decisions.

It is most likely that in their unreceptive, unaware and unawakened spiritual state, they will lose their greatest love. As a result, their true love suffers their own wounds that need healing. This creates a never ending cycle of love stories that require lifetimes to actually experience what they seek: a true manifestation of harmonious, spiritually and vibrationally aligned soul union that facilitates optimal ascension of both souls.

THE CONGESTED ENERGY FIELD OF FRICTION

This is similar to you allowing a stranger to come into your house. They may come and visit, but are you allowing them into your bedroom with dirty shoes? Or are you keeping the bedroom door locked, and they must remove their shoes before even stepping thru the main doorway of your home?

Whenever your soul intuitively and for the purpose of self-preservation, partially locks the access to the most sensitive energy field of your heart, you cannot expect it to be easily unlocked. If you have interacted with someone and know their energy was not supportive of yours, you need to consciously work on cleansing your energy field and re-establishing a healthy dynamic that reflects you and not the leftover traces of their negative energy imprint.

> **A HARMONIOUS PARTNER WILL NEVER MAKE YOU FEEL LESS THAN CHERISHED AND LOVED FOR WHO YOU ARE.**

An example would be hanging on to a bad intimate experience and negative belief system that an inappropriate person embedded in you, in the past. Perhaps you harbor feelings of low self-esteem, feeling unattractive, undesirable, inadequate in lovemaking, comparing yourself to someone else, or carrying on with a negative, destructive, self-sabotaging dynamic that occurred with a previous inappropriate partner.

If a bad dynamic creeps up in your intimate physical experience, know that this is not what you deserve, need, want or should tolerate. When you are getting over a past relationship, that left you feeling insecure in your physique, it is up to you to recognize, heal, and reclaim your sexual confidence and power. If this remains a struggle, you need to openly communicate to your new, hopefully compatible and harmonious partner, so they may understand that your hesitation or inability to open up has nothing to do with them, but it is an element of your own personal past trauma and ongoing healing.

> **DO NOT PLACE THE RESPONSIBILITY TO HEAL YOUR OLD WOUNDS ON YOUR NEW PARTNER'S SHOULDERS.**
> **LEARN TO HEAL YOURSELF.**

Likewise, don't constantly dwell in victim mode about all the sorrows and pain or misfortune that you carry from your miserable past. Instead, focus on new beautiful experiences and let go of the old emotions, that belong to yesterday.

Very often, we don't have the awareness to consciously heal all the past wounds, or they may require more time, and as result we carry these scars with us into the new relationship and allow them to linger there for many years. This will bring you absolutely no benefit. Quite to the contrary. It will keep your subtle energy field congested, suffocating with old attachments and preventing you from opening up and ascending into your new harmonious relationship. You have to make space for healthy emotions, consciously let go, and forgive the old, less joyful experiences. We touched on forgiveness earlier in the book. Sometimes, the practice of forgiveness demands regular conscious efforts, to extract all the old, unnecessary and detrimental energy attachments that you need to release.

DETACHING THE CORD

Detaching and separating the subtle energy cord between two people that are emotionally connected is quite challenging. The energy is mighty strong, regardless of the nature of the emotion that connects them, be it love or hate. The stronger the emotions that bind you two together, the stronger the cord. Not to be overlooked is also the fact that the energy cord can remain in existence for a very long time. An example would be meeting a person from many years ago, with whom you think you resolved your feelings of love, yet when you meet them again, all the emotions come back as if no time has passed at all. In subtle energy filed, time indeed does not play a role, and feelings can live on for lifetimes.

When old unresolved feelings of love sink into lower frequency regimen and become feelings of anger, fear or hate, your old energy cords can become quite draining, damaging and are literally sucking the life out of you. This is especially obvious if you were engaged in a dynamic of a giver and a taker. If you were the giver, you can expect the taker to remain attached to your energy field, well beyond the time when you separate. In the case of a taker, this would mean they keep thinking and lamenting and rehashing about a dynamic with that person, and are literally almost holding them hostage with their energy sucking grip. This is not healthy for obvious reasons. The big and pressing question here is, how to detach an energy draining cord with a person that you are no longer in a relationship with, and don't want them in your life? This is not an easy matter and requires tremendous awareness, focus, mind power and determination. There must be no hesitation or false hope on your side. If you expect them to change, hope for a reunion or even just daydream wishing how lovely it could have been, had things turned out differently, you remain connected and accessible to them.

Disconnection will not occur by remaining angry, fearful, or attached to them in any kind of emotional way. And it will not happen unless you establish a state of inner calm, peace and confidence. You cannot get rid of someone with anger and hate, but you can let them go with love and forgiveness. And as difficult as this may seem, that is what needs to be done.

> **DETACHING THE CORD REQUIRES FORGIVENESS, COMPASSION, AND A CONSCIOUS RELEASE OF ALL NEGATIVE FEELINGS. THIS PROCESS IS LIKE FINE TUNED ENERGY SURGERY.**

You can visualize releasing the cord between you two, sending the other person clear intention of forgiveness and then surrounding your own energy field with a shield of bright protective light, so the cord can not reattach itself to you. Pay special attention to your back area, in other words, you need to surround your entire body with light, not just your front. This is easier said than done, but if you persist and are absolutely unwavering in your heart and mind while doing so, you can certainly accomplish it. Rest assured, that by hiring an energy worker who may claim to magically remove or cut the cords for you, this will remain effective only temporarily at best.

Your emotional state and attachments will quickly reestablish the unhealthy connection, almost in an addictive and helpless way. You carry the responsibility for creating the cord, it is your responsibility and duty to undo it, if you so wish. It's like you would ask someone else to pay off your karmic debt. Unless you are asking this of a true master of the highest order, who consciously decides to take it upon themselves to grant you this release, there will be no-one in this world who can do it for you, but you alone.

And such an occasion would be extremely rare, because true masters are very, very few and far between. If you created a cord with another person, it is part of your karmic evolutionary process to learn how to maintain or undo it. Once you accomplish letting them go, you are healed and free of undesired cords. And while this may sound a bit challenging to accomplish, I hope it inspires you to be supremely cautious whom you mix your energy field with, and carefully preserve your sacred energy space. And this requires spiritual maturity, self-awareness, and a healthy dose of self-love.

THE HONEST STATE OF YOUR RELATIONSHIP

When you take intentional, loving steps towards understanding each other and respecting the absolute world of subtle energy dimensions, your relationship has incredibly good chances of thriving and surviving thru anything that comes your way. One of the strongest principles to follow is honesty. Of course this is easier said than done, but honesty will always work much better than hiding and pretending. Eventually everything will catch up to you. It is also perfectly normal that many of us carry past scars or wounds, therefore an open relaxed conversation will help you maintain your relationship on a level of deep trust and confidentiality. Make a conscious effort to overcome any old habit of allowing bothersome things to accumulate, until they become a big great ball of resentment or unhappiness.

> **IT IS NEVER TOO LATE TO BE HONEST.**
> **IT IS ALWAYS TIME TO PURSUE THE TRUTH,**
> **YOUR NATURAL ORGANIC AND TRUE SELF.**

Speaking up, whatever it may be, will always help you diminish the potential for conflict and maintain a fluid, open flow of energy between the two of you.

One particular aspect that you may continue to encounter, are certain topics that will always seem to cause havoc or misunderstanding. No couple is entirely friction or conflict free, it just depends on how they go about it. If you allow friction to explode, because it took you a long time to speak up, then you both know that you could have prevented it and handled it better.

Make it a habit to begin your day together in a most peaceful and loving way. No matter what happens during the course of the day, conclude your evening with the same peaceful, loving, and kind disposition towards each other. Never carry a conflict into the dreamland, it won't do anyone any good, no matter how stubborn you feel in proving your point. Harmony before sleep is a non-negotiable must.

RECOGNIZING OLD HABITS AND CONQUERING TRIGGERS

When the two of you embarked on a relationship, you began to fulfill the essential part of your spiritual agreement. The fact is that as human beings, we can learn from each other. And for that we need relationships, interaction, but most of all, we need interplay with people that resonate with our hearts.

Two people that dislike each other will also learn something, but in a different way. Learning thru love is the most promising concept. You will endure much more, not easily give up and fight to survive thru various life's test. When you are sent a partner that you love and they accompany you on this journey of life, you are both learning from each other and begin to understand the main concept.

> **LEARNING YOUR LIFE LESSONS IN COMPANY OF THE PERSON YOU LOVE, HAS THE BEST CHANCES OF PRODUCING POSITIVE RESULTS.**

Everything in life is undergoing a constant change. This is the only way to make progress, move forward, learn and ascend higher. Your mission together as a couple most likely contains unfinished elements from your past. How will you remember them? By inexplicable and wonderful acts that you excel at, the mutual likes, familiarity with each other, ease of cohabiting, and similar views of life. Maybe you share a goal that fulfills you, makes you happy and brings you together. Perhaps having children was always your big desire, and this lifetime you get to finally enjoy doing precisely that. Perhaps you wanted to work together, create, invent, travel, explore, research, discover, investigate, develop, manage, protect, or teach…who knows? You get a chance to do it in this life. And there will be also the unusual odd habits between the two of you, and certain familiar aspects that may irritate, upset, scare and trigger you. This may be an old reflex, a reminder of your past challenges, something you can learn from each other this time around.

Instead of making an elephant out of a mouse, try and figure it out. Perhaps a battle for control, fear of abandonment, possessiveness, an inexplicable sense of betrayal, continuous unreasonable conflict…all these kinds of challenges could be a sign of old scars, unfinished patterns from a past life, that are present once more, ready for your healing. The best remedy for these challenges that present disharmony in your relationship is to recognize them and look at them as a third person. Instead of pointing the finger, and getting defensive or afraid, look at the problem as an undesirable entity that keeps interfering in your good communication and great love, that you have or one another. And then remove it together with intention and full awareness.

Examine yourself and see what is the most powerful trigger that makes you respond in a defensive way?

IF THERE IS A CHALLENGE THAT SEEMS TO BE ESPECIALLY BURDENSOME, IT MAY BE AN ANCIENT OBSTACLE THAT YOU HAVE AGREED TO OVERCOME THIS TIME AROUND.

What is the word, action, missing element, or statement that sends you into an unreasonable tailspin of reactive emotions? These are your triggers.

Now become a real detective and examine yourself, how far back does this go?
Why, and when does this provoke or agitate you the most?

Then share these observations with each other and tackle them together in a more mature, explorative way. Less characterized by personal sensitivity, but more as an element that you can and will overcome together. Communicate, assure each other, reinforce your bond, and face every nuance that needs to be addressed. Now, you have weakened the challenge and strengthened your love.

RESOLVING CONFLICT AND HEALING

A conflict that keeps lingering requires deeply committed work. First, work on your own, calmly observing what is the most upsetting element that triggers discord. Then communicate with each other, exploring why something is challenging and how you can find peace, calmness and resolve. You would be surprised how sometimes a seemingly profound issue dissolves with the simplest of remedies.

Perhaps letting go of a stubborn expectation will open up the doors for peace. Maybe things will greatly improve by just taking a break from each other with daily time in solitude, sharing home duties in a more balanced way, paying attention to careless communication with others. Most often, priorities create an unnecessary issue of resentment between two partners, especially if there are seemingly countless other concerns, ahead of your relationship. Become a negotiating diplomat, develop the ability to ask for what you need, and voice your unhappiness. Learn to say no to others that may be demanding your attention, while the partner feels forgotten and left out.

Sometimes communication may be impossible. Passion seems to be forgotten in the sea of duties, obligations worries and lack of time. Moments of tenderness are evasive, we feel deprived and neglected. You don't receive the attention you desire, feel unappreciated and resent feeling like the least important person to your partner. Perhaps you feel taken for granted, and sense the newness and freshness is a thing of the past. The length of your relationship may make you wonder, if your love reached a plateau and there is nowhere else to go, nothing new to discover, no exciting new possibilities on the horizon for the two of you.

All these situations can appear out of nowhere and then attempt to ruin your perfectly balanced, long-term resilient and deep love. You need opportunities for rediscovering yourselves, overcoming unnecessary doubt or lingering unhappiness, just because you feel disconnected, overwhelmed with family obligations, financial burdens, working duties, or responsibilities to your relatives or larger family dynamics. It seems that a quick solution is evasive, since time, energy, finances or even sheer enthusiastic energy are hard to find.

> **YOU NEED TO REMEMBER HOW VERY FORTUNATE YOU ARE TO HAVE FOUND EACH OTHER, TO LIVE THE DREAMS, DESIRES AND LONGINGS OF YOUR SOUL.**

Remember, how very rare your unique love bond is, how much you endured together and still persevered. Know that your love is like a most precious, tender flower, an exotic plant that requires proper care, a delicate level of humidity in the air, sunshine for certain amount of time, and most of all, the one irreplaceable key element – each other's attention.

When the two of you have little time for each other, you need to adjust the schedules, so you have alone time, no matter how many things and obligations are waiting in the wings. You two can only drive this adventure forward by spending quality precious time together to reconnect, breathe and magnify your subtle energy Love Matrix in a most positive, energizing and invigorating way. And while physical intimacy creates a unique opportunity for closeness, it may lack the element of deep soul communication in stillness. The kind of stillness where you feel each other's heartbeat and really truly look into each other's eyes.

> **CONFLICT IS RESOLVED AND HEALED WHEN YOUR BOND IS REPLENISHED, CULTIVATED AND CARED FOR.**
> **YOU NEED TO HEAL AND RE-ESTABLISH YOUR CONNECTION.**

Mudras will offer you most fantastic tools to work on this aspect and nurture each other's souls with a high level of energy communication between the two of you. This may bring you incredibly close and often evoke a profound experience of blending your two souls that recognize, understand, and cherish the deep bond of love between them. Conflict appears when this bond is neglected.

MISUSE OF PHYSICAL INTIMACY

There is an interesting occurrence that can happen when couples have a conflict. Quite often, the only remedy they can think of, is to engage in physical intimacy. Let's look at this from a subtle energy perspective and reflect on the consequences. When two people argue and are filled with anger or fear, they are functioning from Chakra 3 level. By deciding to use physical intimacy as the remedy to escape the conflict, they will move their frequency away from the Chakra 3 energy field, possibly to Chakra 2 or Chakra 4, depending on their general disposition. Keep in mind, that the negative manifestation aspect of Chakra 2 is manipulation, jealousy and envy, so whenever someone is using intimacy for such a purpose, they have descended to Chakra 2 energy level. When a person remains at Chakra level 3, they will abuse power and be ruled by the ego while engaging in intimacy. Using this kind of distractions may seem effective for short term, but will not eliminate or permanently resolve the main issue that caused their conflict. Sooner or later discord will reappear. But by consciously approaching it from an elevated frequency level, the partners have a better chance of dissolving and healing it right away.

With Mudras this is expedited, emotions and blockages are released, thus elevating your frequency. Mudras will protect and prevent you from sliding downwards into coarser frequency field, where friction resides.

> **YOU CANNOT POSSIBLY RESIST AN EMOTIONAL RELEASE WHILE PRACTICING MUDRAS.**
> **THIS WILL HELP YOU ESTABLISH A LOVING CONNECTION AND TAKE YOU OUT OF EGO INTO THE HEART.**

After Mudra practice and sitting in silence, you created ideal conditions for loving, kind hearted communication. You will speak from the heart with utter honesty. It will remove your defense mechanisms, eliminate your fear, and reconnect you on heart level. All guards are down, what remains is love. This is the most pure and intimate kind of conversation. It is also an ideal time to voice a resolution, a decision, or a promise that will help you navigate thru the future and beyond.

MERGING OF YOUR ENERGY FIELDS

The interaction between two people in love is loaded with powerful frequency exchange on the finest subtle level. This exchange can't be seen and is often not even sensed. If you are attuned and highly aware, you will certainly recognize these powerful energy shifts. You are aligning and recharging your mutual energy field, and developing an incredibly powerful protective energy shield of light force around the two of you. This will make you immune to outside disturbances, and in a certain way you will become invincible. In addition, you will attract positive energy, people, interactions and increase your magnetism.

No matter what challenges of life you endure, by practicing Mudras you are creating and maintaining a fortress of your love, resilient, and long lasting, serving as a most reliable safe haven for your precious love.

YOUR PHYSICAL CONNECTION AND SPIRITUALITY

The expression of physical intimacy enters a whole new arena when you become aware of the delicate and immensely powerful aspects of energy exchange with another person, especially where emotions of love play a decisive role. Understand that there are ways to elevate, uplift and transcend your physical merging into a truly transformative experience, but you need to elevate your individual frequency so that a manifestation of higher love can occur.

Think about this from the energy perspective; by blending your physical desire with the aspects of pure heart and love – Chakra 4, following by a truthful communication exchange – Chakra 5 and entering a zone of synchronized intuitive psychic attunement – Chakra 6, you are creating a relationship where worldly matters and disturbing frequencies can not affect you as much.

> **BY TRANSCENDING YOUR LOVE TO A LEVEL OF TRUE SPIRITUAL PARTNERSHIP, YOUR SOUL'S POTENTIAL IS MAXIMIZED AND YOUR EVOLUTIONARY PROCESS IS ACCELERATED.**

This way you can successfully prevent many possible delays or setbacks that you are otherwise susceptible to. The only way to eliminate suffering, is to move beyond the material and worldly overwhelmingly challenging dynamics, and learn to live with an unwavering inner balance. Always see an easy solution for every challenge that comes your way, and a peaceful and positive outcome, no matter what you face. Challenge only remains, if your disposition slides into a state of despondent pessimism and allows the lower frequencies to drag you into a despair and discontent of negativity.

Until both of you learn to consciously uplift your individual and relationship disposition, you are vulnerable to external destructive forces. The moment you ascend beyond this vulnerable state, to strengthen and solidify your union in higher principles, your journey an intention should be clear. When you are both ready, willing and able to do so, you will overcome all obstacles and live the love-filled life you both desire and rightfully deserve. Only you decide when you are ready to pursue a relationship of the highest possible manifestation. No outside element or force will disrupt what you have and you will truly become invincible, filled with light and love for all. Your union will inspire others and help them strive for what they see is possible.

YOUR ASSIGNMENT

AFFIRMATION

> NOBODY KNOWS
> WHAT GOES ON IN A RELATIONSHIP
> EXCEPT THE TWO SOULS IN IT.

DIARY

This week you are called to reflect upon your disposition towards physical expression of love. Examine your ability to expand and uplift that experience into a spiritual celebration. Each one of us has a different view, past, emotions and mental dispositions towards intimacy. By consciously healing your old wounds, knowing yourself and your desires, you can learn to communicate with your partner in an honest, most loving way, fearlessly, free, while cultivating trust and devotion to each other's hearts.

PROCESS

Work thru the questions, come back in a few days, see if anything changed, add it on, clarify, clean it up, and self-discover through the process.

PRACTICE

Work with the diary, answer the questions and practice the Mudras listed. Write down how you feel before and after the Mudra practice. Observe the shift in your energy field.

> THE EXPRESSION OF PHYSICAL LOVE
> IS A SACRED RITUAL OF YOUR SOUL'S
> NATURAL ASCENSION PROCESS.

Your Workspace

YOUR PHYSICAL RELATIONSHIP

HOW DO YOU FEEL ABOUT THE PHYSICAL ASPECT OF A RELATIONSHIP?

This is a reflection upon your disposition towards intimacy, sex, and physical connection. Instead of avoiding this topic, reflect on it and diminish any unnecessary belief systems that may affect you in a negative way. Disregard all presumed expectations or feelings of insecurity and try to view this topic from a new, spiritual perspective in knowing, that the right partner accepts and loves you precisely as you are.

If you are single, this is a wonderful concept to keep in mind when you meet your future partner.

If you are in a relationship, you can both explore ways of consciously raising the frequency of your interaction and most loving disposition towards each other. We are always changing, as do our bodies, our minds and our emotions. And finally with time, our spiritual maturity gains more space and attention in our lives, as we follow the natural way of ascension.

Create a most comfortable, confident, respectful and loving space, where you experience physical intimacy as the highest form of loving communication.

Your Workspace
DRAINING ENERGY CORDS

DO YOU SENSE ANY ENERGY CORDS THAT ARE DRAINING YOU?

This does not relate only to previous romantic relationships, but all energy cords you may have with any person other than your partner, that has an emotional influence on your life.
It can be also your parent, a relative, friend, and truly anyone that is connected to you thru your heart center.
If your heart is open to a person, you allowed them a certain access.

Examine if these heart connections are in any way draining or restrictive. If so, remember that your energy body should be as free as possible of any energy congestion, so that you can create and maintain sufficient space for your love relationship. Your closest family members will always have a heart connection to you, however, do not forget that in order for your love relationship to thrive without disturbances, you need to always keep sufficient space for your love partner, and be clear about priority levels.

Recognize and understand your possible source of energy drain and consciously extract those who demand too much.
Release all unwanted cords from your past or current emotional attachments, and intentionally make room for your heart-love partner.

Your Workspace
CULTIVATING LOVE

CAN YOU AVOID CONFLICT AND CULTIVATE LOVE?

How do you generally handle discord, conflict, difference of opinion, points of view, or desires, actions and beliefs when interacting with others?

What is the main source of conflict in your partnerships?

How do you handle this challenge?

Do you avoid and distance yourself, become unavailable, or use other ways of releasing your frustration, while not communicating in traditional sense?

Do you ever use intimacy as an outlet for your frustration with a conflict?

Intimacy can be a most healing bond that helps you endure thru difficult times and continuously reinforces your loyalty and devotion to each other. Reflect on your past disposition, and review your behavior. Eliminate any source of inner conflict and re-enter your relationship with as little emotional baggage as possible.

If you are single, this is a perfect time to prepare.

Now you can make a conscious choice to resolve conflicts, and attract a new, sustainable and harmonious relationship.

For your Mudra Practice

YOU ARE GREAT, JUST THE WAY YOU ARE

The inner balance of your creative and sexual expression is like a precious bloom that contains your essence. The creative power within us all, has countless expressions. It needs to be shared, seen, cherished and loved. Inner steadiness is required, so that no outside distractions can temper with the pure expression of who you are. What you share must not be a compromised, adjusted, adapted, changed and suffocated version of you. The only way your presence will excite, inspire and ignite love in others, is when you fearlessly share the authentic vibrations of your soul, with all the complex nuances, glowing sparks and mesmerizing hues that are unique to only you. You are one of a kind, take your place in the spotlight, this is your time to shine.

MUDRA FOR FEELING YOUR ENERGY BODY

Sit with a straight back and keep your shoulders down, nice and relaxed. Bring your hands in front of you, facing each other. The tips of the fingers are pointing away from you, all fingers are together. Keep a relaxed gaze on the area between your palms, without clearly focusing on your hands. Observe the subtle energy movement. Hold for Three minutes and relax.

BREATH
LONG, DEEP AND SLOW THROUGH YOUR NOSE

MANTRA
EK ONG KAR *(One Creator, God Is One)*

CHAKRA
THIRD EYE - 6

HEALING COLORS
INDIGO

AFFIRMATION
I AM AN ENERGY FIELD OF LIGHT

MUDRA FOR CREATIVITY

Sit with a straight spine. Connect the thumbs and index fingers, keeping the rest of the fingers straight. Bend your elbows and lift your hands to your sides with palms facing up at a sixty-degree angle to your body. Concentrate on your Third Eye center and meditate for at least three minutes.

BREATH
Short, fast breath or fire from the navel

MANTRA
GA DA *(God) variation elbows in or out 60 degree*

CHAKRA
Third Eye - 6, Crown - 7

HEALING COLORS
Indigo, Violet

AFFIRMATION
I AM CREATIVELY INSPIRED, INVENTIVE AND ORIGINAL

MUDRA for DIMINISHING WORRY

Sit with a straight back, shoulders down, nice and relaxed. Bring the hands up in front of your heart with palms facing up. The sides of the little fingers and the inner sides of the palms are touching. Now bring your middle fingers tips together, and extend the thumbs away from the palms. Keep the fingers stretched as little antennas for energy. Hold for Three minutes, then relax and be still.

BREATH
Long, deep and slow through your nose

CHAKRAS
Heart - 4, Throat - 5, Third eye - 6

HEALING COLORS
Green, blue, indigo

AFFIRMATION
I RELEASE ALL WORRY AND FEEL ASSURED

MUDRA FOR INNER SECURITY

Sit with a straight spine and place your hands in reversed prayer pose: hands touching back to back at the level of your heart and solar plexus. Hold the pose for a beat, then repeat with palms pressed together in a prayer pose, thumbs against the chest. Hold for a beat and repeat. Practice for Three minutes, then relax.

BREATH
LONG, DEEP AND SLOW THROUGH YOUR NOSE

MANTRA
AD SHAKTI AD SHAKTI

(I Bow to the Creator's Power)

CHAKRA
SOLAR PLEXUS - 3, HEART - 4

HEALING COLORS
YELLOW, GREEN

AFFIRMATION

I AM SAFE AND SECURE, I AM SHELTERED AND PROTECTED

MUDRA FOR SEXUAL BALANCE

Sit with a straight back. With your elbows slightly to the sides, clasp your hands together. The fingers are intertwined. The right thumb on top of the left will empower the male side of your nature and the left thumb on top empowers the feminine, emotional side of your nature. Practice for three minutes.

BREATH
LONG, DEEP AND SLOW THROUGH YOUR NOSE

MANTRA
AD SHAKTI AD SHAKTI
(I Bow to the Creator's Power)

CHAKRA
REPRODUCTIVE ORGANS - 2

HEALING COLORS
ORANGE

AFFIRMATION
MY SEXUALITY IS VIBRANT AND HARMONIOUS

MUDRA FOR REJUVENATION

Sit with a straight back. Place both palms directly on your ears. Massage your ears in a circular motion away from your face – counter clockwise. Listen to the sound of "the ocean" you create with the palms of your hands and continue for at least three minutes.

BREATH
LONG, DEEP AND SLOW **through** YOUR NOSE

MANTRA
OM *(God in His Absolute State)*

CHAKRA
THROAT - 5, THIRD EYE - 6, CROWN - 7

HEALING COLORS
BLUE, INDIGO, VIOLET

AFFIRMATION

I AM ONE WITH THE INFINITE POWER OF THE OCEAN

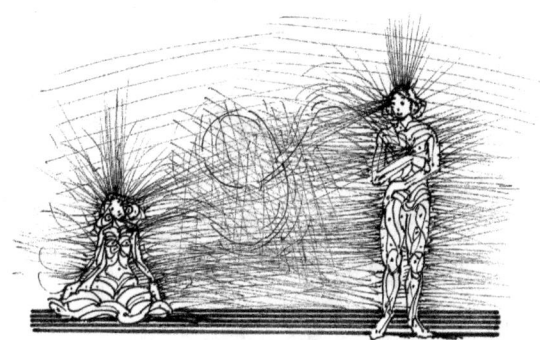

Week Seven

ALIGNING YOUR MINDS AND HEARTS

Some people think and believe that everything happens in the mind. Certainly a lot happens in the mind, but not everything. Your life experiences are a product of your individual balance between your heart and your mind. Some people who function mostly in their mind, see it that way. And for others, who come from their heart, the view differs.

> **IT IS THE PERFECT BLEND OF THE TWO MAJOR POLARITIES OF THE MIND AND THE HEART THAT HELPS YOU NAVIGATE THRU LIFE'S CHALLENGES AND PURSUE WHAT YOU NEED IN ORDER TO FULFILL YOUR DREAMS.**

This delicate and important dynamic is something you need to understand and find out for yourself, before expecting it to work in your relationships. Why?

Well, let's say you are a mind person, always thinking, over analyzing and justifying every choice, decision, and experience. If you are unaware of your disposition and your partner is of the opposite make, you will have a constant block in your communication field. You will push the mental aspect ahead of your heart and be able to layout a logical explanation for every challenge or disagreement you have, while you may be accused that you feel nothing.

As a result, you will feel misunderstood and deprived of intellectual synchronicity, while your partner, who is more heart centered and emotionally inclined, will feel emotionally deprived.

And this can't be simply categorized as a male and female problem. It is much more complex than that, as this dynamic can happen regardless of gender, for you can have a very emotional man and very mental woman or whatever combination you find yourself in.

It has to do with the mind and heart equilibrium of the individual. This balance or imbalance will follow you thru every aspect of the relationship. If you are both overly mental, your union will go to extremes of intellectualizing emotional experiences, which is never a good idea. Why? Because emotions do not work by the rule of logic, practicality or planning. Emotions are free, spontaneous and unpredictable. That is what makes them beautiful and equally challenging in nature.

On the other side of the spectrum, if you are both exclusively heart-centered, you might be emotionally too sensitive, especially when dealing with demanding practical and mental aspects of life. This will present a different hindrance and a continuous challenge.

> **THE KEY IS FINDING A FAIR BALANCE BETWEEN MIND AND HEART, BUT BEFORE YOU CAN PURSUE THIS GOAL IN A RELATIONSHIP, YOU NEED TO WORK OUT YOUR OWN INDIVIDUAL DYNAMICS, INVISIBLE BOUNDARIES AND COMFORT LEVELS.**

Any kind of meditation practice can be helpful in accomplishing this individual inner balance, but Mudras are especially powerful, effective and fast. By selecting Mudras to help you target these very specific subtle energy areas you need to heal, your results are achieved with speed and success. You are consciously and intentionally participating in your healing process. This requires some inner soul searching, in order to understand and discover for yourself what kind of person you are, which is essential for a harmonious union of two evolved souls.

However you function is going to feel normal, but you need to take a moment and truly recognize your natural tendency. Expand your awareness to understand and feel a person that functions in the very opposite way, on the other side of the spectrum of human experience.

An example would be; understanding emotionally and mentally how a person that is the opposite of you, experiences life.

If you are overly thin, and they are overweight or the other way around, can you put yourself into their shoes?
If you are married and they are single or the other way around?
If you are considered successful and they are not, or the opposite?

Imagine their experience of life and expand your ability to truly comprehend this from an entirely different perspective. It will open and develop your ability for deep compassion, profound understanding, void of judgment, harsh criticism and rushed, usually incorrect assumptions. This is also an excellent way to help you blend the exceptional skills of your mind and heart.

> **OBSERVE THE WORLD AROUND YOU AND THEN THINK WITH YOUR HEART AND FEEL WITH YOUR MIND.**

If that seems impossible to do, it is not. Try it. It will help you exercise blending and balancing the two opposites. Of course, understanding how you function, is the first required task at hand. You probably already know what are your natural tendencies, but let's try to make it clearer.

Are you always overanalyzing every emotional experience?
Do you tend to justify your choices and interactions with others?
Do you rehash the same story in your mind, trying to find answers, reasons, causes, and variables how something could have, or should have been, despite results to the contrary?
Do you view a love relationship as a practical, logical, expected and beneficial choice?
Do you approach your relationship as a business deal, a wise decision for your needs, and an overall, society and larger-family pleasing choice?

If any of these possibilities ring true, you are not properly acquainted with deep love. The kind of love that takes your breath away and makes you see the entire life and world from a different, life-altering perspective. In order to experience that kind of love, you absolutely need to let go of the mental grip that you are functioning in.

> **PRACTICALITY AND LOVE DO NOT WALK HAND IN HAND,**
> **THEY DO NOT KNOW OR UNDERSTAND EACH OTHER,**
> **FOR THEY SPEAK A COMPLETELY DIFFERENT LANGUAGE.**

So you need to abandon this limited expectation of a relationship as you imagined, and consciously work on stillness of the mind, while opening your heart. On the other side of the spectrum, if you are a person functioning solely from the heart, you may have a hard time keeping your emotions under control, which could prove to be a real challenge as well.

Are you overly emotionally sensitive, take everything very personally?
Does every event trigger all sorts of inner reactions that upset your emotional balance?
Do you continuously dream about unrealistic romantic expectations of what your partner should be, or have an idea of your ideal partner so removed from reality, that nobody could ever fit such a picture, or fulfill all your expectations?
Do you have a great partner, but continuously expect more than they can reasonably offer?
Are you so overwhelmed with uncontrollable emotional reactions, that you confuse a simple smile and kind gesture as a marriage proposal, and a stern serious face as a personal insult?

This would indicate an emotional inner challenge, and you cannot expect to experience a steady, harmonious, relaxed, fulfilling and balanced relationship. Your emotions need to get settled into a peaceful state of equilibrium, so you experience life's most beautiful moments and not simply exist in a state of tortured suspense and self-inflicted emotional suffering.

If your heart feels ignored and starved for love, this may create and emotional state of neediness and desperation, which is never going to attract a healthy and long lasting partnership. Remember, your desperate state will attract a similar desperation, but perhaps on a more mental realm. Maybe a person starved for mental-companionship will help fill your missing aspects, but just for a short while. After the initial immediate fulfillment of each other's needs, you will begin to want more of what the other simply isn't able to offer. Why? Because your are coming from the opposite side of the spectrum. A mutual sense of frustration will emerge, and suddenly you may feel you have nothing in common anymore. These are complex interactions of highly sensitive nature.

Keeping your emotions in balance will allow you to likewise balance your mental interaction and help you live and love with consciousness and presence. You will compliment and complete each other. But if you keep either your mind or your heart deprived of proper and balanced engagement, they will live in a neglected pattern in your deep subconscious. If and when you will let your guard down, the other side of your nature will come out swinging and you won't even know or understand that part of yourself.

Here is an example:
An overly mental person, incapable of open emotional expression, finds themselves in an unexpected situation where they drop their guard and defenses, and all their controlling mentality goes out the window. They give their emotional side a chance to surface in an unexpected, emotional outburst, a crying eruption, proclamation of unrequited love, or profound sadness, heart's longing, unfulfilled desires…all that suppressed emotional burden, never fully expressed, finally just explodes. As someone, who always had everything under control, they suddenly find themselves in a messy, emotional puddle. The other side of their nature has come out and taken over. The heart finally has a chance to express all that it carried for so long. This will create quite a shock for that person. As a result, they may end up engaging in intimacy with someone that they would mentally never allow themselves to, because of their logical thinking patterns and self-imposed limitations.

Now, if we imagine another person that is precisely the opposite, very emotionally open, who finds themselves in an unpredictable situation that triggers a purely mental response, this may reveal their surprising negative and pessimistic mental block. These are two extreme examples of the consequences when there is no balance between the heart and mind. If you now take this dynamic into a relationship, you can imagine some pretty intense events that may develop as a result of these complex individual unresolved dispositions.

> **THE MORE SELF-REALIZED YOU ARE BEFORE A NEW RELATIONSHIP, THE BETTER YOUR CHANCES OF ATTRACTING A COMPATIBLE PARTNER AND ESTABLISHING A GOOD RELATIONSHIP BALANCE.**

What about the individual energy frequency? Would that play a role in interaction as we learned before? Yes, of course, and in harmony with that concept, if the person is very mental, they function mostly in Chakra 3, where the mind, ego, and emotions of fear and anger rule. But if they naturally function dominantly in Chakra 4, then their overactive mind, which is ruled by Chakra 3, will attempt to pull them down into the state of fear and logic, away from love – Chakra 4.

A good balance of mind and heart is needed for healthy function of all chakras. Let's continue to look at the way subtle energy works with these various possibilities. As you know, Chakra 5 relates to speaking the truth, and communicating with the world around you. If your heart is overloaded with unexpressed emotion, you will speak to those around you. However, if you add a healthy dose of mental energy, your speech will demonstrate a good example of heart and mind balance that is possible.

Knowing who you are is the key. This gives you the option to find and cultivate your unique mind and heart balance, while functioning at your highest frequency possible. Once your individual balance is accomplished, you will become the partner you wish to be. This inner balance will help your partner find their own inner balance as well.

> **AT LEAST ONE PARTNER HAS TO HAVE AN INNER BALANCE IN ORDER FOR YOUR RELATIONSHIP TO HAVE A CHANCE OF MAINTAINING A HARMONIOUS STATE.**

But if the other partner is struggling, and is very fearful with an overactive mind, or overly emotional, then it will be challenging. Your relationship will depend on the evolutionary ability of the weaker partner.

You cannot force someone to grow and evolve faster, since everybody needs their time. This may sound complicated, but all it takes is calm self-assessment, to recognize your disposition. And the good news? Once you understand how you function, you have the conscious choice to shift, adapt, and make the necessary changes that will bring you what you desire – absolute harmony and synchronicity in your relationship.

THE GREAT GATEWAY BETWEEN YOUR MIND AND HEART

Let's reflect on more esoteric views of these two mighty forces, and why the harmony of these two sides is so crucial. From the practical perspective it is pretty obvious, but there is another underlying reason for the importance of balance between these two polarities. As mentioned before, the power of the mind is energetically centered in your solar plexus, the home base of your ego, and mental disposition. This is Chakra 3, where you are still easily swayed and pulled downward into the deceptive illusion of Earthly realm.

Things that matter on material plane are connected to this center of ego temptations and traps, and mental overload. Once you have lived thru the long, necessary and challenging lessons connected to this center and have overcome the Earthly attachments, you begin to naturally move upwards toward the next big centre, your heart Chakra 4.

> **ONCE YOUR CROSSOVER INTO THE HEART IS ACCOMPLISHED, YOU ARE IN CONSIDERABLY LESS DANGER OF BEING PULLED DOWN AND BACK INTO THE WORLD OF ILLUSION.**

Yes, you may make occasional visitations, especially if you are surrounded by people who function solely on that level. But your true nature, your soul natural frequency will no longer be comfortable on the lower level of chakra 3. You will feel out of place, distanced, almost with a sort of aversion to all the distractions and predictable trouble causing addictions that reside there.

Now, an interesting dynamic happens. You will begin to function from the heart, giving unconditionally, with joy and honest generosity. It may take you a bit longer to learn how to receive as well, and this must be also mastered in order to fully function in the heart. But what is interesting, is how you will use your mind and heart as they relate to your general character disposition.

You see, it is entirely possible that you are functioning from your heart, but have a very mind oriented character disposition. This will create an interesting dynamic where you will be generous, kind, open hearted, and aware of heart's essence, but still use your powerful mind to further elevate your overall heart frequency. In other words, you will be able to find the sacred balance within, by keeping a calm mindset and follow the guidance of your heart. This is an excellent combination, that will help you live with a purpose and not be overwhelmed by the general harsh nature of this world.

It will facilitate your further ascension and more positive actions and contributions to the world. In another scenario, if you naturally function at Chakra 4 – Heart level, and are less mental by nature, by experiencing life primarily thru your heart, you will encounter some difficulty in dealing with the reality of this world. You will perhaps naively expect others to be like you, won't know how to tackle existential matters, and embark on a life journey of illusion and daydreaming, while lacking in strength to sustain yourself in the harsh grips of the material world, where you currently reside. In such a case, you will have to learn to activate and harmonize the mind's mighty powers, so that you can sustain yourself, despite your natural heart inclination. This may be one of your life's lessons.

Adaptability, expanding your soul's potential, mastering any environment you find yourself in, and remaining a loving, kind person, despite the challenging circumstances that surround you, regardless of disappointments you may endure – this is our goal. It requires stamina and resilience of the soul, to stay on track and fulfill your mission, no matter what comes your way.

> **REGARDLESS OF WHAT NATURAL FREQUENCY YOU FUNCTION AT, YOUR STATE OF MIND AND HEART BALANCE DEPENDS ON YOUR PERSONALITY AND CHARACTER.**

This is important to know, so that you do not have an idea of randomly dividing people into various categories. Each one of us is a very complex and unique being, that carries evolutionary information, soul's past experiences with sorrows as well as gifts, and the current set of circumstances affected by countless factors, including parents, societal restrictions and expectations, and last but not least, your unique cosmic – astrological aspects. This is why each one of us is a completely unique special being, navigating thru this human experience the best we can, under our individual circumstances. Nobody knows what it feels like to be you. Trying to understand this human complexity with expanded sense of awareness, non-judgment and compassion, is our goal.

SYNCHRONIZING AND PURIFYING YOUR MINDS

This may sound incredibly complicated, but it is all a matter of open and clear communication. If you know yourself, you are always at an advantage, because the process of self-discovery can sometimes prove to be quite painful, and you may rebel against it. Seeing one's own shortcomings is a challenge, and admitting that we are not perfect, can trigger all sorts of defensive reactions. Once you calm down and realize your abilities as well as weaknesses, you will be able to stand in a relationship with confidence and on solid ground. You won't be blaming your partner for something that you don't want to see in yourself, when they force you to face it. You see, your partner is really like a most precise and truthful mirror. Nothing escapes the harsh light of truth. It may not be intentional and they may not be aware of it at all.

> **LOVE BRINGS YOU TO A STATE OF OPEN VULNERABILITY AND TRIGGERS YOU PRECISELY WERE YOU NEED TO GROW.**

Whether you want to or not, you have to face it and see every tiny crack in the mask that you wear around in public. In the world of intimacy and love, your mask falls away sooner or later and there you are, all faults and gifts you may possess, everything is exposed. Once you are comfortable and accepting of yourself, you can stand in front of your mirror – partner. Your surrendered comfortable stance will help you enjoy the moment, instead of struggling to preserve an image that doesn't exist. Synchronizing each other's minds requires the removal of all unnecessary old "baggage," defenses, and masks.

If you carry unresolved conflicts, worries, fears and anxieties, they will disrupt the smooth energy flow between your two minds. Let's look at this from the ever fascinating esoteric subtle-energy perspective. If you have issues with fear – Chakra 3, your heart will not function at its full capacity, because you will carry an energy congestion in the Chakra 3 area, which will prevent a healthy energy flow into the next, Chakra 4 of the heart. This will result in Chakra 4 having less fluid energy, and may manifest as hesitancy before opening your heart, fearful disposition towards love, lack of self-love and fear of commitment. Furthermore, the energy which always moves upwards, will be less fluid in the next center Chakra 5, which rules speaking truth and your ability to communicate. How will this manifest itself?

Well, you will have a hard time expressing your true feelings, you may talk incessantly, but fail to convey how you really feel or what you really need, want or don't want. Keep in mind, saying "no" requires some strength as well. You may just use chatter in an effort to avoid the real, honest kind of conversation. Your talk will carry the nuances of fear, frustration, anger and anxiety, stemming from congested Chakra 3, that will continue to pollute every expression of your personality.

Going further upwards, your Chakra 6 that rules your intuition will likewise receive less energy, so you cannot possibly expect to have unobstructed access. It will be difficult to have a synchrony of the minds if you both lack in fully functioning Chakra 6, and are too busy tending to unresolved issues of lower energy centers, in this case, specifically Chakra 3.

Finally, in regard to Chakra 7, that rules your trust, faith, and connection to awareness of the Universal power, you will lack in clarity because again, your energy current is weak and abnormally drained by the unresolved Chakra 3 issues. This is the way we can easily understand the natural movement of energy upwards thru each chakra center and the consequences on every part of your life. This is where Mudras again bring an irreplaceable tool to help you work on resolving and healing energy congestion in areas that present a personal challenge to you.

> **MUDRAS PURIFY YOUR MIND FOR A FREE UPWARD ENERGY FLOW,
> ENABLING YOU TO FEEL FULLY FROM THE HEART,
> SPEAK WORDS OF TRUTH, HARMONY AND INSPIRATION.**

You will facilitate the synchronicity of the mind, be able to think alike, read each other's mind, and understand each other on such a high level, it will help you experience your relationship on an entirely different realm of existence.

And finally, your mutual connection and understanding as well as ability to receive clear guidance from the Universal power – Chakra 7, will grant you a unique gift of working in synchrony with the Divine will. That is truly a blessed experience. It is when everything feels right, good and is flowing smoothly along. That is a sign of complete, harmonious synchronicity of two people in a relationship and their unity with the Universe.

LISTENING

One of the crucial elements in great communication is your ability to listen. You have to be able to patiently and calmly hear what the other person is trying to convey to you. You need to hear their words and observe their emotions intertwined within their speech. Don't prepare and rush an answer until you've heard everything. You need to listen and hear each other. And before you can do that, you need to be able to hear yourself. Yes, of course you will hear your mind, but you absolutely must strive to always listen to your heart in equal measure.

Now that we have intricately reviewed the way your own challenges can suffocate and dampen the flow of your individual energy and affect your ability to communicate with your partner, you can begin to consciously observe how you act, react, assume, defend and deal with communication challenges that come your way. Speaking with clarity, wisdom, and conveying words of your heart, will always help both of you to establish a kind, peaceful and comfortable zone, where you feel safe to reveal and share your utmost secrets, desires, fears and doubts. Sharing is what life and true partnership is all about.

Nobody is perfect when they meet their partner, but understanding the role your own maturity and self-awareness in a relationship, will offer you an inspiration to strive further, work on yourself deeper, so that you can enjoy what you desire and share your life in a beautiful way. Conquering obstacles becomes a joint mission, for this is one of the great pillars of a fulfilling, equal and harmonious relationship.

SPEAKING ~ VERBAL COMMUNICATION

Words that hold hurtful intentions are more damaging than silence, and words filled with genuine love, carry tremendous healing powers. Words matter, what you say will remain imprinted in the ether and carry on the frequency of your message.

> **WORDS UTTERED IN THE NAME OF LOVE**
> **FOREVER EMBED IN YOUR SUBTLE ENERGY LOVE-MATRIX**
> **AND PERMANENTLY AFFECT YOUR UNDERSTANDING,**
> **OPENNESS AND GENERAL DISPOSITION TOWARD LOVE.**

This is why it is so difficult to undo words we didn't mean, they seem to linger on forever, and depending on the person, some people can never quite overcome what they heard once, no matter how many apologies follow. Forgiveness will help you release the energy of the harmful or negative words spoken, but the memory of them shall unfortunately linger in the background for some time or even forever.

If someone is hurtful with words in the heat of an argument, they can create a lot of considerable damage. Verbal conflict of fiery explosive nature with an air of unpredictability and aggressiveness, is the expression of the lower levels of human nature. Abusive and hurtful words carry long term destructive consequences. Why would someone engage in such a conduct? Because the cannot control the pain, anger, fear and disdain they carry.

These negative emotions may often not have anything to do with the person on the receiving end of the argument. They may have triggered a negative reaction simply by stating the truth. This does not require words, or even actions, sometimes simply the appearance of another person that carries a lot of powerful light, may trigger a volatile person to explode. There is absolutely no gain and only damage as a result of such an exchange. Any person with some level of spiritual awareness, should strive to conquer impulses of verbal aggression, for it does not agree with anything you are longing for. Yes, you can be mad, speak loudly, even scream if that helps you feel better. But do not direct it at another person, that just happens to be closest to you at the moment. Release the pent-up energy that can't be contained in another way on your own, and try to face, resolve and understand what brought you to this state. Work on yourself and your issues until you can control your negative impulses and never abuse another person that happens to be near. It is your issue, so don't let it pollute your relationship. If what angers you has to do with your partner's actions, you can convey this in peace, for you will accomplish much more that way. Any kind of unpredictably angry or explosive behavior that you consider part of your nature, is emotionally abusive and completely unacceptable. If you can not manage to contain your outbursts of temper, therapy or anger management may be your best option.

> **LOVING AND SUPPORTIVE WORDS CAN MAKE THE BIGGEST DIFFERENCE IN THE WORLD. THEY CAN LITERALLY CHANGE SOMEONE'S LIFE.**

Kindness can't be measured. It can be delivered with simple, beautiful, genuine, heartfelt words that will transform your relationship into a beautiful safe haven of trust, mutual support and loving exchange. After Mudra practice, you are in an absolutely ideal space for a wonderful, open-heart and deeply honest conversation. Truth, love, appreciation and honest revelations about each other will forever change and significantly ascend your relationship. The conversation after you have centered and balanced your energy bodies and have created an invisible field of synchronicity and love, will be profound, simple, but powerful beyond imagination. In order to cultivate this kind of verbal exchange, and overcome any habits of discord, cultivate Mudras for Two practice, and open up to spontaneous natural and utterly peaceful conversation exchange afterwards. You can find a rich selection of Mudra sets in my book *LOVE MUDRAS, Hand Yoga for Two*. This is how you will establish a new, beautiful approach of speaking with each other, that will remain with you always, not just for a special occasion. Respectful, supportive and loving words will sustain you thru any challenge and help you find a way back into the space of love and positivity.

SHARING

Your ability to generously share with your partner, is a clear indicator of your state of heart consciousness. Sharing is closely related to giving, so we return to the question of giver and taker. If you are able to share, you are a giver, if you can't share, you need to examine why you feel the need to keep everything to yourself, and can't be generous. Usually it is connected to fear and selfishness, which is based on fear for survival, competition, and results in inability to give. Again, these are all Chakra 3 issues. So quite obviously, if someone does not have the ability to share with a loved one, they have an energy obstruction or unhealthy negative congestion in Chakra 3, that is preventing the natural upwards energy flow and functioning of Chakra 4.

To resolve this challenge, return to the source of the problem and examine what is the main fear that is keeping someone in a selfish or greedy mindset. Communicate about it and see if the issue can be cleared. However, you must not ignore the possibility that a person who functions on Chakra 3 level, is simply not sufficiently emotionally mature and evolved to overcome selfishness and egotism. Their awareness and ability to give and receive has not yet manifested. This leads to a logical and simple conclusion, that if one person is spiritually more evolved and a giver, they will suffer in a relationship with a partner less evolved who is incapable of giving, but is very comfortable with continuous, entitled taking. Recognizing this character trait before you commit to an inappropriate partner, is of greatest importance. If your Love Matrix is incompatible in this aspect, the road to a happy, fulfilling and harmonious relationship will be a tough one, filled with frustration, misunderstandings and disappointment.

> **THE NATURAL BEHAVIOR OF A COMPATIBLE AND SYNCHRONIZED COUPLE IS TO SHARE LIFE'S EXPERIENCES.**

Sharing requires a different skillset than being completely independent and capable of facing and enduring anything that comes your way. It is necessary to have that ability, but likewise, the experience of sharing is utmost necessary.

It is often the case, that a very capable, independent person simply does not find a compatible partner, equally capable as well as spiritually evolved. The experience of sharing simply eludes them and they remain alone, carrying the burden of necessary and total self-reliance in addition to great responsibility for others.

Sharing in a partnership is a blessing. It may not always be easy, but do keep in mind, that humans are meant to be together, helping each other, supporting, loving and expressing their experiences and learning from this union. Sharing is an experience that is necessary, in order to evolve to the highest spiritual level of selflessness and generosity. The ability to receive love, kindness, affection and support is necessary for a full human experience.

> **A COMPATIBLE SHARING COUPLE IS ALWAYS STRONGER THAN ONE PERSON. STRIVE TO FIND THIS IN LIFE.**

If this eludes you, cultivate the experience of sharing through larger family, friends, a spiritual community, animals and nature. Sharing space, the comfort of food and gentle affection can manifest in various ways and will always offer a sense of togetherness, support, inner harmony and joy.

REACHING OUT

If you have been challenged with a conflict in your relationship, it might be beneficial to establish some space for reflection and solitude. Take your time and meditate, practice Mudras and consciously heal your inner conflict. Then, overcome your pride and reach out. True love does not play games and proudly sit in a stubborn tantrum. It is always better to extend your efforts and make known to your partner your genuine caring thoughts of concern, desire for harmony, or simply state your love for them.

ADAPTING

You may have been doing things a certain way all your life, but in a relationship, some things will necessarily have to shift and be a bit different. You may have been "spoiled" by the control your single life has given you, although at that time you may have not seen it that way. But being a couple requires its sacrifices, and adaptability is one of those necessary things. Adapting to your partner while letting them know what is comfortable for you, is the basis for creating such a state of comfort, that you won't have to keep adapting all the time.

However, life will always require you to continue adapting, to a certain degree. Why? Because nothing stays static, it changes continuously and constantly. That's the beauty of life, so that we are never bored.

COMPROMISE AND BOUNDARIES

A compromise does not mean you will have to forget all your favorite things to do, or lose all your freedom. It just means that when you have someone in your life, you should make adjustments, so that there is a mutual field of balance. It can't be all just your way, or all their way. This means that even if you have no trouble making a compromise in order to make something easier for your partner, equally so, you need to have the ability to say "no" when you feel forgotten, ignored and your wishes or needs are not considered. In other words, you need to negotiate a compromise for yourself as well. If you don't make this clear, and expect the partner to guess what you wish, you won't succeed. Communicate and ask for a compromise, and you will most likely harmoniously accomplish what you want. Another big secret to a successful compromise is this: if you behave respectfully, kindly and lovingly toward yourself, you are clearly demonstrating the boundaries and limitations of what is acceptable to you, and what you believe you deserve, and need.

YOU SET THE EXAMPLE HOW OTHERS CAN AND SHOULD TREAT YOU.

If you just exhaust yourself continuously by doing everything for everybody, and then wonder why nobody notices or appreciates you, then you have clearly missed an important point. You have the free will to say yes or no to what you can, and will do.

Of course there are circumstances beyond our control, that may require you to sacrifice in an incredible way, and you may have seemingly no choice, because it is either you or nobody that can do what needs to be accomplished. But that is a different situation. When we are talking about a relationship, there are the two of you that tackle various dynamics and challenges. You should hopefully help each other, the best you can. That requires a sort of compromise as well. How the two of you treat, share and help each other, that is between the two of you.

Set the boundaries, discuss the rules, levels of comfortable compromises, and adjust as situations present themselves. If one of you has to take care of their elderly parents, this is a situation that is going to affect both of you, and you can not leave the partner that has this sudden added responsibility, just because they won't be able to give you as much undivided attention as they used to. If you are a true partner, you will stand by your partner thru thick and thin, thru everything in life, just like the wows of marriage declare. This loyalty is needed regardless of your marriage status. It is simply the required level of respectful, appreciative and unconditionally loving disposition that two souls maintain in a union. It is your soul's promise regardless of legal paperwork. It is a spiritual promise that lasts beyond this life, into the next and beyond.

THE HEART

The heart is where the soul resides. It doesn't reside in your head or your foot. Heart is the first chakra center where you experience a higher awareness of unconditional love. This is where you leave the ego Chakra 3, behind, and embrace yourself as a spiritual being that has a higher purpose. You begin to understand that life is more, than just thinking or caring about yourself. Your heart is where you experience an openness, a sharing, an energy exchange of the finest qualities.

> **NOTHING IN YOUR LIFE IS AS IMPORTANT AS LOVE.**

Love is truly everything. It is a major force to be reckoned with. It is the power that heals, helps you overcome indescribable obstacles, and permanently and forever changes your life, as well as that of others.

And yet, many of us are afraid of getting hurt, feeling the pain, losing love, and experiencing a heartbreak. A broken heart is devastated, crippled, and inconsolable. But that harsh reality is a part of life and helps you understand what it means to feel alive. When you fall in love, you are literally walking on air. When you fall out of love, you feel lost and confused. When you lose your love, you fear that you shall perish and drown in sorrow. A heartbreak can feel like physical pain in your heart and some people die of a broken heart. If and when you find new love again, you are afraid it shall happen all over again. The scar in your heart may heal, but it will never disappear.

No love story is the same, for no two people are alike. Yes, they can be similar, but not the same, not ever. The most important aspect is that you dare to fall in love. And when you happen to meet a soul that resonates with yours, don't let fear destroy the chance of it. This is such a common occurrence. Love has incredible power and when you feel how it takes over your every breath and you lose the control that you so desperately cling to, yes you may decide you will walk away, fearing that everything seemingly valuable will need to be sacrificed. But you my feel this way only because you do not understand and know what true love is. It is not a pre-calculated practical and planned situation. If you perceive it that way, you will always miss the "real deal." You won't even begin to understand what love is.

Love is when you let yourself go with it and don't hold back. Not even an inch. When you don't overanalyze and find fault with the other, looking for excuses how you can run away and avoid your true feelings. When you don't play games to cheat or test the other. When you are 1000% fearless in giving what it takes, to experience the full power of the two of you. That is love.

Can you do that? Can you trust yourself, or are you desperately hanging on to imaginary control, to fear, to rules, conditions, or succumbing to expectations bestowed upon you by the society or relatives? Can you just remove all these fear-based nuances and allow yourself the full experience of love?

> **YOUR HEART NEEDS TO FEEL ALIVE, IT NEEDS TO EXPERIENCE THE TREMENDOUS FORCE OF LOVE.**

Perhaps it also needs to know what it feels like to be broken, lost, deceived, abandoned or betrayed. Why? Because that makes you human, it makes you who you are with all the beautiful nuances, laugh lines, and unique qualities. The best artistic creations are often a result of broken hearts. This is part of life. And life has no guarantees.

We often say; one does not know what they have, until they lose it. Yes, well that's unfortunately true. And this becomes a lesson. And next time, you won't make the same mistake. Your heart holds the capacity to offer all these tremendous experiences to you, the otherworldly sensations and beautiful moments, which there is no other way to know or comprehend. Once you understand the power of your heart, you can balance the delicate relationship between your mind and your heart.

You simply can't balance something until you understand the power, heaviness and massive essence that holds it all together. So until you have truly deeply and madly loved, you are looking at love from an inexperienced perspective, sort of guessing, wondering, imagining and longing. But you don't really truly understand what it is. And in order to experience true deep maddening love, you have to become fearless.

When you are fearless, you will attract an equally fearless partner, and together you will ascend to your heart and experience the mighty power that resides there, the power that lives in every living thing, the power that sustains the entire Universe, as far as we can imagine. Of course this power goes unimaginably further. It goes into eternity. This synchronicity, when two people love each other truly and deeply, goes on indefinitely, for their love will never die. It may go to sleep, into hiding, into waiting…but it will be resurrected when time comes.

The love experiences in this life that you are living thru now, or that still await you, these experiences may be the continuations of your previous long lost, forgotten, missed or destroyed loves from your far, distant past. Reuniting and meeting them again in this life will remind you that no love is ever lost, forgotten, or destroyed.

> **THE DYNAMIC BETWEEN MIND AND HEART IS A MAGICAL ONE.**
> **WHEN THESE TWO ENERGIES DANCE IN HARMONY,**
> **THEY HELP EACH OTHER ACCOMPLISH THE IMPOSSIBLE.**

When they try to compete, there is trouble. You need your mind to have a vision, and you need your heart to love that vision. Cultivate both sides in yourself, and you will have a much easier time finding that perfectly balanced magic, that the Universe gave you.

Love lives on forever. Love is indestructible. And in love, the two of you are indestructible as well.

YOUR ASSIGNMENT

AFFIRMATION

> INSTEAD OF THINKING THERE'S A BATTLE BETWEEN YOUR MIND AND HEART, THINK OF THEM AS THE GREATEST ALLIES...

DIARY

This week you are fully prepared to consciously take the step from your mind into your heart. Practice and recognize how this transition occurs, what different moods during the day may pull you into fear, and how you can maintain your natural state of living from your heart. Observe your state before and after Mudra practice.

PROCESS

Work thru the questions, come back in a few days, see if anything changed, add it on, clarify, clean it up, and self-discover through the process.

PRACTICE

Work with the diary, answer the questions and practice the Mudras listed. Write down how you feel before and after the Mudra practice. Observe the shift in your energy field.

> WHEN MIND AND HEART WORK IN UNISON, LIFE BECOMES POETRY IN MOTION...

Your Workspace
MIND OR HEART?

DO YOU FEEL MORE AT HOME IN YOUR MIND OR HEART?

Perhaps you already know your answer, or believe you know it, but might surprise yourself to realize the opposite.

Observe how you act and respond to situations.
What is your reaction when an emotional decision has to be made, or an emotional choice is required?

Do you analyze all the facts, do you first deal with your fear, do you think, reassess, and waver back and forth consumed by indecisiveness?

Do you fearlessly throw yourself into an emotional response, without thinking?

Do you have an emotionally overwhelming reaction to heart-felt scenes, books, films or everyday events?

You know who you are. Reflect how this plays a role in your relationships and how you could sustain a greater sense of balance and harmony.

Once you find your mind and heart disposition, you can consciously adjust the volume and find a healthy balance.

LISTEN, SHARE & COMPROMISE

CAN YOU LISTEN, SHARE, ADAPT AND COMPROMISE?

These are very important qualities to cultivate.
Why? Because they will always be of great help when you need to reinstate a harmonious, desirable balance with your partner.
Reflect on how you feel about these abilities and honestly review your disposition.

This will help you gain clarity about which qualities you need to develop further or improve, in order to participate fairly in maintaining peace, harmony and love in your relationship.

Your Workspace
EMBRACING LOVE

CAN YOU LET GO OF FEARS AND EMBRACE LOVE?

This is the most essential question.

If you are longing for love but can't open up, you will be waiting for a long while.

If you are single, this shortcoming will prevent you from recognizing and allowing love into your life.

If you are in a relationship, your new level of trust and open heart will magnify your love, take it to a higher level, and grant you the ultimate experience of ascended love.

In order to immerse yourself in love, make an effort to overcome your self-imposed fear-based limitations, and courageously give it all you've got.

Real, deep, and everlasting love requires an "all or nothing" disposition.

Send a clear signal to the Universe that you are ready, willing and able to love unconditionally, and wish to experience the highest possible manifestation of love. Write down your thoughts.

For your Mudra Practice

PUT YOUR MIND WHERE IT BELONGS

Practice Mudras every time you feel your mind is running off with an unproductive habit, and pulls you away from your heart. If you bring a scattered or confused mind into your relationship, your static frequency will obstruct easy flow of energy between yourself and your partner. When you feel more settled, centered, and in command of your thoughts, you can maintain great communication and disposition with your partner.

FREE YOUR HEART

The gate to your heart can be obstructed by various energy clusters, that are all based on fears. Any less desirable disposition, such as holding a grudge, hesitation, anxiety, pessimism, negativity, self-doubt, and inability to open up your heart, needs to be consciously removed, so you can welcome love into your heart and experience the higher manifestation of this powerful force. But this cannot happen, unless you regularly and intentionally release and let go of all negativity that may have gathered, thru various experiences. Cleansing your heart of negativity is not a one-time occasion. It requires regular practice and tender care to sustain a clear, positively charged space, where your self-love and your partner's love can land on fertile ground and successfully thrive. Tenderly tend to your heart each day, and cultivate a heart filled with abundant love, compassion and magnetic healing energy. This needs to be an individual practice, for you want to avoid transmitting your negativity onto your partner at all costs. Instead, release all undesirable emotions into the Universe, so you can be your best, when merging energy with your partner. As a result, together you will be able to create a pristine, clear and high frequency level in your Love Matrix. Always strive to keep it as pure as possible.

MUDRA FOR CALMING YOUR MIND

Sit with a straight spine. Cross your arms in front of your chest, elbows bent at a ninety-degree angle and arms parallel to the ground. The right hand is on top of the left arm and left hand below the right arm. All fingers are together and straight. Hold and keep the arms from sinking. Hold for Three minutes, then relax and be still.

BREATH
LONG, DEEP AND SLOW THROUGH YOUR NOSE

MANTRA
OM (*God in his absolute state*)

CHAKRAS
SOLAR PLEXUS - 3, CROWN - 7

HEALING COLORS
YELLOW, VIOLET

AFFIRMATION

I AM SERENE AND COMPOSED

MUDRA FOR POWERFUL ENERGY

Sit with a straight spine. Lift your hands in front of you at the solar plexus. Place your ring fingers flat and straight together and interlace all other fingers, the right thumb on top of the left. Hold for three minutes and concentrate on your breath.

BREATH
LONG, DEEP AND SLOW THROUGH YOUR NOSE

MANTRA
OOOOONG *(God as a Creator in Manifestation)*

CHAKRAS
HEART - 4, THROAT - 5, THIRD EYE - 6

HEALING COLORS
GREEN, BLUE, INDIGO

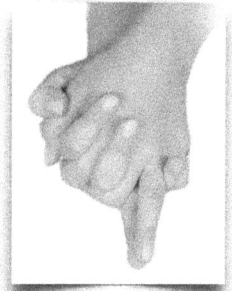

AFFIRMATION

I GATHER MY POWER, I GATHER MY STRENGTH

MUDRA FOR INNER INTEGRITY

Sit with a straight back. Bend your elbows and lift your upper arms parallel to the ground. Bring your hands to ear level, palms facing out. Curl your fingers inward and point the thumbs out toward your ears. Hold for three minutes and relax.

BREATH
Short, fast breath of fire from navel

MANTRA
SAT NAM *(Truth Is God's Name, One in Spirit)*

CHAKRAS
Throat - 5, Third eye - 6

HEALING COLORS
Blue, Indigo

AFFIRMATION

**I AM HONEST AND TRUE TO MYSELF
I UPHOLD MY INTEGRITY**

MUDRA FOR EMPOWERING YOUR VOICE

Sit with a straight back. Bend your elbows and hold them parallel to the ground as you bring your hands up in front of you at the level of your throat. Turn the right palm outward and the left palm toward you. Now bend your fingers and hook your hands together, the left hand on the outside. Pull on the hands as if trying to pull them apart, shoulders down. Hold for Three minutes, then relax.

BREATH
Long, deep and slow through your nose

MANTRA
SAT NAM *(Truth Is God's Name, One in Spirit)*

CHAKRAS
Throat - 5

HEALING COLORS
Blue

AFFIRMATION

MY WORDS INSPIRE, MOTIVATE AND CELEBRATE

MUDRA FOR POWER OF PROJECTION

Sit with a straight back and keep your shoulders down, nice and relaxed. Bring your hands up to the level between your solar plexus and the heart region. Bend the third and ring fingers, and press them together back to back from second to third knuckle. Interlace both index fingers and both small fingers. Press the thumbs against the upper side of the right index finger. Practice for Eleven minutes, then relax.

BREATH
Short breath of fire with continuous rhythm of the Mantra

MANTRA
HAR HAR HAR (*God, God, God*)

CHAKRAS
Solar Plexus - 3, Heart - 4, Third Eye - 6

HEALING COLORS
Yellow, green, Indigo

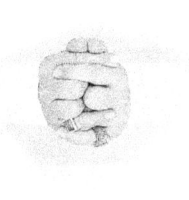

AFFIRMATION
I ALIGN MY FREQUENCY WITH MY HIGHER PURPOSE

MUDRA FOR RELAXATION AND JOY

Sit with a straight back and lift your hands up in front of your chest. Make a fist with your left hand, tucking the thumb inside. Wrap your right hand around the left and place your right thumb over the base of the left thumb. Concentrate on your Third eye area. Hold for Three minutes, then relax.

BREATH
Long, deep and slow through your nose

MANTRA
HAREE HAR HAREE HAR *(God in His Creative Aspect)*

CHAKRAS
Solar Plexus - 3, Heart - 4,

HEALING COLORS
Yellow, green

AFFIRMATION
I AM RELAXED, CAREFREE AND JOYOUS

Week Eight

AWAKENING THE PURPOSE OF YOUR SPIRITUAL LOVE

We have arrived at the last stop on your relationship journey – your spiritual union. The truth is, that this is not the end, but only the beginning. This is where your human entrapments and insecurities end, and your deepest spiritual experiences begin.

> **THIS IS WHERE IT IS REVEALED WHETHER THE TWO OF YOU ARE ABLE TO FIND, RECOGNIZE, UNDERSTAND AND FULFILL YOUR SPIRITUAL DESTINY.**
> **THIS IS ABOUT THE BIG PURPOSE OF YOUR JOURNEY TOGETHER.**

Many of us dream of and idolize spiritual love, but do we know what that actually means? What do you imagine how this concept or idea works? Some people romanticize and imagine sitting together on soft cushions, meditating, and looking at each other blissed out, completely immune to the headaches of everyday life. That's pretty immature and unrealistic. You can do that for a few minutes, even occasional hours perhaps. If you are on a special retreat, cut off from the real world and all its demands, you can live in this bubble for a few days.

Upon your inevitable return "down to Earth," back to reality, things usually slip back into the normal state of affairs. The daily grind, the annoying headaches of material existence and sooner or later, your "spiritual" mood evaporates into thin air. And perhaps in a little while, you become disillusioned, believing that you failed at this idea, or that your partner is at fault, for this "spiritual thing" not working properly. But the real, tangible spiritual love is something entirely different.

The true manifestation of spiritual love is your ability to conquer all Earthly challenges together, loyally stand by each other, and never lose sight of the love and deep bond between you two, while understanding and consciously communicating with the universal power, that is present in each and every one of us. It means total surrender and trust in your love, devotion, and unquestionable support of each other.

> **THE TRUE MAGIC OF A RELATIONSHIP THAT ENDURES THRU THE TESTS OF TIME IS LOVING AND CHERISHING AN EQUALLY LOVING, COMPASSIONATE AND COMPATIBLE PARTNER THAT WILL ALWAYS HAVE YOUR BACK. THIS IS THE SIMPLEST WAY TO PUT IT.**

Imagine if you lived in the ancient times, and you would find yourself in a vicious battle, fires raging all around you, unexpected dangers looming and unpredictable events occurring continuously, a sobering life and death situation.

Who could you count on? Is your partner your unequivocal ally? Can you count on them, trust them with your life? You see, sometimes life can feel precisely like that. But, if you have a truly loving, solid, confident, compassionate partner, the battleground becomes completely manageable and challenges are only temporary.

If this partner is standing by you like a rock, protecting your back, so you can look forward and face whatever may be, knowing full well that your back is safe…well my dear, if you have that, then you are fortunate beyond description, for this is the greatest, grandest thing to find. Because this person understands you, knows how you function, what you need and what you want. You don't have to even say a word, you communicate with your minds and know precisely how to remain in perfect synchrony, simply invincible to the battles of this Earthly realm. You are so strong together, that nothing can touch you. That is what it means to be with your other, perfect half.

Yes, you may find passionate love, fantastic intellect, abundance of laughter and happiness, strength, stamina, irresistible physical attraction, but if the person is incapable of having your back, protecting what you two have, and understanding the inner makings of your soul's essence, well …then what you two have is all very vulnerable, endangered and most likely perishable.

It is like a delicate exotic flower, that shows its tender bud in springtime, and someone steps on it in ignorance. But if you two are synchronized on the same wavelength, your love is shielded from crushing, and it will bloom and mesmerize everyone around you, transforming them in a breathless instant. And with time, you'll help this flower grow into a beautiful, majestic tree, strengthening its roots wider, deeper, while growing more glorious each and every day. Its shade will offer protection and nurturing shelter to the two of you, and perhaps others, if you invite them to share in this rare beauty.

This kind of love is a gift, and a lot to ask for, while not easily granted. Can you find this kind of love? You won't know unless you try, unless you give it all you've got. Life hands you what you agreed to before your return, what you asked for in your dreams, what you deserve, and what you earned…sometimes you may get it much later than you wanted, perhaps even losing hope that you'll ever find it at all. But there might be a good reason for the delay. You may have to travel thru heartbreak or long, dark tunnels of loneliness, but eventually you shall find your love. Why?

Because you are meant to love and be loved. Am I certain of this? Yes, I am, and so should you. And when love does come your way, it will require constant tending to, precious delicate tenderness, attention and effort.

> **NOTHING IN LOVE IS AUTOMATIC, ASSUMED, LOGICAL AND CANNOT BE TAKEN FOR GRANTED.**

Why? Because love will be taken away if not appreciated. And a love lost will hurt, it will pain and suffocate you inside, but it will also teach you to never again let it slip thru your fingers, or take it for granted. It will also teach you not to waste your time succumbing to fear, hesitation, and ignorance. Keep in mind, that even if you find yourself alone at this very moment, we all have marvelous partners that have accompanied us thru lifetimes. Perhaps even the same partner, lifetime thru lifetime, meeting you again and again.

You were not always and forever alone, perhaps you happen to be alone right now, but by striving to understand yourself better and listening to your heart, you have opened a gateway, a magnetic field has been activated, and you will attract a new, perhaps very different person into your life.

> **MAYBE YOUR ANCIENT LOVE IS ABOUT TO APPEAR AND RECOGNIZE YOU IN AN INSTANT. WHO KNOWS, JUST ALLOW THE UNIVERSE TO SURPRISE YOU, FOR MAYBE THIS PERSON IS ALREADY HERE, IN THIS WORLD, PRECISELY AT THE SAME TIME AS YOU ARE.**

The only thing that needs to be coordinated is the place where you two shall meet. It could be tomorrow at the corner bakery. So you see, time is already on your side. Which means, you need to pay attention to where you are, what you do, and whom you surround yourself with. But this is not the point of this book, because you can read such endless suggestive articles, each and every day.

The truth is, you have to meet yourself first. Then, you become consciously and energetically open to meeting someone. And if you are in relationship right now, this is the perfect time to take it deeper into your heart, further into your Spirit, and confidently lift your love into a higher frequency, one measure at a time.

If you are in a relationship, but are the only one on a spiritual quest, and your partner seems to be in another world entirely, take it upon yourself to introduce them to this other world, this new, marvelous, deeper connection that you can experience. Just do it the right way, without too much noise or a big, demanding, intimidating announcement. Just like when you take a baby swimming for the first time. You hold them in your arms and stand in water and they are with you. They feel safe and marvel at this new field of new sensations. And then, before they know it, you submerge with them in the water and they love it, feeling safe because they are in your arms. It's kind of similar to that. Sooner or later, they will want to master this water world on their own, enthusiastically squealing at the sheer joy of it.

If you are a good, sensitive and attentive teacher, they will love it. If you are impatient and critical, well then, you are just a bad teacher. Take it as an assignment, and you will see the difference. It will bring you joy as well, and you will elevate your relationship to an undiscovered and fascinating new level. Your partner may surprise you, be very receptive and swim like a fish in this new environment. And then there is the third possibility, that you are both on this journey simultaneously and here you are! This is of course quite a special rare occasion.

As I mentioned previously, the reality in the present time is that the majority of people are alone, there are currently more single people on the planet than there are couples. Especially rare are people who are in relationship that truly complements them and is a pairing of two equals. You have decided to evolve higher, pursue more knowledge, and explore love in ways you never thought imaginable. Or perhaps you have soldiered on your journey strongly, joyfully and lovingly, but need more tools to battle the unexpected obstacles that stand in your way.

> **EVERY OBSTACLE HAS A REASON AND A PURPOSE,
> EVENTUALLY BRINGING YOU A GIFT.**

After you climb over the impossibly high mountain peak, a beautiful field of peace and serenity awaits, where you can rest, take a deep breath and look around you. You might find your soul partner, a new manifestation of your beautiful love. But before arriving at such a rewarding position, you still have a lot to learn, explore, and fine-tune whatever prevents you from realizing your optimal relationship potential. But here is the good news; you are absolutely on your way to enter the field of attunement and synchronicity with clarity of your purpose. Your Love Matrix is aligned.

ATTUNE YOUR SPIRITS

The most challenging test you shall meet in your relationship is the concept of synchronizing the inevitable changes. Change is something that will happen. Why? Because life is a journey of constant change. Each and every day brings unexpected elements and new developments. Of course sometimes life feels stagnant, and you are stuck in one place, restricted by circumstances beyond your control. But even in such a case, you are changing. You may change your level of contentment, you become restless and find new interests, and there you go, you are changing even at a seemingly perfect standstill. Your insides are changing, your perceptions, your longings, your ideas, your hopes, your patience, everything is constantly changing.

You may become unhappy and discontent for no apparent reason. Perhaps you will even create conflict, simply because you are restless. You may battle your partner, when in fact you are just stir-crazy. You may say they are boring and unadventurous, simply because you are boring yourself.

And let's not forget how absurd is the idea that someone else has to entertain you, and diffuse your boredom. If you are an interesting, self-sufficient person, you are able to entertain yourself on your own, with no assistance. Could you entertain yourself on a deserted island? No?

How about lying on the beach and counting the clouds, listening to the birds, collecting seashells? Or do you need someone else to be constantly maintain your state of entertainment? Have you thought of this?

> **IT IS SO IMPORTANT TO DO SOME DEEP WORK ON YOURSELF, BEFORE EXPECTING TO SUSTAIN A DEEPLY SPIRITUAL RELATIONSHIP.**

And there is also the question of expectations. What is your idea of a spiritual relationship? What are your expectations and actual ability to consciously participate in an exchange on that level? Be honest, be clear and ask yourself all these questions. A clarity may emerge that you have unreasonable expectations from your partner. They should entertain you, inspire you, maintain you, protect you, stand by your side, support you and also spiritually guide you.

The spiritual clarity that you may long for, needs to be cultivated within you. It is like breathing. No one else can do it for you.

As a couple, synchronicity, attunement, similarities and compatibility are your strengths and gifts. But this also changes with time. You may be compatible for a while and then not. And then perhaps later, again. In other words; it is not written in stone that just because you two are so incredibly compatible and love each other to the highest level, that everything will go on smoothly forever. Perfection is also conflict, friction, discontent, fears, arguments, peacemaking, truce, and as a consequence – your growth, maturity, evolution. That is humanly perfect.

It can only happen this way. You will not necessarily grow, if there is none of that. Yes, you will grow old, but not in an evolutionary sense. So you see, there is no easy way, shortcut, recipes or secret combination to open the gates and sneak thru unscathed.

The moment you arrived in this world, you were thrown into an existence of illusion, time restriction, and Earthly limitations. You forgot all about your immortal Spirit, and the sustaining resilient power of timeless, everlasting love. Because if you knew all this right from the start, you would never let anything throw you off, succumb to doubt, fears, jealousy, obstacles and loneliness. You would know without hesitation, that you are never alone, are forever loved, and that destiny will always bring you the person you are supposed to love, who will equally love you in return.

How can you remember all this ancient information stored in the depths of your soul? You can do so with Mudra practice. You can call upon your destined mate and consciously work thru the many countless challenges and lessons that come upon you. It will harmonize you, bring you on the same energy level with your partner and help you recognize in each others eyes, the other, hidden side of your being – your soul connection. The human side is what you see every day, the Soul is what you find inside yourself and each other.

> **WHEN TWO PEOPLE INTRICATELY RESONATE IN LOVE,**
> **A UNIQUE PAIRING OF LIGHT, POWER AND DIVINITY IS ESTABLISHED.**
> **DO YOU UNDERSTAND THE POWER OF SUCH INFLUENTIAL FORCE?**
> **THIS IS THE ATTUNEMENT OF YOUR BEAUTIFUL SPIRITS.**

ACCEPTANCE

The world we live in is in many aspects very limited. We have a limited sensory ability to see, hear, smell, feel and taste. But do not let that discourage you.

> **IF YOU UNDERSTAND AND ACCEPT YOUR LIMITATIONS,
> YOU CAN ACTUALLY OVERCOME THEM.**

You learn to navigate around them, to look beyond them. This way, you expand and go above the norm. Lifting your relationship beyond what others consider a regular, normal relationship is one of these pursuits. Yes, you can be perfectly content having the same daily routine and not changing one bit of your schedule, for years to come. And you can have the Sunday barbecue or summer vacations or whatever you two do, that makes you feel and look like you belong to the average, "normal" population. You do and live by what's expected. But on the other hand, you have a choice to be a bit different, try things your unique way. Look at each other and explore more, ask, respond, find out, research, discover and get excited about something nobody knows. Something otherworldly.

What if you had a special formula that would guarantee to sustain your closeness at a most delicately intimate level, and help you love each other in a more profound, deeper way, each and every day? What if there was a way to be excited about a mutual pursuit, something that is just yours and very unique? Would you want to know about it? Mudras will help you enter an entirely new dimension of communicating, understanding and loving each other.

Learn about acceptance of each other's differences, shortcomings or perhaps, imperfections. Instead of looking at them as deficiencies, look at them as beautiful specialties. Unique beauty marks, and secret hideaway puzzles that you can unravel together or on your own. But no matter what these individual unique quirks are, accept them and embrace them in a loving, compassionate way. You will instantly reduce their negative power and open the door to finding the hidden treasure that they may offer. Quite often a seeming flaw can unveil the greatest treasure.

> **ACCEPTANCE OF EACH OTHER'S IMPERFECTIONS
> WILL OPEN A NEW GATEWAY TO EXPERIENCING
> THE GREATEST TREASURES OF UNCONDITIONAL LOVE.**

AWARENESS

This is a golden rule to help maintain a state of harmony. What is the opposite of awareness? Ignorance – the greatest enemy of our evolutionary process. Many people may be quiet, even hurtful in ignorance, when all they need is to enter a state of awareness about themselves and others.

An example would be someone who is completely unaware of their own negative disposition and continues to blame others, projecting their own mood, accusing everyone around them of something they are fighting within, while in state of ignorance. Nowhere is this more obvious than at the core of a personal relationship.

> **THE CLOSENESS THAT AN INTIMATE RELATIONSHIP REQUIRES, WILL EVENTUALLY BLOW OFF THE COVERS HIDING ONE'S UNRESOLVED ASPECTS, AND REVEAL THE NAKED TRUTH BENEATH.**

If someone is acting all brave and strong, but underneath it all, they feel small, insecure and frightened, this will come to light sooner or later. If you recognize this weakness in your partner beforehand, you are aware of their challenge or obstacle. You can help navigate thru this journey of inevitable revelation and vulnerability, simply because you are aware. Likewise your partner who is aware of your Achilles' heel, can be gentle, kind and supportive, when you are personally challenged.

Ideally, your own awareness will bring you self-realization and self-understanding. But it is almost guaranteed that your partner will unintentionally push an invisible button, and trigger something that needs to be healed within you, that will resurface and create and unexpected cloud or a fearful conflict.

Remember, relationships are here to teach us, and clearly for obvious reasons certain lessons can only be learned when you are in a twosome. Being aware and present will help you sail thru this growing process in a most painless, and perhaps even exciting way. The less you resist, the easier it's going to be. You may finally discover the source of your deep grief, fear or self-doubt. Your life may profoundly change as a result. Awareness of the value of this growing process will hopefully help you approach every challenge with reflection, confidence, patience and unwavering support for each other. This is the growing process.

Again, I remind you, there is no perfect man or perfect woman out there, that has absolutely no flaws. This does not exist, so don't fool yourself into entertaining such a futile, immature expectation. The question is only this: how strong is your love, and how willing are the two of you to work thru these phases of a relationship and growing process? If your desires for making it work are compatible, you are in luck and will conquer whatever comes your way.

If your positions and abilities are incompatible, it will require more work. Being aware and honest with each other about compatibility while synchronizing your needs, is the key to sailing thru life's unpredictable waters and stormy challenges. Fearless honesty will be highly rewarded.

TRANSFORMATION

Life will present you with repeated opportunities and it is entirely up to you, how you navigate thru them and what kind of choices you make. Some opportunities may only come once, and love is fickle that way. So your choices matter, a whole lot.

Are they your usual, safe choices, or are they daring, courageous choices?
You will be inclined to go the way you have always gone in the past. This is your habit, safe bet, and even if it continuously brings you an unhappy outcome, this is how you have done it before and may do it again. Or you will have the strength and the ability to open up to a transformation and allow new energy into your life. Once you do this, you will have entered the zone of profound positive evolutionary transformation.

> **TWO SOULS ON A UNIQUE JOINT JOURNEY OF LOVE WILL BE TRANSFORMED WHETHER THEY LIKE IT OR NOT.**

It is funny, because when we are happy in a relationship, we often have a tendency to want everything to remain in a standstill, as in: "It is perfect right now, please make it last forever, and remain precisely like it is!" Well, human life does not work that way. We are born and we die and in between is our life. And this is a non-negotiable fact. So we can't make it stand still.

So the question remains: Are you able to enjoy the transformative process from day to day and really make the very best of your life?

If this is a challenge, and you resist the natural process of transformation, you will remain in a state of regret, complain, victimhood, negativity and pessimism. You'll be lamenting about the past and wishing for something that was, and will never be again.

Why? Because greatness can not be repeated. A wonderful day will never be duplicated. An amazing kiss will never be redone. It is a once in a lifetime occurrence. Even movies that get redone are usually a bleak, watered down version of the great creative accomplishment that happened in the original version.

> **YOU SIMPLY CAN'T COPY OR REPEAT THE MOST BEAUTIFUL AND PRECIOUS MOMENTS OF LIFE.**

BUT here is another option: you may enjoy differently wonderful days, a variation of a differently fantastic kiss, and a new experience of loving communication. It will be different, and perhaps even more wonderful than the day before. If you want to copy and repeat what was, you will entirely miss what is.

Life is an ongoing process of transformation. That is actually the whole idea. It's rather counterproductive to live a life where you fear the transformative process like aging, for example. Guess what, the baby that is born this precise second is getting older with each passing minute, just like you. It is transforming, just like you. What you do within your time schedule while in this world – that is up to you. Transform and grow as much as possible, and you'll get the right idea of it all. Stay stuck and stagnant, hiding under the table, and you'll miss the entire point.

Nobody is having a grand time all the time. You may happen to see someone having their grandest time in life and say, "Gosh how lucky they are!" But you won't see them when everything is falling apart and say, "Gosh how lucky am I?"

If you are alone, your inner transformation will eventually bring you a destined partner. How you transform yourself and how open you are to change, will play a decisive role in whom the Universe sends your way.

Obviously until this very present moment, you perhaps did not pay so much attention to this aspect, or you paid the wrong kind of attention. If you are single and feel incomplete, less worthy, lonely, forgotten and a failure at relationships, then there is an urgent, immediate need to transform! That's right, for in this sorry state you will attract a very confusing potential partner. Certainly not someone that knows the real you. So as a single person, embark on this transformative journey with an enthusiastic outlook for all marvelous possibilities that await.

And as a couple, you will uncover new enthusiasm and welcome the transformative change with open arms. Because every challenge that you overcome, is a challenge conquered. Every doubt, friction, mishap and wound that you heal, will bring you closer to where you want and need to be in order to ascend together. Look at your past as a glorious road to victory, for you are here now, together, unified and consciously aware of your choices ahead.

Discuss what you miss and long for, open all the doors and windows and air out the dust. Transform yourselves and rediscover an even deeper, more profound connection that binds you two together. Now, take all that you've learned, accomplished, overcome and excelled at, and apply it to your journey ahead. You'll see, each day will become more beautiful and lovely than the day before. It is up to you how you maintain this precious gift of love. Pay attention and recognize the beautiful new nuances, the precious most valuable wisdom that resides within your hearts. The pure love between two people is worth preserving at any price.

FIND YOUR KARMIC PURPOSE

This is of course the big, most fascinating mystery to be uncovered, it is the pursuit of your truth, of your assignment and of your reason for being. There is an astrological approach to look at your celestial map and see some very revealing elements that may help you uncover your deeper past, and the purpose of your journey. But while some of you can't see that information, there are other ways to find out these mysterious facts. In fact, Mudras will offer you precisely this.

> **TO HAVE A GLIMPSE INTO THE GREAT BEYOND,**
> **TO UNDERSTAND THE INVISIBLE YET MIGHTY ENERGY STRINGS**
> **THAT BIND YOU TOGETHER STRONGER THAN STEEL,**
> **THIS REQUIRES A VERY RECEPTIVE MIND AND AN OPEN HEART.**

When you practice Mudras together, your energy magnifies while your joined frequency rises. You connect thru your merged energy field that opens an invisible gateway of information. A quick glimpse, a thought, a feeling of recognition and often a deep heart-felt revelation will occur, and you will remember your purpose together.

Many times, the connection you have, has endured profound obstacles, hardships, challenges and all of that past is blended with a powerful emotion of old, indescribably connected and deep sense of profound inner longing for your love to live, breathe and be together. You will receive the information you are looking for bit by bit, and the next step required is going to be bringing this information into the light, to examine and reflect upon it together.

The Karmic purpose is revealed within your deepest longing for each other.
What is this longing? Is it simply to be together, is it to create a family, pursue a mission, launch an impactful project, or travel, discover, teach, guide, or justify, be peaceful and calm enjoying the simplest of life in a most private way.

What is your desire in regard to each other?
At the deepest level of your heart is the basic emotion that you feel for each other. Is your love weighed down with fear and worry of losing each other, is it a sense of completion, unfounded danger, jealousy, fears of all kinds and flavors? What is it?

This is a puzzle that needs resolving, as it contains an answer that only you know. Once you do, speak to each other and be as honest as possible. This is the best way to heal what's burdening you from the past. If you lost each other ten times before, and are now finally together, it is perfectly understandable that you'll be still carrying that fear, no matter how unfounded it may seem. If there was a situation of jealousy, it may still sit with you and disturb your peace in most unfounded ways. Where is this old unrest coming from? Acknowledging your other feelings besides love, will actually make your love indescribably stronger.

PART OF YOUR KARMIC PURPOSE IS TO HEAL, ACCOMPLISH, FULFILL.
ONLY YOU CAN UNRAVEL THIS MYSTERY.
WHEN SEARCHING WITH INTENTION
PROGRESS WILL BE FAST, POWERFUL AND LIFE CHANGING.

RECOGNIZE YOUR SOUL CONTRACT

This is of course awfully close to your karmic purpose, but not the same. Your karmic purpose may be healing, forgiving, experiencing a desire, a path that you both wish for and must travel.

A spiritual contract is something you promised to each other. It is a mutually agreed upon mission, project, goal that you want to pursue and complete. While you may not completely fulfill your karmic purpose of healing, you may on the other hand, fulfill your spiritual contract of offering help to each other in pursuing your joint goal. Your karmic purpose may require a few lifetimes to heal, especially if you endured suffering or were prevented from being together.

> **YOUR SPIRITUAL CONTRACT HAS A DEFINED DESCRIPTION
> OF WHAT YOU TWO WANT TO ACCOMPLISH,
> PURSUE AND CONTRIBUTE TO EACH OTHER AND THE WORLD.**

How can you understand your spiritual contract? This would be revealed in more internal work with each other. Beneath the triggered emotions that make your react to each other like you do, beneath the fears, old scars, old attachments and long lost love, there will be a higher purpose. Your spiritual contract won't entail sitting on a couch and drinking lemonade while watching movies together. That would perhaps represent a way of a healing, relaxing and enjoying the daily aspect of your union.

Your spiritual purpose would require a conscious action, a pursuit of something you can accomplish. What are you both good at that you also love to do? What is your unique ability as a team that is much more powerful and defined while together?

What is a venue that would offer you two to manifest this?
Is it an orphanage, support group, rescuing mission, an enlightening offering to the world?
Is it having a family and raising conscious beings that will eventually change the world?
Is it saving a troubled clan?
Is it discovering a new medical procedure?
Is it inventing a new format of entertainment and healing thru arts?
Is it teaching others about healthy food and nutrition, new kind of lifestyle in nature?

Think, explore together, find a mission that resonates with you and appeals to you both while making sense. And then work on it and see if doors open. If they do, you are on the right track. If they don't, you need to define your mission better, refine your search and work on it from a different angle. This is your way of finding and fulfilling your spiritual contract. Once you are on the right track, it will feel really good and right, and your passion will be contagious. Things will move along and you will experience an openness of the Universe, to help you manifest and accomplish what you desire.

But it is very important to keep in mind, that while you each try to fulfill your spiritual contract, you might be still battling your old wounds, which will make you weaker, doubtful, fearful and somewhat hesitant on your path. As a response, the Universe will automatically send you challenges in order to strengthen you. Do not see moments of small obstacles as the end of the world or a clear sign that you are moving in the wrong direction. You can't and mustn't be discouraged in two-seconds. But do pay attention and see what triggered you, and then put your heads and hearts together and get thru the obstacle with a conscious, fearless disposition. This will offer you the potential for tremendous progress. The moment you recognize this, a big shift will occur, for you will heal your karmic past and embark on the path of fulfilling your spiritual contract and purpose.

OVERCOME EARTHLY LIMITATIONS

The imaginary Earthy limitations that seem to be blocking your progress are only there to help you find a better way, refine your search, avoid pitfalls and be selective about who you allow into your private orbit.

> **DO NOT ALLOW OTHERS INTO YOUR PRIVATE RELATIONSHIP ORBIT, SINCE THEIR OPINIONS MAY STRICTLY REFLECT THEIR OWN PERSONAL INTERESTS AND DESIRES.**

You must be mature enough to understand and know, that when two people are supremely happy and in love, there may be others who will experience a sense of jealousy and competitiveness towards you. It may even be in your closest family unit. It is truly naive to expect the average person who is generally discontent, to be genuinely happy for two people who are a strong pairing. They will feel jealous, envious and upset at the sheer sight of the two of you. This is human and understandable, especially if they are in an unhappy place in their life. But don't let any negative energy come into your personal space. You can't allow that. The space between the two of you is sacred and the moment you allow an outsider access, you are vulnerable and opening yourselves up to other's influences.

> **THE RELATIONSHIP BETWEEN THE TWO OF YOU IS BETWEEN THE TWO OF YOU AND PRECISELY NOBODY ELSE. YOUR LOVE IS PRIVATE, JUST YOU TWO IN YOUR SACRED SPACE, UNTOUCHABLE AND OFF LIMITS TO ALL OTHERS.**

This kind of love bond will help you overcome the usual Earthly limitations and obstacles. You will be able to feel each others energy, thoughts, calls and answers when you are apart, or in need. This is clearly overcoming the Earthly limitations. Remember, when you reawaken the love between you, that may be ancient and has survived thru death, you are operating within a system that is beyond Earthly limitations. You are using a program that is unique, special and simply out of this world. Keep that in mind and don't limit yourself to this particular dimension.

Understand and know that love is from beyond this place of space and time. When you vibrate on this level, you move into the dimension beyond our sight, despite the fact that you are seemingly still living and breathing here and now. You move in two worlds simultaneously. This is what overcoming Earthly limitations is about. How exciting!

ASCENSION OF SOUL UNION

No matter how harmonious and evolved you may be, there is always a higher ground, an evolutionary seemingly unattainable realm, where you two could and can go. In other words, the field of ascension is limitless and ever present. It is impossible to ascend, if you are still attached and bound by lower chakra entanglements with ego, power and the mind. Your heart is the doorway, and merging your souls thru your hearts, will open up a gateway for you to ascend and evolve to dimensions that the world is limited to understand.

How can you describe the overwhelming emotion of true unconditional love?
You can try, but won't quite duplicate the experience in your listener.

How do you describe swimming in the ocean, merging with the great power of the current?
How do you describe the hypnotizing aroma of a rose, evoking far away memories?
How do you describe the feelings when two people meet for the first time?
How do you describe the experience of skydiving?
And how do you describe the transformation through birth or death?

You can try, but it is not the same as living thru it. Similarly, I cannot adequately describe the sensation or two souls ascending thru the power of soul union in love. I can only convey to you, that when two souls unite on their highest frequency and equal energetic disposition of the heart, they transcend time, space and limitations of human body.

They enter a field of otherworldly existence, where the rules of the Earth dimension don't apply. We all leave this Earthly realm at our designated time, and exit thru the sacred gateway that granted our entry, when we arrived.

> **OUR TIME IN THIS WORLD IS LIMITED, VALUABLE, PRECIOUS,
> AND FILLED WITH ASSIGNMENTS.
> IF WE ARE FORTUNATE TO MEET OUR SOULMATE,
> WE HOPEFULLY ALLOW THIS LOVE TO THRIVE IN ITS FULL POTENTIAL.**

If we have chosen to travel on our own, and reunite with our mate in a different dimension of existence, there surely is a reason for it. Perhaps we depended too much on them before, and agreed to travel solo for a bit. The reunion will be that much sweeter. And whomever we meet while here, each person carries a tiny key to the puzzle this life presents. Do not dismiss a hidden treasure just because you are impatient, unable to discern or recognize a heaven-sent messenger that can accompany you thru this life. If you want a companion, they will appear, trust the Universe to send you someone you know from before, and it shall be so. If you have found them and are lucky to hold their hand and look into their eyes first thing in the morning and lastly before you leave for dreamland, than make sure, you don't hold back, but open up your heart and allow the power of the two of you to thrive through the engine of ascension.

Your imperfections are perfect and you are beautifully lovable, precisely as you are. Know and love yourself with all your faults and wrinkles and you will understand, that even if at times you feel alone, your greatest love is the Universe itself. The Universe has protected and nurtured you thru every second of your life, and it shall continue to do so, till the end of time.

> **MUDRAS CAN HELP ACTIVATE THE HEALING JOURNEY OF YOUR HEART. YOUR HEART'S TRUE HOME IS UNCONDITIONAL DIVINE LOVE.**

This is the final chapter of our journey into your heart. It is a very intense exploration of advanced manifestations of your Love Matrix.

Remember, that everything and anything is possible, and love is something you can attract into your life. If you recognize it, and manage to sustain it, you will navigate thru the unexpected hurricanes and overcome any obstacle that might be in your way. You deserve love, for it is your birthright.

Sail ahead with confidence in your heart, and awareness of your soul and always remember; LOVE is immortal, LOVE is everlasting, LOVE overcomes all limitations of time, death and space.

> **LOVE IS TRULY EVERYTHING AND THE ONLY THING THAT MATTERS IN THE BEGINNING, MIDDLE AND THE END OF YOUR LIFE.**

I pray your journey thru and towards love continues with renewed faith, courage, hope and confidence, that you are loved beyond your wildest dreams. The love that the Universe carries for you is unconditional and omnipresent. Feel it, breathe it, and call it upon yourself with each Mudra that you practice. The power to do so lies in your beautiful hands. Use them with grace, devotion and faith.

YOUR ASSIGNMENT

AFFIRMATION

LOVE IS EVERYTHING AND EVERYTHING IS LOVE...

DIARY
At this time of your love-intensive journey, call upon the deepest knowledge and awareness of your spirit-self, to awaken and provide the answers you need. All you ever wanted, needed and desired is locked away, until you open your Spirit to love. Once this gate is opened, you can begin to understand the most complex elements of your life's purpose and its various assignments. This incredibly fascinating and equally important topic is something you can research and examine throughout your life. Always explore the next chapter as your life unfolds and various relationship experiences occur. Keep writing these insights, inner journeys and answers that are revealed, and carefully tend to your self-exploration. Your diary work should continue throughout your life, for it will help you catch your answers, before they escape into the abyss of timelessness.

PROCESS
Work thru the questions, come back in a few days, see if anything changed, add it on, clarify, clean it up, and self-discover through the process.

PRACTICE
Work with the diary, answer the questions and practice the Mudras listed. Write down how you feel before and after the Mudra practice. Observe the shift in your energy field.

> **CONTINUE THE DAILY MUDRA PRACTICE AND CONSCIOUSLY TEND TO YOUR HEART, EACH AND EVERY DAY OF YOUR LIFE.**

Your Workspace

YOUR SPIRIT'S LONGING

HAVE YOU ASKED YOUR SPIRIT WHAT IT LONGS FOR?

These are deep intimate conversations with yourself regardless of your relationship status.

Nobody can or will answer this question, only you.

In order to find true contentment with your partner, you need to hear, respect and consider your soul's longings.

This will hold the key to how the two of you can find that perfect balance to travel together with magnified power, towards a merged spiritual force to find your joint venture.

Anything the two of you truly need, want and wish to create, will have a great chance of manifesting, when your love-infused mission comes from your hearts.

This is an evolving journey, so the answers change, develop further than you never imagined.

This is your Spirit truth.

Your Workspace

TRANSFORMATION AND CHANGE

ARE YOU WILLING TO TRANSFORM AND CHANGE?

Embrace change, welcome it, for it brings with it the endless field of possibilities.

How do you feel about this?

If you are resisting, ask yourself, why?

Describe the scenario you desire, and outcome you wish for, a vision you dream of completing.

Now accept and recognize that in order to accomplish and realize it, a transformation needs to occur.

Now you see, that fighting change is like fighting life.

Go with the flow and get on board with change in every possible way, for it will bring the answers and realizations of all your dreams.

Now you can **conquer your resistance to change.**

Your Workspace
KARMIC PURPOSE & SOUL CONTRACTS

DO YOU RECOGNIZE YOUR KARMIC PURPOSE AND SOUL CONTRACTS?

This is possibly the most interesting and important detail of your love journey.

Be an objective observer, a detective, take into consideration all seemingly unimportant small elements and details, and you will unlock the mystery of your sacred contract.

Look at your past and find compassion, higher understanding of perhaps painful love experiences, recognize the necessary growing process and needed lessons your learned.

Now apply them to your present life and consciously find clear signs and revelations of your contract.

They can be simple, like healing old wounds, enlightening others, or simply overcoming the loss of each other in the far away past.

But now, you are here, together and ready to enjoy the fruits of your battles, the beautiful parts of your journey, and the rewards that you earned.

Trust and confidently move forward with hearts full of abundance and love.

Now you can recognize there is a perfect order of purpose for everything.

For your Mudra Practice

GLORIOUS VICTORIOUS LOVE

Whenever you feel the challenges of life sway your confidence, or try to plant the seeds of doubt and fear within you, stand stoic, strong, confident in resilience of your unbendable faith and courage. Your love is in your heart, in the essence of your soul, and in every cell of your physical body. Fill your mind with awareness and conviction that love is victorious, and finally, call upon the Universe to protect you and envelop you with an impenetrable shield of love. Remember, that love magnifies in the presence of a confident Spirit.

RECLAIM YOUR POWER

What is attractive, is the real you. What is confusing is the adapted version of you, when you are trying to please everybody else, except yourself. If a butterfly would hesitate before reemerging into the light, it would never get the chance to fly. If it would hesitate to fly, it would never experience life and feel the wind under its wings. If you are afraid to come out of your shell, love will elude you. If you will hesitate before sharing your love, your heart will whisper a sad melody, and not sing in it with full power. Your daily Mantra begins in the morning when you see yourself for the first time in a new day and say:

> "HELLO MY BEAUTIFUL, PRECIOUS SOUL.
> I ADORE AND LOVE YOU,
> AND TODAY YOU AND I SHALL BE A HAPPY PAIR."

MUDRA FOR DIVINE WORSHIP

Sit with a straight spine. Place your palms together in front of your chest. Sit still and concentrate on your Third Eye for at least three minutes.

BREATH
Long, deep and slow through your nose

MANTRA
EK ONG KAR *(One Creator, God Is One)*

CHAKRAS
All Chakras

HEALING COLORS
All Colors

AFFIRMATION

I ALIGN MY FREQUENCY WITH MY HIGHER PURPOSE

MUDRA FOR ILLUMINATING YOUR HEART

Sit with a straight back and keep your shoulders down, nice and relaxed. Cross the hands in front of your heart, right hand over left. Both palms are turned towards your chest. The thumb fingers are straight and hooked together, all fingers are straight, right small finger is held apart. Hold for Three minutes and relax.

BREATH
Long, deep and slow through your nose

MANTRA
OMM *(God in His Absolute State)*

CHAKRAS
Heart - 4, Third eye - 6, Crown - 7

HEALING COLORS
Green, Indigo, Violet

AFFIRMATION

I AM A BEACON OF LIGHT

Mudra for Evoking Your Intuitive Voice

Sit with a straight back and keep your shoulders down, nice and relaxed. Intertwine your fingers leaving the index fingers straight and pressed against each other at full length. Bend your elbows and lift your hands up, hold them at the level of your throat with outstretched index fingers in front of, but not touching your lips. Index fingers point up towards the sky, thumbs are crossed. Practice for Three minutes and relax.

BREATH
Long, deep and slow through your nose

MANTRA
OMM *(God in His Absolute State)*

CHAKRAS
Throat - 5, Third eye - 6, Crown - 7

HEALING COLORS
Blue, Indigo, violet

AFFIRMATION
I CALL ON MY INTUITION

MUDRA FOR HEIGHTENED AWARENESS

Sit with a straight back and keep your shoulders down, nice and relaxed. Lift your hands above your head. Palms are pressed together, elbows to the side. Inhale, stretch your elbows and raise your hands as if someone is pulling them up. Then exhale, bend your elbows and lower your hands to the beginning position, a few inches above your head, palms always pressed together. Practice for Three minutes and relax.

BREATH
Inhale slowly when lifting hands, exhale when lowering hands

MANTRA
SAT NAM *(Truth Is God's Name, One in Spirit)*

CHAKRAS
Throat - 5, Third eye - 6, Crown - 7

HEALING COLORS
Blue, Indigo, violet

AFFIRMATION
I RAISE MY AWARENESS, I REACH FOR THE LIGHT

MUDRA FOR UNIVERSAL ENERGY & ETERNITY

Sit with a straight back, keep your shoulders down, nice and relaxed. Bend your elbows, bring your hands up and away from your body to form two V's. You can keep your arms slightly closer and lightly touching your body, to establish a stronger sense of powerful energy in your chest area, or leave some room between elbows and your body. Raise your palms to your heart level, keeping all fingers together. Feel the nurturing energy flowing into your hands. Hold for three minutes and relax.

BREATH
LONG, DEEP AND SLOW THROUGH YOUR NOSE

MANTRA
HAR HARE HAREE WAHE GURU
(God, the Creator of Supreme Power and Wisdom, the Spiritual Teacher and Guide Through Darkness)

CHAKRAS
BASE OF SPINE - 1, CROWN - 7

HEALING COLORS
RED, VIOLET

AFFIRMATION
I CALL ON MY INTUITION

MUDRA FOR VICTORY

Sit with a straight back and keep your shoulders down, nice and relaxed. Make gentle fists with both hands. Lift up your arms and cross them in, over your upper chest, left over right. This powerful Mudra is seen in many sculptures of Egyptian Pharaohs. Practice for Three minutes, then relax.

BREATH
LONG, DEEP AND SLOW THROUGH YOUR NOSE

MANTRA
OMM *(God in His Absolute State)*

CHAKRAS
ALL CHAKRAS

HEALING COLORS
ALL COLORS

AFFIRMATION

I AM VICTORIOUS AND SUCCESSFUL

MUDRA INDEX

Balanced Speech…187
Balancing Yin & Yang…190
Calming Your Mind…246
Contentment of Your Heart…186
Creativity…216
Developing Meditation…56
Diminishing Worries…217
Divine Worship…276
Emotional Balance…57
Empowering Your Voice…249
Evoking Your Intuitive Voice…278
Facing Fear…94
Feeling Your Energy Body…215
Happiness…124
Healing a Broken Heart…120
Heightened Awareness…279
Help With a Grave Situation…121
Illuminating Your Heart…277
Inner Integrity …248
Inner Security…218
Love…123
Mental Balance…91
Nurturing Your Heart…149
Opening Your Heart…122
Overcoming Anxiety…92
Patience…188
Power of Projection…250
Powerful Energy…247
Powerful Insight…152
Preventing Stress…95
Receiving Universe's Law…154

Rejuvenation…220
Relaxation & Joy …251
Releasing Negative Emotions…60
Self ~ Healing…61
Self ~ Reflection…58
Self ~ Confidence…96
Self ~ Identification…151
Sexual Balance…219
Taking Away Hardships…59
Tranquilizing the Mind…93
Trust…150
Two Hearts…191
Universal Energy & Eternity…280
Uplifting Your Heart…125
Victory…281
Willpower of Manifestation…153
Wisdom…189

ABOUT THE AUTHOR

SABRINA MESKO Ph.D.H. is a recognized Mudra authority and International and Los Angeles Times bestselling author of the timeless classic *Healing Mudras - Yoga for your Hands* translated into fourteen languages. She authored over twenty books on Mudras, Mudra Therapy, Mudras and Astrology, Meditation techniques, Spirituality and Holistic Care.

Sabrina was born in Europe where she became a classical ballerina at an early age. In her teens she moved to New York and became a principal Broadway dancer and singer who turned to yoga to heal a back injury. Eastern-trained but Western-based, she completed a several-year intensive study of teachings with world renowned Masters, one of whom entrusted her with bringing the sacred Mudra techniques to the West. She is a Yoga College of India certified Yoga Therapist.

Sabrina holds a Bachelors Degree in Sensory Approaches to Healing, a Masters in Holistic Science, and a Doctorate in Ancient and Modern Approaches to Healing from the American Institute of Holistic Theology. She is board certified from the American Alternative medical Association and American Holistic Health Association.

She has been featured in media outlets such as The Los Angeles Times, CNBC News, Cosmopolitan, the cover of London Times Lifestyle, The Discovery Channel documentary on Hands, W magazine, First for Women, Health, Web-MD, Daily News, Focus, Yoga Journal, Australian Women's weekly, Blend, Daily Breeze, New Age, the Roseanne Show and various international live television programs. Her articles have been published in world-wide publications. She hosted her own weekly TV show educating about health, well-being and complementary medicine. She is an executive member of the World Yoga Council and has led numerous international Yoga Therapy educational programs. She directed and produced her interactive double DVD titled *Chakra Mudras*, a Visionary Awards finalist. Sabrina also created award winning international Spa and Wellness Centers and is a motivational keynote conference speaker addressing large audiences all over the world. Sabrina recently launched Arnica Press, a boutique Book Publishing House. Her mission is to discover, mentor, nurture and publish unique authors with a meaningful message, that may otherwise not have an opportunity to be heard.

She is the founder of MUDRA MASTERY ™ the world's only online Mudra Teacher and Mudra Therapy Education, Certification, and Mentorship program, with her certified graduates and therapists spreading these ancient teachings in over 26 countries around the world.

WWW.SABRINAMESKO.COM

www.ingramcontent.com/pod-product-compliance
Lightning Source LLC
Chambersburg PA
CBHW080240170426
43192CB00014BA/2504